HISPANIC SUBSTANCE ABUSE

HISPANIC SUBSTANCE ABUSE

Edited by

RAYMOND SANCHEZ MAYERS, Ph.D.
Rutgers University

BARBARA L. KAIL, D.S.W.
Fordham University

THOMAS D. WATTS, D.S.W.
The University of Texas at Arlington

Foreword by

Juan Ramos, Ph.D.
Deputy Director for Prevention and Special Projects, OD
National Institute of Mental Health

CHARLES C THOMAS • PUBLISHER
Springfield • Illinois • U.S.A.

Published and Distributed Throughout the World by

CHARLES C THOMAS • PUBLISHER
2600 South First Street
Springfield, Illinois 62794-9265

© *1993 by* CHARLES C THOMAS • PUBLISHER

ISBN 0-398-05849-0

Library of Congress Catalog Card Number: 92-43848

Printed in the United States of America
SC-R-3

Library of Congress Cataloging-in-Publication Data

Hispanic substance abuse / edited by Raymond Sanchez Mayers, Barbara
  L. Kail, Thomas D. Watts ; foreword by Juan Ramos.
     p.   cm.
   Includes index.
   ISBN 0-398-05849-0
   1. Hispanic Americans—Substance use.   2. Hispanic Americans—
Substance use—Prevention.   3. Substance abuse—United States.
I. Kail, Barbara Lynn.   II. Watts, Thomas D.
HV5824.E85H57   1993
362.29'12'08968073—dc20   92-43848
                                                                        CIP

CONTRIBUTORS

ANTHONY ALCOCER, Dr.P.H.
California State University, Northridge
Department of Health Science

MANUEL BARRERA, JR., Ph.D.
Arizona State University
Department of Psychology

LUIS H. CARIS, M.D., M.P.H.
University of Chile
School of Mental Health

RICHARD C. CERVANTES, Ph.D.
University of Southern California
School of Medicine

MARIO DE LA ROSA
National Institute on Drug Abuse
Epidemiology and Prevention

MELVIN DELGADO, Ph.D.
Boston University
School of Social Work

CARANN FEAZELL, M.S.W., C.S.W., CEAP
Human Resource Consultant

GEERTRUIDA C. DE GOEDE, M.L.S.
The University of Texas at Arlington
University Libraries

M. JEAN GILBERT, Ph.D.
Kaiser Permanente
Organization Effectiveness Department

DENISE HUMM-DELGADO, Ph.D.
Simmons College
School of Social Work

BARBARA L. KAIL, D.S.W.
Fordham University
School of Social Work

ALBERTO G. MATA, Ph.D.
The University of Oklahoma
Department of Human Relations

JUAN RAMOS, Ph.D.
National Institute of Mental Health
Prevention and Special Projects

FINETTA REESE, Ph.D.
Virginia Commonwealth University
Department of Psychology

ARTURO T. RIO
University of Miami
Department of Psychiatry

SYLVIA RODRIGUEZ-ANDREW, Ph.D.
Texas Lutheran College
Department of Sociology and Social Work

BEATRICE A. ROUSE, Ph.D.
National Institute on Drug Abuse
Division of Applied Research

RAYMOND SANCHEZ MAYERS, Ph.D.
Rutgers University
School of Social Work

DANIEL A. SANTISTEBAN, Ph.D.
University of Miami
Department of Psychiatry

FERNANDO I. SORIANO, Ph.D.
University of Missouri
Department of Behavioral Science

FEDERICO SOUFLEE, JR., Ph.D.
The University of Texas at Arlington
School of Social Work

JOSE SZAPOCZNIK, Ph.D.
University of Miami
Department of Psychiatry

THOMAS D. WATTS, D.S.W.
The University of Texas at Arlington
School of Social Work

For
Carann, Jordan, and Sara Caitlin Sanchez Mayers
Mi hermano, Richard Sanchez
Louis Kail
Ilene, Rebecca, and Jeanine Watts
James W. Callicutt and Jean H. Liebman.

FOREWORD

The pain and suffering experienced by individuals, families, and communities due to substance abuse will almost certainly continue as efforts to develop prevention and treatment remain ineffective, resources diminish, and the sense of urgency fades. While values sustaining our meager efforts come into question, and the political influence and scientific base to mobilize and inform interventions does not materialize, program efforts falter and the clients/victims are labeled treatment-resistant, noncompliant, or disinterested in their own well-being. The substance abuser population group and their family members are not organized to advocate in their behalf, and whatever advocacy is mobilized is on the part of the providers who look out after their own narrow interests and not the client groups. Scientific research is also not being undertaken on a systematic basis and usually conflicts arise as to its value, leading to non-action. Most importantly, the social institutions and helping professionals with responsibility in this area are not held accountable, either for their failure or for the negative consequences of their actions.

In this era, becoming culturally competent is beginning to be seen as an integral part of professional competence. Increasing recognition is being given to developing multicultural human services and to assess the cultural aspects of services delivery. But neither the intended or unintended consequences of the organization, financing, and delivery of human services to culturally diverse populations has received serious attention. Human service organizations and their infrastructures, surrounded by walls of indifference and ethnocentrism, remain almost immune to any discourse on their effectiveness with culturally diverse populations.

Discourse on these critical issues will become even more important as the helping professions advance through the 1990's. Specifically, the dramatic increase and changes in the culturally diverse populations in the United States will bring about new and exciting challenges to the human service infrastructure, including services provided by public and private social welfare agencies, research, and training programs. While some responses will be a reaction to the increase in population as reflected in the client caseloads, there is an urgent need to take initiative in addressing the impact of societal mechanisms on the human services infrastructure. Thus, the challenge to the helping professions is not limited to the assessment of the impact and consequences of their assumption and concepts on culturally diverse populations or the identification of strategies to change the human services infrastructure so that it can respond appropriately to their growing needs. While these are crucial, they are not sufficient. The most influential agents with jurisdiction over the human services infrastructure have been traditionally overlooked and taken for granted in the change process: these are the legitimizing and authorizing bodies with responsibility for accreditation of facilities providing inpatient and outpatient care, accreditation of educational institutions and specialized training for the helping professions, accreditation of services for families and children, licensing and certification of human services professionals, and the sanction and support of diagnostic and assessment tools extensively utilized by the helping professions. These self-governing bodies are parties to the social contract with society designed to protect it from quacks and incompetents. Yet, there has been no visible effort to incorporate the needs and specific characteristics of the culturally diverse populations in the criteria established by these authorizing bodies. As experience indicates, present policies and procedures have had mostly negative impact on culturally diverse populations since they do not reflect criteria representative of these groups. The much-needed policy analysis and evaluation in these areas has not been done. Due to budgetary constraints, we are now experiencing considerable activity resulting in a significant impact on populations which have not representation or data base to counter the actions taken against them. In fact, the challenge to these authorizing bodies to negotiate a social contract with culturally diverse population groups to protect them from quacks and incompetents is long overdue, and may result in a higher degree of adherence to changes than all the conferences and workshops on culturally diverse populations.

Recognizing the negative impact of the value base of the human services infrastructure and how that infrastructure negatively affects various culturally diverse populations, we can begin the process of overhauling the infrastructure according to a different set of assumptions. Although such work will require considerable effort and time, it is imperative that the reform process include several key tasks. Retraining helping professionals through continuing education, changing and improving the effectiveness of the service delivery system as it pertains to culturally diverse populations, adding multicultural content to certification and licensing examinations, and including multicultural criteria in the accreditation process are all initial steps in improving services for culturally diverse populations. These tasks must be incorporated in the processes of the legitimizing and authorizing bodies. Such changes require ongoing commitment as well as a passion for justice on the part of helping professionals and institutions. These initial steps must be followed by a comprehensive overhaul of the assumptions underpinning the value frameworks of the legitimizing and accrediting bodies. While there has been some significant work in modifying criteria in the accreditation of educational institutions, this significant step must be followed up in other sectors.

It is the work of institutional change that must take place as a next step to the voicing of concerns. Unfortunately, the helping professions prefer to change individuals rather than the legitimizing bodies that hamper their work with culturally diverse populations. So the rhetoric of institutional change has not been followed up with action on systems change. The goal is to ameliorate the symptoms, consequences, and outcomes generated by this indifference. The human services infrastructure needs to be challenged; strategies must be designed to open the process to evaluation and to important work that is currently being done. We look forward to the time when services will be provided by licensed or certified helping professionals who have passed examinations with sections on multicultural content and who have been trained in accredited programs that incorporate multicultural content as required by accreditation criteria. We also look forward to the time when treatment facilities and the helping professions will have to meet accreditation standards and criteria that incorporate multicultural content. The time for action is at hand.

The articles in this book are like cries for help in a forest of indifference and skepticism and, at times, outright hostility. They represent the best, yet they are not heeded, and for the most part, the work goes unnoticed. It is the hope that concerned readers will join to raise their voices and call attention to the plight of the substance abuser, the families, and the community.

JUAN RAMOS
Deputy Director for Prevention and Special Projects, OD
National Institute of Mental Health

PREFACE

Substance abuse is a major public health problem in this country. It has significant adverse affects upon the lives of millions of people: those who abuse alcohol and drugs as well as their families, employers, and communities. It is a complex problem that cannot be easily ameliorated.

Recently, substance abuse and the myriad of problems related to it have generated much public interest. There are a number of reasons for this. One of them is the federal government's initiatives in combatting drug abuse; another has to do with concern over IV drug use and its relation to AIDS. This mounting concern is reflected in increased funding for substance abuse prevention and treatment.

Those who work in the health and mental health fields come into contact with persons of diverse cultural backgrounds who have substance abuse problems. This book is concerned with substance abuse among Hispanics, the fastest growing minority group in the United States. The purpose of this book is to address the concerns of students and professionals who work with this population. It brings together in one place the current and most up-to-date research on this problem by well-known experts in the fields of alcohol and drug abuse. It is hoped that this information will be of assistance to an array of audiences which include scholars and researchers, professionals in the human services, and the general public.

The book is divided into two main sections: epidemiology/etiology and prevention/treatment. The first section presents an overview of the extent of substance abuse problems in Hispanic communities, differences among the various Hispanic subgroups, and some causal factors that may be involved. The second section presents strategies for prevention and approaches to treatment for this population. The book concludes with an Appendix that lists further resources that can be drawn upon by students and practitioners. This resource list is an added strength of the book, as it helps human services professionals find additional information from one source.

The editors wish to thank all of those who gave their time and assistance to this effort, especially the authors. They have contributed their considerable scholarship and expertise to this book, and we are grateful for their doing so. We also appreciate the comments of Dr. Juan Ramos, who points out in his foreword the systemic changes needed for substance abuse treatment and prevention to be truly effective in minority communities.

Dr. Mayers wishes to thank his co-authors, Federico Souflee and Carann Feazell, for their help in reading and writing numerous drafts of Chapter Twelve. In addition, he wishes to pay tribute to the memory of Dr. John Spiegel, professor emeritus of Brandeis University and past president of the American Psychiatric Association, for his ceaseless research in the area of ethnicity and its relationship to behavior, especially manifestations of mental health and illness.

CONTENTS

xvii

PART IV. APPENDICES

PART V. BIBLIOGRAPHY

HISPANIC SUBSTANCE ABUSE

PART I
INTRODUCTION

Chapter 1

HISPANIC SUBSTANCE ABUSE: AN OVERVIEW

RAYMOND SANCHEZ MAYERS AND BARBARA L. KAIL

The Hispanic* population is a heterogeneous group made up of a wide variety of Spanish-origin peoples with varying historical experiences, length of residence in the United States, and level of acculturation. The 1990 Census counted more than 22 million Hispanics in the United States, comprised mostly of Mexican Americans, Central/ South Americans, Puerto Ricans, and Cuban Americans (Census Bureau, 1990). Mexican Americans make up the largest percentage of Hispanics (63%), followed by Central and South Americans (14%), and Puerto Ricans (11%) (Census Bureau, 1991). Cubans consisted of 5% of the Hispanic population, while "Other Hispanics" were 8% (see Figure 1-1).

Yet the use of the term, Hispanic, creates many problems for researchers, as it refers to all of these peoples and often ignores the intracultural differences among them. There are wide disparities between Mexican Americans, Puerto Ricans, Cubans, Central and South Americans on indices such as educational attainment, socioeconomic status, and labor force participation. There are also disparities in patterns of drug use because there is a clustering of the various Hispanic subgroups in different parts of the country, just as types of drug use vary around the country. For example, Mexican Americans tend to be clustered in the Southwest, Puerto Ricans in the Northeast, and Cuban Americans in the Southeast. Yet, even with the differences, Hispanics often have more in common with each other than with the larger Anglo population because Hispanics share a common Spanish heritage.

Surprisingly, while there is much anthropological literature, there is little solid data on this group called Hispanic. One of the areas in which there is a dearth of literature is in the area of substance abuse—its extent

---

*The term "Hispanic" refers in general to all persons of Spanish origin. It will be used interchangeably with "Latino."

5

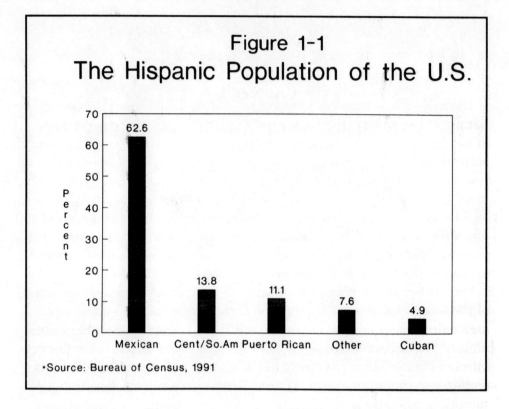

Figure 1-1
The Hispanic Population of the U.S.

*Source: Bureau of Census, 1991

in Hispanic communities, causal factors, prevention and treatment approaches.

Not only is the Hispanic population a complex, heterogeneous one, substance abuse itself is a complex issue imbued with political and moral overtones. When we use the word "substance abuse" we are referring to the use of a wide range of substances whose chemical composition, physiological effects, and legal consequences vary greatly. An important characteristic of substance abusers, however, is that they are often "polydrug" users, that is, they combine use of many substances at one time or over their abusing careers. The authors in this volume have contributed to our existing knowledge by synthesizing existing data and bringing to light new data to help in our discussions of substance abuse patterns among Hispanics.

PATTERNS OF ALCOHOL AND DRUG USE

Epidemiology

In many respects drinking patterns within the Hispanic community parallel those within the larger population. Alcocer reports frequency of alcohol use appears linked to gender, age, socioeconomic status, and acculturation. As in the general population, Hispanic women drink less compared to men. Many studies report Hispanic women are much more likely to abstain and those who do drink, drink less. This pertains to both the Mexican American and Puerto Rican communities. Drinking also decreases with age within the Hispanic community although at a slower rate than within the White or Black community. Drinking appears to increase with income and education.

With acculturation, drinking patterns change and approximate those of the mainstream culture. First generation, and hence less acculturated, men exhibit a pattern of low abstention, low frequency of drinking and high consumption on each occasion of drinking. The typical pattern is infrequent drinking to intoxication. The more acculturated second generation increases the frequency of drinking but retains the high consumption per occasion typical of the Mexican pattern. These patterns appear to reflect expectations and beliefs about alcohol. Gilbert, in her chapter, reports that among Mexican Americans, men hold more positive expectations about alcohol than women. They are also subject to fewer normative restrictions on the settings for drinking and the amount of consumption compared to women. Norms and restrictions on consumption become more permissive with acculturation as well.

There are also intracultural differences in drinking practices among Hispanics, often obscured by epidemiological studies. Puerto Rican men and women appear to adopt the pattern of low abstention and frequent drinking found among the larger population but retain the old pattern of drinking to intoxication. Mexican American men appear to have higher rates of abstention, but those who drink, drink heavily compared to other Hispanic men. Hispanic Health and Nutrition Examination Survey (HHANES) data also suggest this sub-group holds more permissive norms toward drunkenness than Cubans and Puerto Ricans. Dominicans stress moderation in drinking with time in the U.S., favoring social control.

Among Hispanic youth, some studies suggest higher levels of drink-

ing compared to Whites and Blacks while other studies do not find
ethnic differences. The literature does suggest that alcohol is part of a
larger substance use/abuse phenomena, a gateway drug, among all ethnic groups studied.

As with alcohol, patterns of drug use do not differ greatly among
Whites, Blacks, and Hispanics, reflecting patterns in the larger community.
Household surveys both nationally and in Texas suggest marijuana is
the most commonly used illicit drug with much smaller percentages
using stimulants, tranquilizers, inhalants, cocaine and heroin. Whites
use all drugs at greater levels than Hispanics, with cocaine being the one
interesting exception. Among the youngest Hispanics (12–17 year olds)
included in the national household survey conducted by the National
Institute on Drug Abuse (NIDA), the rate of cocaine use by Hispanic
males and females exceeds that of their White and Black counterparts
(see Figure 1-2). Data based on the Hispanic Health and Nutrition
Examination Survey (HHANES) suggest that except for inhalants, drug
use is most prevalent among the Puerto Rican community and least
prevalent among the Cuban community.

Inhalant use in the Hispanic community has been the subject of
intense study. The bulk of this research consists of local/community/school-
based studies. In this volume, Mata and colleagues classify users as
experimental, social, or chronic. These authors also note a high noncontinuation rate of inhalant use suggesting that the bulk of inhalant users
are either experimental or move on to other drugs. In fact some of the
unique aspects of inhalant use as the low cost, relative availability, and
early onset of use make this activity a gateway to other illicit drug use.

Analyses reported in this volume by Kail suggest predictors of use
also follow patterns of the larger community. Socioeconomic status,
gender, and peer use are all related to self use. Within the Mexican
American community, males with friends who use drugs are particularly likely to use drugs themselves. However, entry into drug abuse
among Mexican Americans may have two unique aspects: the role of
familial drug use, and acculturation. Reported parental abuse of alcohol
and drugs is lowest among Mexican Americans. Yet the expectation
remains that this variable would be related to self use. This is not so
in the data reported here, in sharp contrast to other studies focusing on
the role of family disruption and discord in drug use. Acculturation also
appears to play a mediating role. Acculturation increases the likelihood
of acquiring drug using friends and when combined with low education

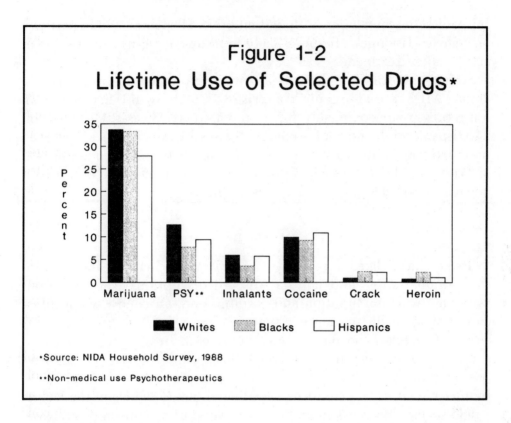

Figure 1-2
Lifetime Use of Selected Drugs*

•Source: NIDA Household Survey, 1988

••Non-medical use Psychotherapeutics

and income greatly enhances the likelihood of drug use. Acculturation accompanied by inclusion in the mainstream economy decreases the probability of use.

There are at least two consequences associated with drug use by Hispanics: crime and AIDS. Chapters by De La Rosa and Caris and Soriano explore these themes. De La Rosa and Caris report that Hispanic addicts are particularly likely to be involved in drug dealing and violent crime compared to White and Black addicts. In fact, Hispanics are particularly likely to be both perpetrators and victims of drug-related violent crime, at least based on police reports. Gang involvement may nurture such activities through socialization into norms, especially that of "locura" (being a "wild and crazy guy"). However, Moore (1990) argues drug-related criminal activities are more a product of individual gang member involvement rather than activities sponsored by the gang as a group. When not involved in narcotic use, crime among Hispanics and Whites drops. Methadone treatment does appear to have a short term effect in reducing criminal activities and narcotics use. Yet, among

Hispanics, treatment appears to less effective. Hispanics, and in particular female Hispanics, are more likely to resume drug use and criminal activity after treatment.

Soriano reports that there is an over representation of Hispanics among AIDS cases; Hispanics comprise 8.4% of the total U.S. population but represent approximately 16% of reported AIDS cases. Over half of all Hispanic adult and adolescent AIDS cases are associated with intravenous drug use. This is a startlingly high rate when compared to the 14% of White non-Hispanics who appear to have contracted AIDS through behavior associated with intravenous drug use.

Etiology

Two themes related to etiology emerge from the material included in this volume: stress and familial discord/disruption, especially that associated with immigration and acculturation. Of course, yet a third consideration is the influence of the peer group.

Both Cervantes and Barrera note the role of stress in the etiology of substance abuse. Cervantes notes the following stressors: lack of English-speaking ability; lack of job skills; living in poor neighborhoods with high crime rates; and concerns over liberal family beliefs of the larger Anglo society. Barrera's model of social support systems and drug use includes stress as a mediating factor which social support systems reduce, therefore reducing the probability of substance use and abuse. He suggests that stress interacts with such potential predispositions to drug use or stress may contribute directly to negative affective states which the individual tries to self-medicate with psychoactive substances.

Three different chapters authored by Cervantes, Barrera, and Santiesteban and colleagues all consider familial stress and disruption as a primary contributor to substance abuse. Cervantes, based on his sample of Mexican Americans, reports a relationship between family disruption such as parental illness, absence, or drinking, and high levels of emotional distress among his sample of Mexican Americans. Leaving friends and relatives when migrating is also a source of distress.

Cervantes also notes the role of familial disorganization and acculturative stress. He finds that families at greatest risk consist of a son who rejects the culture and an under-acculturated mother who shows neurotic patterns of behavior. Santiesteban and colleagues also suggest that differential rates of acculturation among family members creates stress.

Intergenerational conflicts between adolescents and their parents often intermingle with behavioral and value conflicts stemming from the differential rates of acculturation. Several characteristics of families that protect against problem behaviors are good family management skills; communication characterized by directness, reciprocity and specificity; flexibility in handling intra-familial and extra-familial stressors in adaptive ways; and conflict resolution skills.

Within the Hispanic community, peer use of drugs remains a consistent and important predictor of drug use. Within the Puerto Rican, Mexican American, and Cuban American communities, the peer group typically introduces the youth to the drug and provides instructions on drug use as well. Among regular drug users the peer group provides support in obtaining funds as well as obtaining the substance itself.

PREVENTION/TREATMENT

All the material in this section on prevention and treatment stresses the notion that services must be culturally sensitive to be effective. Several common themes emerge when attempting to implement this directive: the importance of family—"familismo"; the value attached to collectivism/cooperation as opposed to competition; the notion of "personalismo"; expectations of "simpatia"—getting along well with others; the role of "respeto" in dealing with individuals; and an action orientation to problem solving.

As mentioned by Delgado and Humm-Delgado, and Santiesteban, et al., a distinctive characteristic of Hispanic culture is the importance of the family. "Familismo" expresses a vision of the family as the center of social support characterized by solidarity, harmony, cooperation, strong emotional ties and reciprocal kinship obligations. Problems are to be handled and kept within the family as much as possible so as not to dishonor the family name. While a strength of this community, this characteristic can also at times discourage help-seeking. To be effective, preventive and treatment efforts need to include the family as a whole whenever possible.

Personalismo, simpatia and respeto are likely to characterize interaction between provider and client. Personalismo refers to a preference for individualized treatment rather than rules which might prevent arbitrary treatment and discrimination but appear rather cold. Personal relationships must be based on simpatia and respeto. Simpatia refers to the importance placed on manners, courtesy, and cooperation. Just as interpersonal conflict is discouraged, one must also strive to be pleasant in interactions. The "small talk" and socialization prior to engaging in any group or individual treatment/preventive intervention are important components of simpatia. Respeto refers to respect both provided to the provider—disagreement is not expressed directly—and expected by the recipient. A simple example might be that the provider might anticipate when conversing in Spanish to use the more formal "usted" rather than the informal "tu."

Delgado speaks of a preference for an action orientation to problem solving in the counseling situation. This connotes the use of a more directive and action-oriented approach rather than a focus on historical insight into problems and changing cognitions. The mutual aid/self-help group uses this directive approach in trying to meet the needs of individuals. In fact, since self-help groups emphasize face-to-face interactions and reject the impersonality of large bureaucratic systems, they can be a useful adjunct to more traditional treatment, especially in the after-care phase of treatment.

Delgado and Humm-Delgado say that while there have been barriers to use of self-help groups by Latinos in agency settings, there is a long tradition of mutual aid in Latino communities. This tradition may make Hispanics well-disposed to using such groups. For acceptance of agency-based self-help groups by Hispanics however, the cultural characteristics outlined above must be taken into account, as well as an understanding of attitudes towards substance abusers. A well-accepted agency in the Latino community can be a referral agent, a resource, an advocate, or even provide institutional legitimacy for such groups.

Involvement of the whole family has been a preventive approach described by Cervantes in the Hispanic Family Intervention Program. This program tries to enhance individual and family coping skills in order to strengthen ties to important social institutions and reduce the risk of later substance abuse in Hispanic children. It uses a psycho-educational approach which includes coping skill enhancement, substance abuse education, and academic skill building.

Also using the cultural characteristics of Latinos described above, Santiesteban et al. describe a conceptual model and therapeutic approach found effective in the engagement and treatment of Hispanic substance abusing youth. In contrast to the population described by Cervantes as pre-clinical, the youth in Santiesteban et al.'s study have already become involved in substance abuse. Some obstacles to effective treatment for these youth include identification of the user, and resistance to entering treatment. They detail a procedure called Strategic Structural Systems Engagement (SSSE), developed to engage adolescent abusers and their families in treatment. They have also developed an innovative approach to working with individual family members when the rest of the family is difficult to engage in treatment. This approach, called One Person Family Therapy, proceeds when only one person comes to therapy. The design of these therapeutic approaches is specifically for Latino populations. What is significant about them is that they are based on empirical data in a clinical setting.

Mayers et al. present an approach to working with Latinos within the workplace. They suggest that employee assistance professionals, mental health counselors, and others interested in developing prevention programs aimed at Latino populations need to borrow the market research strategies of business. This means that prevention planners must familiarize themselves with the target market, they must develop appropriate strategies for that market, and they must keep appropriate data on the effectiveness of their approaches.

Treatment facilities, especially for-profit private agencies, make millions of dollars a year in providing in-patient and out-patient treatment of various kinds. Unfortunately, because many Latinos are among the working poor and often lack health insurance, they are unable to afford these more costly types of treatment. Even when referred for treatment, it may not be of a culturally appropriate nature and thus may not have the most positive outcome for the substance abusing client. Mayers et al. point to some measures mental health or employee assistance professionals can use to help coordinate culturally sensitive substance abuse treatment for Hispanics. This includes a thorough inventory of community resources available, such as bilingual/bicultural counselors, and religious leaders.

CONCLUSION

Even given the major contributions of the authors in this volume, there is much work to be done, for there is much we do not know. There is a paucity of research on substance abuse among Hispanics. The Hispanic population tends to be either entirely overlooked, or all the subgroups are aggregated so that it is impossible to make distinctions between them. One of the major problems in the substance abuse literature is the lack of standardization of data collection instruments that prevents meaningful comparisons across studies. Often studies use small sample sizes that make generalization difficult. It is critical that researchers expand their efforts, especially in the areas of prevention and treatment of substance abuse with Hispanic populations. We therefore set forth a research agenda for those interested in effectively attacking the problem of substance abuse among Hispanics by applying strategies based on empirical evidence.

Epidemiology/Etiology

While there have been studies on the epidemiology of substance abuse cited in this chapter and in this volume, etiological questions are more difficult to study and generalize from. Yet there is much we do not know. For example, what role do the following factors play in use/misuse of addictive substances: acculturation, gender socialization, natural/social support systems, peer groupings? And what might be some of the intracultural differences among Hispanics in these processes?

Prevention

Much money is spent on preventive efforts. However, it is often difficult to show results from such efforts since they sometimes are not manifest until some years after. For example, to evaluate the success of smoking prevention aimed at elementary school children one would have to do a longitudinal study over a number of years. The same applies to prevention aimed at changing attitudes or behaviors involving alcohol or drugs.

For primary prevention to be successful, it must combine knowledge of a target population with marketing skills. Often agencies involved in prevention have one component but not the other and they do little evaluation. To refine knowledge of the target population we need to know: for what segment of the population are the traditional Latino values most meaningful? In what ways can these values be used to transmit positive preventive behaviors and attitudes? What is most effective with the more acculturated Latino youth?

Prevention programs should have a rigorous evaluative component built in to them or the time and money involved may not achieve desired results. To acquire useful data, a pre- and post-test research design is most suitable. A comparison of a baseline of target behaviors or attitudes with behaviors or attitudes after the introduction of a prevention program may yield important change data. While results of prevention efforts often do not show up for years, short-term changes may result and need documentation. In addition, even short-term changes in behavior or attitudes can be the bases for future efforts.

Treatment

While we have recently learned much about the epidemiology of Hispanic substance abuse, we still know little about what is effective treatment for this problem. For example, what factors enter into decisions to seek treatment, to stay in treatment, and maintain new lifestyles after treatment? What are the differences between those Latinos who seek treatment and those who do not? What are the critical factors or predictors of successful adjustment after treatment? What role does gender play in treatment decisions? And how are the responses to these questions unique to Latinas as compared to Whites, and what intracultural differences exit?

Treatment centers need to build in more efficient monitoring and evaluating systems to measure the results of their efforts. More effort needs to take place in the long-term follow-up of treatment effects among Hispanic abusers. While it is often difficult to do long-term evaluation of treatment for a variety of reasons, chief among them the dispersal of the treatment population, there is no other way that we can know if there is any efficacy to treatment.

Finally, there should be more inclusion of Latinos as a separate category in substance abuse reporting at all levels. Not only should Hispanic data be separated from White and Black, there should also be separate analyses of the major Hispanic subgroups. Oversampling of Hispanics should be done, if necessary, to ensure adequate representation of Hispanics in substance abuse data. Finally, there is a need for broader dissemination of results to familiarize those working in the human services of successful approaches to prevention and treatment of Hispanic substance abuse. Additional topics and areas for further research are enunciated by our authors.

As stated by Ramos in the Preface to this volume, there are few organized, institutional-level approaches to dealing with Hispanic substance abuse. While the much-touted war on drugs focused on interdiction in Latin America, we were, and still are, losing the war at home.

PART II
EPIDEMIOLOGY/ETIOLOGY

Chapter 2

PATTERNS AND PREDICTORS OF DRUG ABUSE WITHIN THE CHICANO COMMUNITY

BARBARA LYNN KAIL

INTRODUCTION

Drug use appears to be a growing problem, at least within some segments of the Hispanic community. Yet our knowledge remains quite limited. This chapter hopes to fill two gaps within the current literature. First, much of the epidemiological literature subsumes different Hispanic communities under one label (e.g., the NIDA household surveys). These data offer a seemingly meaningful, but in fact muddy, picture of drug use within the Hispanic community. A second gap in the literature is the lack of information on availability and accessibility of drugs. Other epidemiological studies, even those that do consider differences among Hispanic groups such as the Hispanic Health and Nutrition Evaluation Survey (HHANES), focus on actual measures of use. These data sets do not include measures of availability or other aspects of use beyond simple incidence and prevalence, such as source of drug, source of funds and setting in which drugs are used.

This chapter attempts to address these two issues based on a secondary analysis of data collected by the Texas Commission on Alcohol and Drug Abuse. These data contain measures of availability for ten substances or classes of substances. The Hispanics in this study are almost exclusively of Mexican ancestry, allowing for a closer examination of patterns within one portion of the Hispanic community. The analysis begins with comparisons of Whites, Blacks and Mexican Americans on measures of drug use and availability. The chapter then goes on to consider ethnic differences in predictors of use and availability. Naturally, the variables considered are limited by the constraints of the data. However, there is good reason to believe that peer group, familial substance abuse, gender, socioeconomic status, and acculturation may all play an important part in the extent to which an individual may have access to and use drugs.

19

Each of these factors and the relevant literature will be considered in turn below.

Patterns of Use and Access

De la Rosa (1991) and De la Rosa, Khalsa, and Rouse (1990) comprehensively review patterns of use and access based on available epidemiological literature. National surveys generally report lower levels of lifetime use within the Hispanic community, compared to Blacks and Whites, for all drugs considered here. However, the number and proportion of Hispanics who have tried illicit drugs at least once appears to be increasing (De la Rosa, 1991). It also appears that for those who go on to heroin use, the typical sequencing of drugs does not differ greatly from other ethnic groups; marijuana is still the first drug used (Anglin, 1988; Kandel, 1975; Maddux and Desmond, 1981). There are some indications that while national data has not found Hispanics more likely to use inhalants, there may well be pockets of more extensive use in circumscribed areas (Mata & Andrews, 1988; Padilla, Padilla, Morales, Olmedo & Ramirez, 1979). In certain high risk Hispanic subgroups and families, drug abuse may well be a serious chronic multigenerational problem (Booth, Castro & Moore, 1990; Morales, 1984).

Peer Group

Within the literature there is a long history of association between peer use and self use. Many theories of use include the peer as a component (e.g. Jessor & Jessor, 1980) while some make it the centerpiece (e.g. Sutherland and Cressey, 1978; Johnson, 1980). There is a wealth of literature documenting the relationship between friends use of drugs and own use of drugs beginning with some of the earliest research in the area; this relationship is perhaps the most consistently reported within the field.

Within the Hispanic community, there are indications that the same relationship holds. Booth, Castro and Anglin (1990) in their review of the literature report that, among Hispanics, friends' use is the strongest single factor influencing initiation and continued drug use. Both Fitzpatrick (1990) and Page (1990) describe a subculture within the Puerto Rican and Cuban communities in which the peer group introduces the youth to marijuana, usually the first drug of experimentation, and provides rudimentary smoking instructions as well. Moore (1990) describes the phenomenon among Mexican Americans. She notes that loyalty to age peers is an important value and saying "no" to a member of that group may jeopardize the adolescent's standing. Long (1990) and Mata and Jorquez (1988) describe a continued reliance among addicts within the Mexican American community on personal social support networks for learning to use drugs, obtaining drugs, and generally coping with the chaos and exigencies of a life committed to heroin use.

Family

Before discussing the impact of the family on drug use, the unique role the family occupies within the Hispanic community must be considered. Cohesiveness and emotional closeness are typically used to describe the Hispanic family. Valle and Bensussen (1985) identify kinship networks, including individuals entering the family by birth, adoption or marriage, as important naturally occurring support systems within the Hispanic community. De La Rosa (1988) and Rio et al. (see their chapter in this book) note this phenomenon within the Puerto Rican and Cuban communities. Alvirez and Bean (1976) describe this aspect of the Mexican American community in depth and point to familism as one of the most salient characteristics of the Chicano culture. Sabogal and colleagues examined three components of this concept: familial obligations, perceived support from the family, and the family as referents. These authors found that even the most acculturated of their Hispanic sample continued to perceive the family as a strong source of support (Sabogal, F. Marin, G. Otero-Sabogal, VanOss Marin & Perez Stable, 1987).

The literature around family and drug use may be characterized by three themes: The presence of both mother and father and an extended family decreases the probability of drug use; discord in the family is conducive to drug use, perhaps because of differential rates of acculturation; use by family members is conducive to drug use and when combined with peer use has a synergistic effect on self use. The first two themes will be considered briefly while the last one will be considered in greater depth because of its importance in the analysis.

There is a wealth of literature which suggests that the presence of both parents and an extended family may provide support to the adolescent and decrease the likelihood of experimentation with drugs. Within the Hispanic community there are indications that support from, and involvement with, both proximate and extended family is associated with lower levels of stress and substance abuse (e.g. De La Rosa, 1988;

Valle and Bensussen, 1985). Other qualitative studies more specifically suggest that family disruption and a lack of extended family may predispose adolescents to drug use. On the other hand, such strong familial ties may actually permit the maintenance of an addiction as Mexican American, Puerto Rican, and Cuban families are likely to protect their members who are in "trouble" (Fitzpatrick, 1990; Morales, 1984).

Discord may also be associated with substance abuse within the Hispanic family. Several authors (e.g., Rio and colleagues in this book) note that among the families they work with around substance abuse issues, there seems to be a high level of conflict and discord. The extent to which this conflict is explicitly related to issues of acculturation will be considered later.

Drug use by family members may have the same effect on youth regardless of their ethnicity. Within the White community, there are indications that drug use by parents and siblings increases the probability of self drug use. When combined with a peer group that also uses drugs, there may be a synergistic effect greater than the impact of either one alone. Samples of Mexican American drug users also suggest family use may have an impact on self use. Maddux and Desmond (1981) found their sample of Mexican American heroin addicts reported drug use by one-third of their siblings and alcoholism for one-third of their fathers. Long (1990) in his qualitative study of a drug-using barrio gang found these youth had models within the family of drug-taking and drinking. Fully two-fifths reported that at least one member of their childhood family had a problem with alcohol. However, Moore (1990), based on her study of a female barrio gang, describes what she terms a "cholo" family characterized by longstanding gang involvement by several members, illegal income, usually from drug dealing, and imprisonment. This exposure did not kindle an early personal interest in heroin among these girls but was actually off-putting.

Gender-Related Differences

As within other communities, Hispanic males use illicit drugs at a higher rate than females (e.g. National Institute on Drug Abuse, 1991). However, these gender-related differences appear to be even more extensive among Hispanics compared to Whites and Blacks. Hispanic women are much less likely to use all illegal drugs compared to Hispanic males. The one exception appears to be cocaine use among the youngest cohort of teenagers where the gender-related differences disappear. Within the

Hispanic community, gender differences appear to be smallest among Puerto Ricans and largest among Mexican Americans (National Institute on Drug Abuse, 1987).

Socioeconomic Status

De La Rosa (1990) and others have suggested that poverty, limited school and employment opportunities and discrimination all contribute to a propensity toward drug abuse. Poverty is generally associated with greater substance abuse, regardless of ethnicity (Booth, Castro & Anglin, 1990). Racial and linguistic barriers when placed in the context of deindustrialization and changes in the occupational structure may well relegate many Hispanics to an "underclass" status described by William Julius Wilson (Glick & Moore, 1990). There is an association between poverty, low educational attainment and addiction which, along with local Hispanic connections to Latin American drug sources, may make entering the underground economy particularly attractive (Morales, 1984). However, De La Rosa and colleagues note that based on their review of the literature, recent findings suggest Hispanics with somewhat higher incomes report more frequent use of illegal drugs (De La Rosa et al., 1990).

Acculturation.

A number of researchers have suggested theoretical and treatment models which focus on the stresses of acculturation. The "agringado" may be caught between two cultural worlds. The discrepancies may then lead to misunderstandings and behavioral problems. Booth, Castro and Anglin (1990) note that the level of acculturation may be an important moderating variable in understanding differences among Hispanic subgroups in the use of various drugs. Acculturation may also occur differently for Mexican Americans, Cubans and Puerto Ricans.

Among the Cuban community, several authors link substance abuse to the disruption caused by immigration and acculturation within the Cuban community (Booth, Castro & Anglin, 1990; Page, 1990). Rio and colleagues in their work (see their chapter in this book) consider acculturation a central issue in their treatment model, focusing upon the differential rates at which parents and children acculturate and the impact upon family dynamics.

Within the Mexican American community, several studies suggest that there is a direct relationship between acculturation and substance abuse, and that those more acculturated are more likely to abuse drugs. Amaro, Whittaker, Coffman and Heeren (1990), based on HHANES data, find that the use of marijuana and cocaine is higher among Hispanics of all groups who are more acculturated. Overall, acculturation into U.S. society, as reflected by language use, is related to a higher prevalence of illicit drug use, independent of socioeconomic status. Acculturation appears to have the greatest effects on drug use among those who are least educated. Those highly acculturated but not educated are most likely to report drug use. Barrett, Joe and Simpson (1991) suggest acculturation may have an indirect influence on inhalant use through the differential impact of socializing influences such as family, school, peer relationships and the psychological status of the individual. Caetano (1987a) reports a similar relationship between alcohol use and acculturation. He finds that those Mexican Americans who are more acculturated drink more frequently in a greater number of different settings, a pattern closer to the majority culture.

Acculturation also appears to vary by sex in its relationship to drug use. Amaro and colleagues (1990) find among Mexican Americans that acculturation is more highly related to marijuana use among women. This is consistent with findings that acculturation is more strongly associated with alcohol use among Mexican American women than men (Caetano, 1987a). There may well be, then, an interaction between acculturation and SES and gender.

Based on the literature above, one would expect that:

1. There might not be great differences in the types of drugs used among the three ethnic groups considered here, but that Hispanics would have lower levels of use. Depending on whether localized groups of drug users were captured, Mexican Americans in this sample might show some differences, for example, in inhalant use.

2. The relationship of peer group to use and access to drugs will be strong among all three ethnic groups.

3. Family use may be more strongly related to use and access among the Mexican Americans in this sample compared to Whites and Blacks.

4. Gender and socioeconomic status will be strongly related to use and access among all three ethnic groups.

5. Among Mexican Americans in this sample, the relationship of these predictors to access to drugs will be mediated by acculturation.

METHODOLOGY

Design and Sample

This analysis is based on a household survey conducted by the Texas Commission on Drug and Alcohol Abuse in Spring of 1988. The design is modeled primarily after the household surveys conducted by the National Institute on Drug Abuse.

The sample was selected from randomly generated telephone numbers and stratified for three racial and ethnic groups (Anglos, Blacks, and Mexican Americans), three age groups (18–25, 26–34 and 35+), and eight geographical regions. A total of 5,096 interviews are included in the data set. The cooperation rate was 75%. By design, the study over-sampled racial and ethnic minorities, younger age groups, and particular geographic regions so that analysis on sub-groups could be conducted at later points in time. So that estimates would reflect the population of Texas, a multistage weighting procedure was used. Weights were developed by comparing the distribution of age, ethnicity, and residence in the sample to Texas Department of Health population projections for 1988. Respondents were then assigned a weight according to their age, ethnicity and residence. These weights tended to decrease the value of oversampled observations and adjust final estimates to reflect more accurately the actual demographic distribution of the adult population of Texas. (Spence, Fredlund & Kavinsky, 1989).

The sample on which this analysis is based excludes two groups: individuals who consider themselves something other than White, Black, or Hispanic and individuals aged 35 and older. As a group the "other" category, largely Asian, was too small to include in an ethnic analysis. Use of illicit substances was very low among those aged 35 and older and after some initial exploration the most productive route appeared to be limiting the sample to those aged 18–34. A total of 1,146 Whites, 513 Blacks, and 660 Mexican Americans are included in the analysis presented below.

Readers are cautioned that the sample does contain several biases. By design, data were collected among Texans living in households with telephones. Of course, this limits generalization to other parts of the country. The geographic location and data also suggest that the Hispanics in this sample are almost exclusively of Mexican descent, again limiting generalization to other groups of Hispanics. Approximately 10% of Texas households without telephones are not included. It appears unlikely that the addition of these households would change estimates by more than 1% because of their relatively small size. Texans not living in households (e.g. the homeless, the institutionalized) are also not included in the sample. Again this is a small component of the general population so that even large differences in substance use patterns of these groups would produce little change in estimates for the overall population (Spence, Fredlund & Kavinsky, 1989).

Measures

Respondents were interviewed over the telephone. Detailed questions about the following 10 substances or classes of substances concerning access and use were included in the instrument: tobacco, alcohol, marijuana, inhalants, cocaine and crack, stimulants, sedatives and tranquilizers, heroin, opiates other than heroin, and psychedelics. In addition, the instrument also contained questions regarding substance-related problems, opinions about drug use, drug and alcohol treatment centers, law enforcement issues and general demographics. The format was such that individuals who have used relatively few substances were asked relatively few questions. A Spanish version of the questionnaire was administered as needed by bilingual interviewers (Spence, Fredlund & Kavinsky, 1989).

Use and availability: For each of the ten substances or classes of substances listed earlier each respondent was first asked "About how old were you when you first had the opportunity to try _____." Unless the respondent reported never having the opportunity to try the substance he/she was asked "About how old were you the first time you actually used/tried _____." The one exception is inhalants where age at first opportunity was not asked.

A number of surveys have established the utility of self-reported information in estimating the incidence and prevalence of substance use. For a study of this nature indeed self-report appears to be the only feasible means of collecting data. For the study as a whole ($N = 5,096$) the Texas Commission on Alcohol and Drug Abuse estimates the following confidence limits. For all adults, sample estimates of incidence and prevalence would vary from rates for the total population only $\pm 2\%$, 95% of the time. Within each age grouping, estimates of incidence and prevalence would vary only $\pm 3.9\%$, 95% of the time (Spence, Fredlund & Kavinsky, 1989, p. 42).

Several other variables measuring patterns of use are included in this analysis. Those respondents who reported using at least one of the ten classes of drugs listed above were asked the source of the drug: family member, friend, dealer, doctor, or someone else. A second question asked about the source of funds for drug purchases during the period of first use. A final question asked "Around the time you *first* tried one of the drugs you have had for non-medical purposes, where were you most likely to be? Were you more likely to be: at school, at a party, at work, at home, at the home of a friend, in a motor vehicle or somewhere else."

Peer group use: Respondents were asked the extent to which the friends or people they associate with frequently used each of nine substances (marijuana, inhalants, cocaine, crack, uppers, downers, heroin, other opiates and psychedelics). Available responses were most, some, or none. These responses were coded from 2 to 0 and added so that a 0 represents no use at all by friends and an 18 indicates most of the respondent's friends use all of the drugs listed.

Parental use: Parental history of drug or alcohol use is based simply on the respondents report of mother or father using drugs, drinking heavily or having a drinking problem. The variable is a dichotomy simply indicating 1 for the presence of such a history and 0 for absence. Answers were added for both mother and father for a composite measure.

Acculturation: The acculturation index was calculated only for self-identified Mexican Americans and consists of three items. Respondents were asked what language was used most often in the household, coded 0 for English or 1 for Spanish or bilingual Spanish/English. Respondents were also asked the number of years they had lived in Texas coded 0 for "all life" and 1 for having lived elsewhere at least a portion of one's life. Those who had not lived in Texas their whole life were asked where they had lived before moving to Texas, coded 1 for Mexico and 0 for another state within the U.S. The "0" category also includes 21 Hispanic individuals who reported coming from a country other than Mexico as well as those reporting life-long residency in Texas. These items are highly correlated with one another; the phi-coefficient for language use and length of residence is .342.

Responses to these three items were added so the scale has a range from 0 to 3. A 3 represents those who came from Mexico prior to living in Texas and spoke Spanish in the home. A 0 represents a Mexican American individual who has lifelong residency in Texas and speaks primarily English at home. This latter group is clearly first, if not second, generation American.

Other measures of acculturation highlight the strengths and weaknesses of the available scale. Marin and colleagues (1987) combined length of residence, generation, and self identification into an acculturation index similar to the one used here. This index was then used to assess the reliability and validity of an acculturation scale that consists of 12 items measuring preferences for speaking a given language in a number of settings, use and preference of English/Spanish language media and preferred ethnicity of those with whom the respondent interacts. The acculturation index correlated highly with the 12 item scale and the 5 items indicating language preference performed almost as well as the full scale. Reliability coefficients for the shorter 5 item scale were also comparable to those of the full 12 item scale. Other studies cited by Marin (1987) highlight the significance of language in acculturation and the importance of language in self-identification as Hispanic. The measure used in this study does indeed contain one item concerning language preference but would have been stronger had it contained more items in this area. There does appear to be some rationale for including the rough measures of residence and generational status, and this author believes such inclusion increases both the reliability and validity of the measure.

FINDINGS

Patterns of Substance Use

There are significant differences in the use of the drugs considered here among the three ethnic groups (data not shown in tabular form). Whites report significantly higher rates of use for all substances. Mexican Americans are somewhat more likely than Blacks to report use of inhalants, uppers and psychedelic drugs. Mexican Americans are least likely of all groups to report use of marijuana, cocaine, downers and other opiates. On an overall measure of any illicit drug use, Mexican Americans report the lowest rate of the three groups (data not shown in tabular form). A more extensive discussion can be found in the report of the main findings from this survey (Spence, Fredlund & Kavinsky, 1989).

Whites in this sample also report having marijuana, cocaine and uppers available at younger ages (see Table 2-1). Blacks report the oldest age of availability of these substances with Hispanics in the middle. Surprisingly, there are no significant differences in age of first use of the drugs considered here with the exception of marijuana (See Table 2-1). Blacks report a substantially higher age at first use of marijuana compared to Whites and Hispanics.

Table 2-1   Mean Age Of Availability and First Use For Selected Drugs By Ethnicity

	N	Whites	MAmer	Black	F
Mean age of Availability for:					
Marijuana	1707	16.02	16.40	16.83	10.22**
Cocaine	826	19.70	19.92	20.56	4.33*
Uppers	804	17.58	17.40	18.48	3.87*
Downers	596	17.55	17.02	17.94	1.18
Psychedelics	594	17.83	18.07	18.17	1.18
Mean age of first use for:					
Marijuana	1023	16.63	16.62	17.52	5.90**
Inhalants	191	16.32	16.41	14.76	.53
Cocaine	350	20.20	20.44	20.52	.80
Uppers	424	17.96	17.94	18.71	1.20
Downers	214	17.83	18.06	18.37	.65
Psychedelics	269	17.91	18.69	18.91	2.64

* $p < .01$
** $p < .001$

Because usage of these drugs are highly intercorrelated with one another, a multiple discriminant analysis was conducted to determine if these three groups exhibit distinguishable patterns of drug use at the multivariate level (See Table 2-2). The data suggest that there is one function worth considering, and that function discriminates only very weakly; the squared canonical correlation is .03 and the eigenvalue for this function is .03. It appears that this function discriminates a White

pattern from a minority group pattern. The former is characterized by
the use of uppers, marijuana, and psychedelics while the minority pattern is more likely to include inhalants and cocaine. However, these
patterns do not discriminate very well among the groups.

Table 2-2   Multiple Discriminant Analysis for Whites,
Mexican-Americans, and Blacks with Reported Drug Use

Squared Canonical Correlation = ..03
Wilkes Lambda = .96
N = 2282

Standardized canonical coefficients
Use marijuana	.22
Use inhalants	.11
Use cocaine	-.04
Use uppers	.60
Use downers	.20
Use psychedelics	.23

Centroids
Whites	.15
Mexican-Americans	-.25
Blacks	-.26

* $p < .01$
** $p < .001$

Other Patterns of Use

Other measures describing usage patterns do not appear to differ
greatly among the three groups, with the exception of economics. All
three groups secure their drugs primarily from friends and typically use
the drug at a party or friend's home. This would appear to be a pattern
of recreational use dominated by marijuana. Over half the sample report
using funds from illegal activities to purchase drugs. Whites *are* significantly more likely to report a legitimate source of funds compared to
Mexican Americans and Blacks (data not shown in tabular form).

Mexican Americans in this sample report lower levels of parental and
friend use compared to Whites and Blacks. Roughly one-quarter of the

Blacks and Whites report abuse of drugs or alcohol by parents while one-fifth of the Mexican Americans report such use. Mexican Americans also report a significantly lower mean on the measure of friends use compared to the other two groups considered here (data not shown in tabular form).

Predictors of Substance Abuse Among Mexican Americans

Friends' use is strongly correlated with the use of each of the illicit drugs considered here (correlations range from .24 to .43; see Table 2-3). As expected, this is true for Whites and Blacks as well.

Parental use is perhaps the most interesting and surprising of variables considered in this analysis. Use of drugs and/or abuse of alcohol is not significantly related to the self-reported use of any of the drugs considered here (see Table 2-3). This is in stark contrast to findings for Whites where parental use is significantly related to self use of all illicit drugs included in the analysis. Findings for Blacks also report parental use is significantly related to self use of marijuana and uppers. Parental use is also not related to friends' use among the Mexican Americans and very weakly related among Blacks in this sample while these variables are strongly correlated among Whites. This suggests the synergistic relationship described in the literature above may exist largely among Whites.

Socioeconomic status may be more highly related to drug abuse among Hispanics compared to Blacks and Whites but this relationship is, at best, moderate. Income, education, and working are all positively related to marijuana use. Education is also positively related to the use of a number of other illicit substances (see Table 2-3). These variables are not nearly as extensively or strongly related for Blacks and Whites in this sample. Among these two ethnic groups, neither income or education are significantly related to any of the drugs considered here. It may be that among the Mexican-Americans, socioeconomic status is acting as a proxy for acculturation.

Gender differences in drug use do appear to be somewhat more pronounced among Mexican Americans and Blacks in this sample. Mexican American women are significantly less likely to report use of marijuana, cocaine, and uppers. Black women report less use of marijuana, inhalants and uppers compared to men. White women report less use of only marijuana and cocaine.

Table 2-3 Correlation Matrix of Drug Use and Selected Predictors for Mexican-Americans (N = 665)

	1	2	3	4	5	6	7	8	9	10	11	12	13	14	15
1. Use marijuana	1.00														
2. Use inhalants	.35**	1.00													
3. Use cocaine	.43**	.37**	1.00												
4. Use uppers	.41**	.24**	.46**	1.00											
5. Use downers	.28**	.23**	.46**	.43**	1.00										
6. Use psychedelics	.36**	.45**	.59**	.43**	.43**	1.00									
7. Source of drug	.24**	.03	-.16*	-.11	-.03	-.01	1.00								
8. Source of money	-.10	.22**	.37**	.30**	.32**	.40**	-.23**	1.00							
9. Setting	.17*	.08	.12	-.04	.07	.03	.24**	.04	1.00						
10. Parental use	.05	.05	.05	-.03	.00	.05	.01	.03	.01	1.00					
11. Extent friends use	.36**	.24**	.41**	.36**	.29**	.43**	.00	.19**	.13	-.00	1.00				
12. Income	.10*	.10	.04	.02	.06	.10	.08	.05	.08	-.05	.02	1.00			
13. Education	.17**	.04	.11*	.12*	-.09	.12*	.02	-.07	.01	-.05	.13*	.37**	1.00		
14. Working	.13*	.05	.01	.06	.01	-.04	.19*	.00	.06	-.01	-.03	.17**	.14**	1.00	
15. Sex	-.22**	-.08	-.11*	-.10*	-.02	-.08	-.04	-.11	-.07	.06	-.16*	-.06	-.00	-.22**	1.00

* p < .01
** p < .001

The Role of Acculturation on Access to Marijuana

To assess the role of acculturation on patterns of drug use, a multiple regression of the predictor variables was conducted on age at which marijuana was first available. This dependent variable was chosen for two reasons. The first is that this is typically the first and only one of the illicit drugs to be used. The second reason is that, because of its greater distribution among the sample, this measure of drug use has better statistical properties for analysis compared to other measures of drug use.

For Mexican Americans in this sample, the strongest variables are acculturation, gender, working, and friends' use. All have a significant independent impact on the availability of marijuana. Highly acculturated males who are not working and have friends who use drugs have most access. Once acculturation is taken into account, education no longer has a significant independent effect. Parental use is not related (see Table 2-4). However, the reader is cautioned that together these variables are not strong predictors and account for only 12% of the variance in availability of marijuana use.

The pattern above is in stark contrast to that of Whites in this sample. For this group, all variables in the equation have a significant independent impact on availability. Again, together these variables are only relatively weak predictors accounting for 10% of the variance in availability. For Blacks, the analysis is weaker yet. Only 7% of the variance is explained by the two variables with a significant independent effect; gender and working. Surprisingly, friends use and parental use are not independent predictors.

DISCUSSION

The findings described above are largely as expected and consistent with existing literature. Mexican Americans report lower levels of drug use personally as well as by friends and parents. As anticipated, patterns of Mexican American drug use are not terribly different from those of Whites or Blacks. In fact, a multiple discriminant analysis shows only weak discriminatory power. The levels of use and patterns found in this Texas sample are comparable to those found nationally, with the exception of cocaine and crack-cocaine use. National data report higher levels of use among their Hispanic sample (National Institute on Drug Abuse, 1991). This probably reflects the higher levels of use within the Puerto Rican community.

Table 2-4   Multiple Regression of Selected Predictors on Age of Availability for Marijuana

For Mexican-Americans (N=387)

$R^2 = .12$**

Predictor	Standardized Beta Weight
Extent friends use	-.130**
Acculturation	.192**
Education	-.06
Working	.169**
Gender	.177**
Parental use	-.06

For Whites (N=868)

$R^2 = .10$**

Predictor	Standardized Beta Weight
Extent friends use	-.151**
Education	.169**
Working	.101**
Gender	.159**
Parental use	-.07*

For Blacks (N=309)

$R^2 = .07$**

Predictor	Standardized Beta Weight
Extent friends use	-.045
Education	-.013
Working	.143**
Gender	.227**
Parental use	-.074

* $p < .01$
** $p < .001$

The predictors of use and access tell a more interesting story. As anticipated, friends' use is highly related to use and access among all three ethnic groups. Socioeconomic status appears to be a more important predictor for use among the Mexican Americans in this sample compared to Blacks and Whites—those with higher SES (more educated, working, higher income) are more likely to use marijuana. This is also consistent with the more recent findings in the area and brings into question the role poverty might play in the etiology of drug abuse (De La Rosa et al., 1990). It may be that the impact of discrimination, limited opportunities and poverty is more evident among those who engage in heroin use. In the sample considered here, the typical pattern is that of recreational marijuana use which may be a more middle-class phenomenon.

Acculturation, as expected, is related to drug use; the more acculturated are more likely to report access to marijuana at a younger age. Acculturation appears to mediate socioeconomic status and friends use, although working and having friends who use drugs both retain an independent effect in the analysis. These findings would appear to be consistent with existing literature. Amaro and colleagues (1990) find a similar pattern of interaction with acculturation and socioeconomic status. The acculturated but not educated show higher levels of use in her data; the acculturated but not working show higher levels of access to marijuana in these data. These groups may be particularly marginalized and the younger age of access—and possibly younger age of use—may well mean that for this group the pattern may not end simply with recreational marijuana use.

The most interesting and surprising finding is clearly that of parental drug use and its impact on self drug use. While the measure of parental drug use included in this analysis is significantly related to the use of a number drugs among Whites and Blacks, this is not the case for Mexican Americans. These findings may be suggestive of several potential underlying processes. The first is that the parental drug use, especially among the Mexican Americans, is almost exclusively alcohol use and so modeling and access to drug-using networks through parents is not likely. Another potential explanation is hinted at by Moore (1990). Those individuals reporting substance abuse by family members may be part of what this author terms "cholo" families. These families have a long history of gang involvement, illegal activities and imprisonment which may have the opposite impact on younger members resulting in little or no use of psychoactive substances. Perhaps the strongest explanation lies in the cultural tradition of "familismo." In those Mexican

American families where substance abuse is present, the extended family may step in and be strong enough to mediate the impact of this abuse on younger members. This pattern may not exist among the other ethnic groups considered in this analysis.

The findings described above and suggested interpretations raise several implications for policy. The first is that friends appear to provide access to drugs and with acculturation one accumulates friends whose drug-using patterns approximate those of the mainstream culture. It is this relationship and the availability that makes the use possible. As pointed out by Amaro and colleagues (1990), acculturation is very much associated with the social and economic environment one inhabits. It may be that acculturation without participation in the educational system and labor force marginalize the individual placing him/her at greater risk. When this happens to a young women, the risk may in fact be multiplied. This propensity may well be countered by the strength of the Mexican American extended family. The cultural characteristic of "familismo" remains. Despite changes in acculturation, the family continues to be perceived as a strong source of support and a solver of problems (Sabogal, et. al, 1987). This strength should be incorporated in both the anti-drug messages received by the young and treatments to assist troubled youth.

Future research might profitably take several directions. The first would be to explore differences in acculturation among various Spanish-speaking communities as they relate to substance abuse and availability. One would imagine a pattern of back-and-forth migration such as found among "New-Yoricans" would result in different experiences from a one-time irreversible migration such as experienced by the Cubans. A second direction would be continued exploration of the family dynamics. Why is there no relationship between self drug use and parental use among the Mexican Americans in this sample? Several explanations are proposed. To what extent are these dynamics at work? To what extent would the relationship hold—or not hold—if one looked at alcohol or drug use by siblings and cousins of the same generation? Finally, these data pose some interesting questions around availability and use; what are some of the predictors of a short lag time between age of availability and age of first use? Are these predictors different for the three ethnic groups considered here?

Chapter 3

PATTERNS OF ALCOHOL USE AMONG HISPANICS

Anthony M. Alcocer

INTRODUCTION

This chapter reviews the literature on drinking patterns of Hispanics living in the United States. However, prior to reviewing this literature there are several issues relevant to it which the reader should consider. These issues include the use of the term, "Hispanic," the paucity of definitive research, the problem of comparability of research results, the lack of hypothesis and theory building, and questions about the reliability of survey results.

Hispanic

The term, "Hispanic," as used in the literature on alcohol drinking practices, is a broad, encompassing label. It is a term of convenience. Alcocer (1982) noted that such a stereotypical term simply fails to describe the great variety of people that are labeled, "Hispanic." Gilbert and Cervantes (1986) called it a catch-all phrase. In another context Gilbert (1989b) referred to it as a designation of bureaucratic convenience. Further, Caetano wrote:

> It has also been suggested that the all-encompassing label of *Hispanic* is "misleading, stereotypical and racist," confounding the aim of civil rights legislation passed to correct discrimination against disadvantaged people of Latin American Origin (Caetano, 1986, p. 332).

The term is meant to include the diverse nationalities from North, Central and South America, as well as the Caribbean area, that supposedly share a common heritage. But it is a very unsatisfactory term since these people are, in fact, quite diverse and not easily comparable. Gilbert (1989b) stated that national aggregated data for Hispanics mask important differences for those groups at risk and are of very limited utility for program planning in regions dominated by a specific subcultural group. Gilbert and Cervantes found that this sort of aggregation is

37

problematic because, although Hispanic groups may be similar in some ways, " . . . research shows that they differ substantively in terms of drinking patterns and alcohol problem incidence" (Gilbert & Cervantes, 1986, p. 4).

The literature on alcohol drinking patterns reflects this situation. Early studies included a variety of respondents under such labels as Hispanic, Latino, Spanish Speaking, Spanish Surname and others. However, more recent research has focused on specific groups by country of origin. In this regard, Mexican Americans, the largest Hispanic group in the United States, have received the most scrutiny. Meanwhile, little survey research has been conducted on Puerto Ricans, Cubans and other Hispanics.

Paucity of Research

Research on alcohol use in the United States began almost one hundred years ago while general population studies of drinking patterns and problems began in the 1940's. However, it was not until the 1960's, when Hispanics first achieved political recognition, that surveys began to mention Hispanics. Early studies that included Hispanics typically used samples too small to yield significant differences for the various Hispanic subgroups (e.g., Cahalan et al., 1969) or simply aggregated subgroups, failing to differentiate at all between them (e.g., Rachal et al., 1975). It was not until 1984 that a national survey of Hispanics was conducted and reported by Caetano (1985). Unfortunately, this survey was also limited by the small sample sizes in some of the categories.

Problems of Comparability

Comparisons between studies are problematic as well because of the many different indices or measurements used for drinking behavior and related factors. Typically, alcohol use is measured as a quantity-frequency variable with a number of categories included. Few studies use comparable quantity-frequency variables. For example, the 1976 California study of Hispanics (Alcocer, 1979) used four quantity-frequency variables in an attempt to obtain data that was comparable to other studies. In another example, Gilbert and Cervantes (1986) pointed out that the term "abstainer" defined as one who has never consumed alcohol is very different from an abstainer that has not consumed alcohol in the last six months.

Published epidemiological data presents problems as well. Caetano

(1983) noted that regular publications on vital statistics for the United States do not recognize Hispanics as a racial or ethnic group. This is true of morbidity and mortality data as well as crime statistics. Engmann (1976) reported similar problems in collecting epidemiological data on his sample of Spanish Speaking persons in California.

Lack of Hypothesis and Theory Building

The nature of the research reported for the most part does not lend itself to theory building. Gilbert and Cervantes (1986) found that most of the research they reviewed was exploratory and descriptive in nature, designed to generate epidemiological data rather than to test hypotheses. The authors maintain that the result is an absence of sophisticated, multidimensional models for Hispanic drinking patterns.

Problems of Reliability

Finally, drinking behavior is a sensitive topic and there is reason to question the validity of survey responses pertaining to it. This writer's experience in the 1976 California Study (Alcocer, 1979) indicated the possibility of problems in this regard. In reporting on a segment of the survey that dealt with respondents' reports on "close friends that drank quite a bit" this author wrote:

> Such heavy reporting of heavy drinking among friends suggests the possibility of underreporting in regards to self-reported drinking. This becomes even more of a possibility when symptomatic drinking problem results are taken into account. The question which arises is, "If so many people have so many friends who drink quite a bit, why doesn't it show up more clearly on self-reported data?" (Alcocer, 1979, p. 202).

Similarly, anthropologist William Rathje found underreporting of drinking by household respondents when he compared the contents of their trash cans to their reported drinking (Williamson, 1976). This issue has not been satisfactorily addressed in the literature.

ADULT HISPANIC DRINKING PATTERNS

Caetano (1985) pointed out that prior to 1979 most of the information on Hispanic drinking patterns was derived from research in which Hispanics themselves were not the focus of study but, rather, were included as part of a larger sample. In 1979 both Alcocer's study of Hispanics in California and Maril and Zavaleta's study of low-income

Mexican American women in the Lower Rio Grande Valley of South Texas were published. Although these studies were the first large-scale general population studies focused on drinking among Hispanics, they have limited applicability because they were representative of the locales studied.

However, Caetano's (1985) study of Hispanic households in the 48 coterminous United States was the first survey of drinking practices using a national sample of U.S. Hispanics. Data was collected by means of face-to-face interviews, averaging an hour in length, within the homes of the respondents, utilizing a standardized questionnaire administered by bilingual interviewers. The author stated that a measure of the study's success in recruiting Hispanics is the large percentage of respondents (43%) who chose to be interviewed in Spanish.

Caetano used a seven category quantity-frequency index to measure drinking patterns with the categories arranged as follows:

Frequent heavy drinker: Drinks five or more drinks at a sitting once a week or more often. A drink is defined as one ounce of spirits, four ounces of table wine, or 12 ounces of beer, each of which contains approximately nine grams of absolute alcohol.

Frequent high maximum: Drinks once a week or more often and occasionally (at least once a year) has five or more drinks at a sitting.

Frequent low maximum: Drinks once a week or more often but never consumes five or more drinks at a sitting.

Less frequent high maximum: Drinks one to three times a month and has five or more drinks occasionally (at least once a year).

Less frequent low maximum: Drinks one to three times a month but never has five or more drinks at a sitting.

Infrequent: Drinks less often than once a month but at least once a year; may or may not drink five drinks at a sitting.

Abstainer: Drinks less frequently than once a year or has never drunk alcoholic beverages.

This index has the advantage of including both frequency and quantity measures of drinking in seven succinct categories that are easily compared. It has the further advantage of having been used in previous surveys both with the general population sample (Cahalan, 1975; Cahalan, Roizen & Room, 1974) and with a Hispanic regional sample (Alcocer, 1979).

Differences by Gender

Caetano reported that a striking difference was found between the drinking patterns of Hispanic men and women. Women appeared to drink less. About half (47%) of the women reported they were abstainers while another 24% claimed to be infrequent drinkers. Only 22% of Hispanic men described themselves as abstainers while 10% viewed themselves as infrequent drinkers. On the other hand, 17% of males (but only 3% of females) reported frequent heavy drinking.

This was not an unexpected result. Several studies have reported such differences. Cahalan et al. (1969) found that among their national general population sample men drank more frequently and heavily than women. Also, in a California general population sample Cahalan et al. (1974) reported a similar pattern. Klatsky et al. (1983) similarly found that self-reported drinking in a California sample of Whites, Latins, Japanese, Black, Chinese, and Filipinos, men of all races reported more drinking than women.

Haberman (1970) reported higher non-drinking among Puerto Rican females than males (4.6 to 1) and in another study (Haberman, 1986) found greater alcoholism problems for Puerto Rican men than women. Among California Hispanics Alcocer (1979) found that Hispanic women reported abstinence two to three times more often than Hispanic men depending on locale. Maril and Zavaleta (1979) found that in a large sample of low income Mexican American women, in the Lower Rio Grande Valley of South Texas, 86% reported no drinking during the previous year. Paine (1977), Belenko and Kehrer (1978), Johnson and Matre (1978), Markides and Krause (1987), Mendes and Markides (1986), and Markides et al. (1988) similarly found that Mexican American men drank more than women. Caetano (1984a) in a sample of Northern California respondents found that Hispanic women reported higher abstention rates than Hispanic men across all age categories. Holck et al. (1984) stated that the proportion of abstainers among Mexican American women in the U.S.-Mexico Border area was significantly higher than that for Mexican American men.

Differences by Age

Caetano's data suggested that drinking decreased with age. He found that among men the rate of abstention remains stable until the age group 50–59 after which time it increased. Infrequent drinking also increased after age 60 while the next category (less frequent low maximum) began to increase in the 40–49 age group. From another view, both frequent high maximum and frequent heavy drinking increased from the twenties through the thirties and decreased thereafter.

This was an important finding since it indicated heavy drinking persisted into early middle age. Gilbert and Cervantes (1986) noted that whereas in the general population, heavy drinking, alcohol-related social problems and alcohol dependency symptoms are at their highest in the years between 18 and 29 and decrease from that point with age, such a drop does not take place to the same degree among Mexican American men. Gilbert (1989b) suggested that this high rate among early middle-aged Mexican American men was accompanied by an especially high rate of self-reported, alcohol-related problems reported in several studies.

Caetano also reported that women similarly demonstrated a stability in abstinence through their fifties showing a substantial increase thereafter. The only anomaly appeared to be an increase in both frequent high maximum and frequent heavy drinking among women in their fifties. This represented 30% of women in the 50–59 age group.

Differences by Income and Education

Family income was used to differentiate drinking patterns as well. Caetano claimed a positive association between drinking and income although he cautions interpretation of the highest income bracket because of small sample size. Generally, he found that drinking increased with income. For example, abstention and infrequent drinking decreased as income increased for both men and women. Among women, those in the lowest income group had three times as many abstainers as women in the highest income group. Also, the percentage of female infrequent drinkers and less frequent low maximum drinkers substantially increased with income.

College education appeared to decrease abstinence among male respondents. A substantial increase in frequent high maximum drinking was found among those with high school education and in frequent heavy drinking among those with college education. Among women abstention drops with education while women in the lowest education group (grammar school) drink the least of all groups. However, high levels of heavy drinking (frequent high maximum) were found at both ends of the educational categories.

When the factor of age was used to differentiate drinking patterns by education the author found that age did not seem to affect the high rate of abstention among respondents with the least education. Age did affect the level of drinking of college educated men ages 18–29 and 30–39, accounting for 32% of frequent heavy drinking among men. Similarly, these same age categories (18–29 and 30–39) showed most of the infrequent drinking in the college educated group, as well as the frequent high maximum for those with high school educations.

These results are supported by other studies. Maril and Zavaleta (1979) found that among Mexican American women living in the Lower Rio Grande Valley of South Texas those who drank were young and middle-aged married women who had more than the mean level of education. Holck (1984) linked lower rates of drinking among Mexican American women to their lower levels of education. On the other hand, Caetano (1984b) found that among Hispanic women in Northern California, drinking and heavier consumption were positively and significantly linked with education and income. It was similarly linked with Hispanic males but not significantly so. Finally, Gilbert (1989b), commenting on the anomaly of both frequent high maximum and frequent heavy drinking of Hispanic women in the 50–59 age group, noted that these were California older women with more education and in higher income categories.

Differences by Ethnicity

Differences in drinking patterns were calculated by ethnicity focusing on the three larger national Hispanic groups (Mexican Americans, Puerto Ricans and Cuban Americans) and a single category, "Others," which included all other Hispanics. Caetano (1985, p. 152) found that, among Hispanic men, Mexican Americans had the highest rate of abstention but those that did drink, did so more heavily. Generally, they drank more frequently and in greater quantities than other Hispanic men. For example, the author found that 44% of Mexican American men demonstrated frequent high maximum (those ages 18 through 39 only) or frequent heavy drinkers, compared to 24% of Puerto Rican men, 6% Cuban American men and 24% of men in the "Other" category.

Similar results were found for Mexican American women who also seemed to drink more than other Hispanic women, having a larger portion of frequent high maximum drinkers (12% versus 3%, 7% and 1% for Puerto Rican, Cuban American and Other Hispanic women). Puerto

Rican women are distinguished by their low rate of abstention along with the highest proportion of less frequent high maximum drinkers compared to other Hispanic women.

Gordon (1985) in his study of Puerto Ricans, Dominicans, and Guatemalans in the Northeast found significant differences in the drinking practices of the three groups. Dominican males drank less after migrating to the U.S. and changed the context and style of their drinking. Dominicans stressed moderation in their drinking; they appeared to favor social control. Guatemalan males appeared to drink more heavily, typically drinking to intoxication in situations where there were no interdictions against heavy drinking or drunkenness. Typically, Puerto Rican males are more acculturated. Thus, they have fully adopted U.S. drinking customs but have added them to their traditional drinking customs. They also were both heavy and frequent drinkers. Page et al. (1985) investigated Miami's Cuban population and described their patterns of drinking as generally moderate in nature.

Differences by Generation

Caetano also made comparisons on the basis of birthplace with all U.S. born Hispanics divided into either "first generation" (one or both parents born in the country of origin) and "others" (all other U.S. born). Foreign born were categorized according to Mexico, Puerto Rico, Cuba or Latin America. Caetano (1985) again cautions about the small sample size of all groups except Mexicans and Mexican Americans. The reader should note as well that U.S. born Hispanics were not differentiated by country of origin but were recorded as an aggregate.

The results indicated that first generation U.S. born men had lower abstention and higher heavy drinking than subsequent generations. On the other hand, foreign born Mexicans showed the heaviest drinking with rates six times higher than other foreign born in the frequent heavy and frequent high maximum drinker categories. Other foreign born males showed patterns of drinking in the infrequent and less frequent drinking range.

Among first-generation Hispanic women the rate of abstention also decreased but they demonstrated increases in infrequent drinking as compared to later generation Hispanic women. The later generation Hispanic women had a high percentage of frequent high maximum drinkers but abstention rates similar to foreign born Puerto Ricans and Cubans. Foreign born women had high rates of abstention, especially

Mexicans and Latin Americans of whom two-thirds were abstainers. Those foreign born Hispanic women who did drink, did so lightly.

Neff et al. (1987) found that generation positively correlated with drinking level but was negatively associated with acculturation in his sample of San Antonio Mexican American men. Less acculturated men in each of three succeeding generations (immigrant, first and later) were the heavier drinkers. More acculturated men in each generation tended to conform to the lower quantity but higher frequency patterns characteristic of non-Hispanic San Antonio males.

Other studies on acculturation report similar results. Caetano and Mora (1988) found that within five years of immigration abstention rates dropped for immigrant men while consumption rose. Holck et al. (1984) found a decrease in abstention with acculturation among Hispanic women even when sociodemographic variables, such as age, education and income, are controlled.

Neff et al. (1986) established that the likelihood of alcohol use differed significantly across racial subgroups (i.e., Anglos, Hispanics and Blacks). Abstinence was reported by roughly one quarter of both Anglos and less acculturated Hispanics compared to 34% for Blacks and 9% for more acculturated Hispanics. The authors noted that while the more acculturated Hispanics were sociodemographically similar to Anglos, they had dramatically higher rates of drinking than either Anglos or less acculturated Hispanics.

Finally, Gilbert and Cervantes (1986) in a comparison of Mexican and California Mexican American drinking patterns discovered that California Mexican American males showed a distinct pattern of increase in frequency of drinking, becoming more like other California drinkers than like immigrants or Mexicans in terms of drinking frequency. However, frequency of intoxication across the generations did not decline to match the lower intoxication rates of the general California population. Gilbert and Cervantes concluded that Mexican Americans were not simply substituting U.S. drinking patterns of increased frequency of drinking as they acculturated. They were also retaining the high consumption-per-occasion patterns found among Mexican men. The authors comment that this is not a new phenomena but rather one that has been reported before in the literature on studies of Italian American drinking patterns.

Differences by Region

Caetano (1985) in his discussion of the results of the national survey reported that California Hispanics, both male and female, had lower abstention rates than Hispanic respondents in the national sample. However, he noted that abstention rates were lower for all persons in California. There appeared to be a number of reasons for this, including the large number of light drinkers in that State.

Other examples of regional differences were reported by Caetano. California Hispanic men consumed more alcohol than the national Hispanic sample of men. Hispanic women in the national sample do not drink at all or drink frequently. But those that drink frequently consume more per sitting than California Hispanic women, who for their part have more frequent drinkers (19% versus 12%).

Evidence for regional differences in drinking patterns among Hispanics is supported by other studies as well. Gilbert and Cervantes (1986) compared a number of studies (Trotter, 1985; Alcocer, 1979; Maril & Zavaleta, 1979; Johnson & Matre, 1978; Belenko & Kehrer, 1978; Paine, 1977; Cahalan, 1975; Cahalan & Room, 1974; Cahalan et al., 1969) and found that differences in the drinking patterns of Mexican Americans paralleled differences in the general populations between the two states. Generally, California Hispanic males showed a substantially higher proportion of alcohol use than Texas Hispanic males mirroring the higher drinking rates of California men versus Texas men. As the authors themselves stated:

> The studies just reviewed, while demonstrating a range in the prevalence of alcohol use among California Mexican Americans, in general show them to be considerably less likely to be abstainers than their Texas counterparts. And—although this is somewhat less true of women—Mexican Americans in each state tend to resemble their state's general population more than they do their counterpart group in the other state (Gilbert & Cervantes, 1986, p. 19).

DRINKING PATTERNS OF HISPANIC YOUTH

Prevalence of Drinking

Several studies in the literature have focused on the age of onset of adolescent drinking. Studies have identified various ages of onset, ranging from 11 to 14, depending on the sample and locale (Mata, 1986;

Morgan, et al., 1984; Jackson, et al., 1981). However, across the various studies Hispanic youth, both male and female, seem to start drinking later than their White and earlier than their Black and Asian counterparts. Also, male youths, whether White, Black or Hispanic, start drinking earlier than female adolescents.

Other findings in the literature indicate that adolescent drinking increased with age with males again demonstrating heavier drinking than females (Sanchez-Dirks, 1978; Wilsnack and Wilsnack, 1978; Kandel, et al., 1976; Rachal, et al., 1975). Similarly, Hispanic adolescents demonstrated this pattern in regional studies where the respondents were primarily Mexican Americans (Skager et al., 1986; Estrada et al., 1985; Perez et al., 1979; Belenko & Kehrer, 1978; Padilla et al., 1977) or primarily Puerto Rican (Robles et al., 1979).

However, problems arise when comparing the drinking of Hispanic youth to other ethnic groups. Several authors have reported that Hispanic youth generally drink less than White youth but more than Black youth (Barnes & Welte, 1986; Maddahian et al., 1986; Skager et al., 1986; Morgan et al., 1984; Skager & Maddahian, 1984; Rachal et al., 1982; Trotter, 1982; Robles et al., 1979; Belenko & Kehrer, 1978; Kandel et al., 1976; Rachal et al., 1975; Levy, 1973). Other authors, on the other hand, reported the same or higher alcohol use rates for male and female Hispanic adolescents as White and other youths (Mata, 1986; Guinn & Hurley, 1976).

This discrepancy is not easily explained. One cause may be that some studies fail to differentiate between males and females. In the case of Hispanics, the averaging of males and females would cause serious distortions since Hispanic adolescent females have much higher rates of abstinence than either Hispanic adolescent males, other ethnic adolescent females or adolescent females from the general population (Morgan et al., 1984; Trotter, 1982; Sanchez-Dirks, 1978; Rachal et al., 1975).

Gilbert and Alcocer (1988) pointed out that Hispanic adolescent females may be drinking more, adopting drinking patterns similar to Hispanic adolescent males and the general population, but this is also true of adolescent girls in the general population.

Polysubstance Abuse

The issue of alcohol use among youth is complicated by their use of various other mind altering substances, either singly or in substances available to our youth, Hispanic or otherwise. What is most interesting is the progression of substances used that has been reported by several researchers (Mata, 1986; Newcomb & Bentler, 1986; Skager et al., 1986; Maddahian et al., 1985; Morgan et al., 1984; Skager & Maddahian, 1984; URSA, 1983; Estrada et al., 1982; Jackson et al., 1981; Nutall & Nutall, 1981; Bruno & Doscher, 1984; Dembo et al., 1979; Robles et al., 1979; Guinn, 1978; Padilla et al., 1977; Guinn & Hurley, 1976; Kandel et al., 1976; Levy, 1973; Brunswick, 1969). These studies make it quite clear that drinking is part of a larger substance use/abuse phenomena. Alcohol, along with cigarettes, is one of the earliest and most common substances used by Hispanic and other adolescents. Alcohol was found among Hispanic and other youths to be related to the use of marijuana by several researchers (Estrada et al., 1982; Padilla et al., 1977; Guinn & Hurley, 1976) and was shown to be the best predictor of marijuana use among Hispanic high school students by Estrada et al. (1982).

The use of alcohol as an entry to the use of other drugs was postulated by Kandel (1975) in her 4-stage model of substance use wherein adolescents progress from non-use to the use of (Stage One) beer and wine, (Stage Two) hard liquor and/or cigarettes, (Stage Three) marijuana and, finally, (Stage Four) other illicit drugs. At each stage fewer and fewer adolescents report using the substances typical of that stage. Newcomb and Bentler's (1986) study of the use of beer/wine, liquor, marijuana and pills by Black, Hispanic, Asian and White adolescents in the Los Angeles County area seemed to substantiate Kandel's model. However, the results also indicated that there were differential patterns of stability, progression, regression and patterning among the various ethnic subsamples. Gilbert and Alcocer stated:

> The central role played by alcohol in the substance use pattern of Hispanic youth is underscored by the fact that it is the first drug used by many teens, is the most commonly used drug by single drug users and is at the core of most constellations of multidrug use. (Gilbert & Alcocer, 1988, p. 10)

CONCLUSION

It is obvious from this review of the literature that several issues exist regarding Hispanics and their drinking patterns. The term "Hispanic" itself is suspect when used as a broad label for this group of ethnically diverse people. Also problematic are surveys that generalize from limited sample sizes or that group various sub-categories of Hispanics to achieve significant samples. Further, the lack of standardization in data collection instruments prevents meaningful comparisons of various survey results unless the investigators have taken pains to gather comparable data. Hypotheses development and theory building appear still in the infancy stage. And finally, the inherent inability of survey instruments to determine the veracity of respondents' remarks continues to cast doubts on the best survey research.

The survey literature generally has found that Hispanic men drink more heavily and frequently than the general population and their drinking tends to become less frequent and heavy after middle age. Hispanic women similarly drink more than their general population counter parts although they abstain more and drink less frequently and heavily than Hispanic men. Hispanic youth are similarly affected with their problems compounded by polysubstance abuse.

Gilbert and Cervantes (1986) have hypothesized that the pattern of heavy, frequent drinking among Mexican American men results from acculturation: the heavy drinking typical in the Mexican culture combines with the frequent drinking typical of the American culture. As Gilbert and Cervantes point out, this is not a new phenomena. It has been observed in the drinking patterns of acculturating Italian American drinkers.

This has interesting consequences in terms of causation since the literature has tended to attribute the higher rate of drinking problems among Hispanics to such things as discrimination, poverty, genetic propensity and the like. If, instead, this is simply a behavior pattern that emerges when an ethnic group from a heavy-but-infrequent drinking culture immigrates to a frequent-but-light drinking culture then the ramifications for prevention, treatment and rehabilitation are quite different. Clearly more research is needed to confirm Gilbert and Cervantes' hypothesis.

Chapter 4

INTRACULTURAL VARIATION IN ALCOHOL-RELATED COGNITIONS AMONG MEXICAN AMERICANS

M. JEAN GILBERT

INTRODUCTION

This article will synthesize what is known about how Mexican Americans think about alcohol use. A few cautions are in order before proceeding, however. First, it should be pointed out that it is always risky to make assumptions about what is going on inside people's heads, and it is particularly risky to attribute certain ideations to entire cultural groups. Part of the difficulty is that, while there may be a good deal of consensus around a set of ideas among members of a culture, there is always considerable variation, too. Much of the time variation is systematically linked to identifiable factors, such as demographic (gender, age, place of birth) or structural (social class, economic opportunity) variables. People share cultural ideations somewhat in the manner that they share a language: Around a core of linguistic or ideological conventions, there is a great deal of class, regional and idiosyncratic variation.

In their book, *Drunken Comportment,* MacAndrew and Edgerton (1969) note that people's shared understandings about alcohol use are based on

> ... bits and pieces of "evidence'.... from a wide variety of sources—
> parents, peers, schools, books, magazines, radio and television programs,
> movies and ... everyday experience (p. 1).

People are thus *socialized* into their concepts surrounding the use of alcohol and the consequences of its use, and persons belonging to the same cultural group, insofar as they share similar socialization experiences, most likely will share many understandings about alcohol. A major theme of MacAndrew and Edgerton's book is that understandings about the consequences of alcohol use differ across cultures, and these differences produce or at least are strongly correlated with differences in

51

drinking behavior. As will be seen, these associations are clearly present in the data on Mexican Americans.

A further difficulty in discussing people's thinking about drinking is that it is not always easy to find out what people think, particularly about a subject that may have some problems or strong feelings associated with it. One way is to ask people what they think, of course, and to ask enough people, including persons from different segments of a cultural group, to determine if some ideas are generally accepted within the group and where differences lie. This is the strategy used by survey researchers. There is always the risk here that folks will say what they think they ought to think rather than what they do think, however. Researchers try to get around this by careful item construction and cross validation. Moreover, it is valuable at the very least to learn if there is agreement on the "ought to's" which define cultural norms.

Another way to get some grasp of what people are thinking is to observe systematically their behavior and listen to their utterances, hoping to accumulate enough records of both to draw inferences about the kind of thinking the behavior reflects. This is the strategy used by ethnographers who spend significant lengths of time closely studying (and conversing with) members of a single community within a cultural group. If survey and ethnographic research conducted with the same group yields convergent information, we can feel more secure about the validity of the findings. In the following discussion of alcohol-related cognitions among Mexican Americans, therefore, the findings of both types of research will be considered.

ALCOHOL-RELATED COGNITIONS

Research on Hispanics has focused on three general types of cognitions related to alcohol: *expectations* about the consequences of alcohol use, *reasons* for using alcohol and *norms* governing the use of alcohol. Logically, these three categories of thought might be expected to be closely related to each other. For example, an individual's reasons or motives for using alcohol (or not using) are likely to be based on what s/he has learned to expect as the physical, psychological and social consequences of this behavior. Group norms evolve as social controls over the scope of alcohol use and are shaped to a large degree by understandings about why people drink and expectations about the consequences of consuming alcohol. Expectations about consequences related to alcohol use are influenced both by experience with the substance and by observation of alcohol-related behaviors and societal response to these behaviors. Usually, as in the studies of Mexican Americans to be discussed, just one of these categories of cognition is examined by itself. At this point, research is needed to tease out linkages among the different types of cognition and demonstrate their relative influence on decisions resulting in drinking behavior.

Expectancies

Researchers have demonstrated a keen interest in the relationship between people's expectations about the social, psychological and physical consequences of alcohol use and their alcohol consumption. In studies designed to evaluate whether alcohol reduces socially induced stress in social drinkers (Abrams, 1983), it was found that persons who believed they had consumed alcohol, whether they had or not, behaved in a more relaxed, less inhibited and assertive fashion than subjects who believed they had consumed non-alcoholic beverages, again whether they actually had or not. It has also been shown that the more a drinker holds socially learned, reinforcing expectations that benefits will accrue from alcohol use, either in terms of specific positive effects on social functioning (Lang, 1983), performance evaluation (Yankofsky et al., 1986), unpleasant mood states (Marlatt, 1987) or more generalized positive changes (Brown, Goldman and Christiansen, 1985), the greater the consumption of alcoholic beverages. And at least one study (Christiansen, Goldman and Inn, 1982) has shown that alcohol expectancies develop in childhood prior to drinking experience, lending credence to the idea that these cognitions are the product of social rather than experiential learning. The development of cognitive expectations about the consequences of alcohol consumption prior to its actual use suggests that these expectations may be a factor in the complex set of deliberations which precede use.

Alcohol-related expectations among Hispanic drinkers were examined in a recently completed study (Cervantes, Gilbert, Salgado de Snyder and Padilla, 1990–91). Expectations in a sample of 264 immigrant Hispanics (Mexicans and Central Americans) were compared with those of 188 U.S. born Mexican Americans. Both groups were young adults: The immigrants were enrolled in an adult school to learn English, the Mexican Americans enrolled in a community college. An eight item cognitive expectancy scale, the Expected Benefits Index (EBI), assessed expectations of enhanced social acceptance, physical relaxation, freedom from inhibition, global mood elevation, sexual pleasure, tension reduction, social pleasure and social assertiveness which would result from "a drink or two" (Alpha coefficient = .832). Answers to each item were ordered on a five level Likert response set.

The results showed clear gender differences across both immigrant and U.S. born samples. In each group, men's scores on the EBI were significantly higher than women's, indicating their much higher expectations of benefit from alcohol use. Among the immigrants, male endorsement of all eight items was greater than females' and in the U.S.-born Mexican American sample, men were more likely than women to expect a drink to enhance social acceptance, sexual pleasure and social assertiveness. On no items was there greater expectation of benefit on the part of women than men.

Moreover, although there were no significant differences between immigrant men and U.S.-born men in terms of their evaluation of benefits accruing to alcohol use, U.S.-born women were much more likely than immigrant women to anticipate that use of alcohol would produce some benefits. The former were significantly more likely than the latter to expect that alcohol would produce social disinhibition, mood elevation, tension reduction and enhanced sociability.

Across all groups, immigrant and U.S.-born, men and women, there was a significant positive relationship between scores on the EBI and quantity and frequency of drinking (drinking was indexed on a six category scale that ranged from the infrequent drinker who drinks less than once a month but at least once a year, any quantity, to the high frequency/high maximum drinker who drinks at least once a week, consuming six or more drinks per occasion). This finding is consistent with the results of other research which shows the same relationship between expectancies and alcohol use among non-Hispanic adults (Brown et al., 1985) and college students (Brown, 1985).

Finally, this study showed that among men born inside and outside the U.S., scores on the EBI and scores on the quantity/frequency index were positively correlated with depression scores on the Center for Epidemiologic Studies Depression scale (CES–D) (Radloff, 1977). Men who reported high levels of depressive symptoms were more likely than men who reported few symptoms to expect benefits from the use of alcohol; these men also drank more heavily than others as well. These correlations were particularly strong among U.S. born men. These data suggest that Mexican American men may tend to self-medicate with alcohol out of the expectation that it will relieve depressive symptoms. No associations between depression scores and alcohol expectancies or drinking behavior was found among women, however, despite the fact that women in both groups scored significantly higher on the index of depressive symptoms than men.

These findings are somewhat similar to those of Caetano (1987b) who examined the relationship between drinking patterns and depression (also measured on the CES–D) among 1,453 Hispanics interviewed in a 1984 national Hispanic survey (65% of whom were Mexican American). He learned that drinking or heavy drinking *per se* were not predictive of scores on the CES–D among men or women. However, he found that among men and women drinkers, those who reported having alcohol-related problems had twice the chance of being depressed as did those who did not report problems, with depression most strongly associated with problems indicative of alcohol dependence.

In another study, Neff (1986) examined Hispanic data from the Health and Nutrition Survey, in a predominantly but not wholly Mexican American sample, finding that Hispanics who were *less* acculturated (as measured by language use) showed fewer depressive symptoms but drank more heavily than acculturated Hispanics. He tentatively concluded that less acculturated Hispanics might be using alcohol to palliate negative mood states.

Overall, a major finding of the Cervantes et al. (1990–91) expectancies study is that, for Hispanic men, being born in the U.S. is not a critical determinant of higher expectations about the benefits of alcohol use, but for Hispanic women it is. And while drinking patterns among men were not found to vary by national origin among men, Mexican American women born in the U.S. drank more frequently and at heavier levels than women born elsewhere. These generational changes in drinking practices among women are consonant with those found in several other studies in which drinking patterns across immigrant and native born Mexican Americans have been assessed (Holck et al., 1984; Caetano, 1987a). It appears probable that these important changes in drinking practices among Mexican American females are accompanied by the acquisition of more positive beliefs about the consequences of alcohol use.

The studies cited above provide evidence that there is a link between depression and alcohol use among Mexican American men and possibly among women. Although the direction of the relationship between depression and alcohol needs to be better clarified, it appears likely that it may be mediated by expectations that alcohol will provide relief from depressive symptoms.

Reasons for Drinking

Reasons or motives, as they are sometimes called, direct action-taking. They provide intentionality for behavior and are likely to be formulated on the basis of expectation about outcome such as those described in the preceding section.

In a study conducted in 1976–1977 (Alcocer and Gilbert, 1979) and later submitted to secondary analysis (Gilbert, 1987, 1989a), 1080 Hispanics (predominantly of Mexican heritage) men and women, immigrant and non-immigrant, in three California locations, Fresno County, San Jose and East Los Angeles, were asked a battery of 14 questions which assessed their reasons for drinking. Response sets allowed respondents to evaluate a stated reason for drinking as being "not important," "fairly important" or "very important."

Male respondents were significantly more likely to attribute greater importance to *all* reasons for drinking than women. This was true whether the men were U.S.-born or immigrant. Men were especially more likely than women to attribute importance to drinking to alter mood states (to forget, to overcome boredom, lonesomeness, frustration and anger) and to drink because they had worked hard. Men and women both endorsed relaxation, hot weather, sociability and overcoming shyness as reasons for drinking.

Interestingly, across variables, immigrant women were found to be less likely than U.S.-born women to attribute importance to any of the reasons for drinking (Gilbert, 1987). In only one instance did immigrant women show more support for a reason to drink alcohol than U.S.-born women: Drinking to gain energy. Some support was found in both female groups for drinking to relax, to cheer oneself up, to ease frustration, to cool off in hot weather or for health reasons.

U.S.-born women differed significantly from immigrant women in their greater support for "drinking to be sociable." Only 45% of the U.S.-born women felt that sociability was a negligible reason for drinking compared to 62% of immigrant women. And while only 13% of U.S.-born women felt that sociability was a very important reason, this percentage was twice that of immigrant women. Further, more U.S.-born than Mexican-born women were supportive of drinking after working hard and drinking to forget troubles.

The differential endorsement of rationales for drinking among immigrant and U.S.-born women in the sample described above were reflected in different drinking rates across generational groups among women: While only 38% of the third or later generation women were abstainers, 51% of the second generation and 75% of the immigrant women practiced abstention. Twenty-one percent of the third generation women drank at least weekly, while 15% and 5% of the second and immigrant generation women, respectively, drank this often. On the other hand, while men in the different generational groups demonstrated different drinking patterns, for example, increased high quantity/high frequency drinking and reduced abstention were associated with generational distance from immigrant status (Gilbert, 1989a), there were no generational differences in the importance men placed on the different reasons for drinking.

The great contrast in drinking rates between immigrant and U.S.-born women and in the degree to which they assign importance to reasons for drinking suggests that being socialized in the United States changes the rationalizations which underlie decision making and action taking with respect to alcohol use. It seems likely, as with expectations about drinking outcomes, that these modifications are mediated by culture contact and greater integration into the social structure which shapes the drinking behavior of women in the larger U.S. population. The women in the California sample did in fact show increasingly greater contact with persons not of Hispanic heritage with each succeeding generation. Whereas nearly half the immigrant women had no Anglo friends and the same percentage never got together socially with the Anglos they did know, the corresponding percentages for these situations were 15% and 17% and 12% and 13% for second and third generations, respectively. With regard to media exposure, just 18% of the immigrant women reported watching mostly English-language television, while 61% of the second generation and 79% of the third generation watched English language television.

Neff, Hoppe, Keir and Perea (1987) examined what they termed "motives for drinking" among 149 Mexican American and 164 Anglo men in a San Antonio community sample. From a set of 16 items, they extracted three motivational factors: social drinking, generation of positive mood states and alleviation of negative mood states. They found that drinking to alleviate negative mood states was more common among Mexican Ameri-

cans than Anglo Americans and was particularly notable in the least
acculturated portion of their Mexican American male sample that was
U.S.-born of U.S.-born parents, a group that was generally highly acculturated to U.S. society.

Along these same lines, Caetano in the study referred to above (1987b),
examined the relationship between reasons for drinking and depression
in his sample from the 1984 national Hispanic survey. On a test of
proportions he found significant differences between depressed and
non-depressed Hispanic drinkers in terms of their reasons for drinking.
Among men, more depressed drinkers than non-depressed drinkers
drank because they liked the feeling of getting high (39% versus 10%), to
forget worries (37% versus 8%), to have more confidence (27% versus 7%)
and when they were tense and nervous (41% versus 17%). Among women,
more depressed than non-depressed drinkers drank when they were
tense and nervous (22% versus 11%). On the other hand, non-depressed
drinkers were more likely to report other reasons for drinking: Because
"it's a good way to celebrate" (54% non-depressed versus 37% depressed)
and because they "enjoyed drinking" (63% versus 45%). Based on these
findings and the relationship found between alcohol-related problems
and depression in this population (reviewed earlier in this paper), Caetano
advances the possibility that drinking may be used by Hispanics as a way
of ameliorating depressive symptoms.

Alcohol-Related Norms and Attitudes

Cultural norms differ from expectancies and reasons in that they
comprise a group's (usually unwritten) prescriptions and proscriptions
for what is considered appropriate alcohol-related behavior. In other
words, norms set ideal standards for who may use alcohol, when, where,
with whom and in what amounts. Like other culturally influenced
cognitions, norms are transmitted through precept and example, sanc-
tions and censure, verbally and nonverbally. Among Mexican Americans as with other groups, agreement around a specific norm is never
complete, but research has demonstrated several alcohol-related norms
about which there is considerable concurrence.

Survey data on Mexican American alcohol-related norms is scant and
is limited primarily to two studies: Alcocer and Gilbert's (1979) work
on Hispanics in California and Caetano's (1989a) analysis of the 1984
National Hispanic Survey. Most of the data from these two studies center
on gender and age related norms with a smattering of information on

concepts related to appropriate levels of drinking in specific settings. Data generally aren't comparable across studies because different methods and items were used in obtaining information. There are several areas of overall concordance, however.

Informants in the two studies are in accord about the inappropriateness of early initiation of alcohol use among adolescents. A majority of the men and women questioned in each of these adult surveys indicated no support for drinking among persons 16 years old or younger. Only 9% of the men and 7% of the women in the California survey felt it was all right for drinking to be initiated before age 18. Similarly, just 12% of the men in Caetano's national Hispanic sample felt it was appropriate for 16 year old boys or girls to drink, and even fewer women in the sample, 6%, would agree to adolescents drinking at this age. The Alcocer study showed, however, that 45% of the men and 35% of the women would agree to the initiation of beer drinking between the ages of 18 and 20, while 39% of the men and 28% of the women would support wine drinking at this age. The drinking of spirits was accorded even less support, 30% and 22% of men and women, respectively. This study did not attempt to determine if there were differences in norms for men and women at various ages. However, in the ethnographic segment of this California study (Alcocer and Gilbert, 1979) numerous informants commented on the relationship between the responsibility of holding a full time job and the right to consume alcohol, making the point that if a man is old enough to hold down a full time job, he is old enough to drink. No like comments prescribed an appropriate age or circumstances for women.

Data from the 1984 National Hispanic Survey (Caetano, 1987a) does show some gender bias: While 86% of the men sampled and 81% of the women felt it was all right for men aged 21–40 to drink, just 73% and 68% of the men and women, respectively, thought any drinking was appropriate for women in this age range. Forty percent of the men and 35% of the women felt that men could appropriately drink enough to feel high, contrasted with the 32% and 13% of men and women who felt it was all right for women to do so. Caetano examined the relationship between acculturation (measured on an index which included language factors, media preferences and interethnic interaction) and drinking norms and practices. He found acculturation to be related to more permissive norms for drinking among women and this relationship was evident independent of socioeconomic variables or place of birth. Not surprisingly, these norms were reflected in patterns of drinking prevalence and levels of drinking which showed women acculturated to U.S. society as less likely to be abstainers and more likely to be frequent heavy drinkers than women of low acculturation.

Caetano further analyzed this data set by isolating and contrasting subsamples from California and Texas (1989b) and learned that Hispanic respondents in California were more liberal than Texans in their attitudes toward female drinking. Further, both men and women in California showed more support than their Texas counterparts for the social, "fun" aspects of alcohol use.

An ethnographic study of thirty-six Mexican American and Anglo couples in California (in-depth, open-ended interviews and participant observation of drinking activities) supports the gender-related norms found in these surveys and offers some insights into their complexity (Gilbert, 1984). Among a number of the blue-collar Mexican American men interviewed in this study, the right to use alcohol was frequently stated to be reciprocally linked to the male provider function within a culturally sanctioned configuration of rights and obligations accruing to the adult male role. Many men expressed the notion that as long as they fulfilled their roles as providers, their drinking habits should not be subject to question. The importance attached to this male role configuration varied by class and ethnicity among the couples studied. Blue-collar Anglo males generally took the view that a hard day's work earned them the right to a couple of beers after work, but none expressed the view that work entitled him to generalized, unsanctioned drinking patterns. White collar men and women of both ethnic groups did not ascribe to this set of role-associated patterns for either men or women, but tended to define drinking rights for either sex as being associated with situationally defined comportment norms. For example, a person has the right to drink if s/he doesn't behave foolishly, do embarrassing things or cause danger to self or companions.

Rodriguez-Andrew et al. (1988) call attention to the possible historical basis for a traditional Mexican norm associating alcohol as a reward for work. Hacienda owners rewarded their fieldworkers with alcoholic beverages and landholders reciprocally involved in mutual aid work crews rewarded workers with alcohol when their fields were planted or harvested. Farmworkers in the California fields are also rewarded with cases of beer while doing overtime work (Alcocer and Gilbert, 1979). It may be that as

Mexican American males move away from manual labor into white collar jobs this norm loses some of its salience.

Alcocer and Gilbert (1979) examined normative ideations about appropriate levels of drinking in specific setting with specific companions. Among their California respondents, they found little support from either men or women for drinking while at work or anywhere prior to driving. Settings or circumstances in which light drinking (1–2 drinks) was considered all right included while dining out, while visiting relatives, with friends after work, at lunch with co-workers and at recreational activities. Light drinking after work was supported by two-thirds of both men and women, but light drinking at home alone at other times was approved by only 28% of the men and 21% of the women.

Ethnographic research in Texas (Trotter, 1985) and California (Gilbert, 1984, 1985) shows considerable sex segregation in Mexican American drinking milieus, pointing out the preference of males for drinking in male only groups. Trotter describes, for example, the *pachanga,* an occasion for beer drinking, barbecue and conversation which is a male social event. He notes that males report drinking in all male groups in taverns and bars while women do not. He points out, however, that among younger Mexican American women there is a growing tendency for women to frequent mixed sex settings where alcohol is served, such as nightclubs and dances.

Among the blue-collar California Mexican American men Gilbert interviewed and observed, drinking together with same sex companions appeared to have a different meaning for men than for women. It was frequently described by men in terms that showed it to be a bonding mechanism, intensifying relationships and underscoring a shared masculinity. This researcher points out in this context that in Mexico a male drinking companion is often called a *cuate,* literally a "twin brother," a usage that is common among some Spanish speaking Mexican Americans in California (Gilbert and Gonsalves, 1985).

Gilbert found that sex segregation in drinking milieus, while most characteristic of working class Mexican Americans, was also evident to a lesser extent among working class Anglos as well but was not prevalent among middle class Mexican Americans or Anglos. Rodriguez-Andrew et al. (1988) comment on the fact that public drinking by groups of men (outside convenience stores, in neighborhood parks, around a car being repaired in a driveway) is widely practiced in Texas and California, but women's drinking is restricted to private settings and occasions, usually among family and friends.

Gilbert (1989a) notes that class differences in drinking settings and companions were notable among her Mexican American and Anglo informants: Middle class men and women in both ethnic groups drank in many public settings as couples, there was less sex segregation of drinking sites and men and women consumed alcohol in a wide range formal and informal settings and activities with a wide range of intimate and non-intimate companions. In terms of their drinking practices, middle class Mexican American couples were more like middle class Anglo couples than blue collar Mexican American couples. It appears that with upward mobility and greater acculturation to mainstream norms, Mexican American women have more opportunities to drink and Mexican American men become less sex-segregated in their drinking practices.

Attitudes Toward Heavy Drinking and Drunkenness

Most cultures recognize the effects of alcohol on the body, though there is less agreement across cultures about alcohol's effects on emotion, mood or behavior (MacAndrew and Edgerton, 1969) and possibly even less agreement on the positive or negative value of the changes brought on by drinking large quantities of alcohol. Nevertheless, the majority of alcohol-using cultures recognize levels of use and intoxication, and norms are often formulated about the appropriateness of intoxication level drinking.

In Alcocer and Gilbert's California data, there was some support from both Hispanic men and Hispanic women for fairly heavy drinking in several social settings:

• Nineteen percent of the men and 13% of the women felt it was all right to get *high* while visiting with friends; 4% of the men but none of the women felt it was appropriate to get *drunk* under these circumstances.

• Twenty-eight percent of the men and 22% of the women felt getting high at a party was okay; 7% of the men and 2.5% of the women felt that *drunk* was okay at a party.

• Thirty-five percent of the men and 28% of the women approved of getting high at a bar and 12% and 7% of the men and women, respectively, felt getting *drunk* at a bar was acceptable.

Obviously, there was very little support from these Hispanic men and women for drunkenness in all of these settings. Still, it is clear that for each there was a much higher proportion of men than women to whom drunkenness was acceptable.

Caetano has examined "attitudes" toward drunkenness and self-reported intoxication among several groups of Hispanics in California and the U.S. (Caetano, 1984a; 1988). Contrasting 684 Hispanics (predominantly Mexican American) from the San Francisco Bay area with a sample taken from the general U.S. population, he found that reported frequency of intoxication was greater among Hispanic men and women than among men and women in the general population. His analysis also revealed that while both Hispanic men and women held more liberal views than men and women in the general population about intoxication in a man, Hispanics were more censorious than others of intoxication in women.

Contrasting subsamples of Hispanics in the 1984 national survey, this same researcher (Caetano, 1988; 1987c) found that Mexican American men and women were more permissive in their attitudes toward drunkenness than Puerto Ricans or Cuban Americans. Not surprisingly, Mexican American women and, especially, men, were more represented in those categories of drinking where drinkers consume higher quantities of alcohol per occasion. In analyzing the survey data, Caetano additionally compared subsamples of Mexican Americans in Texas and California and learned that Mexican Americans in the latter state were more permissive in their norms and had a higher prevalence of drinking and heavy drinking than the former. Caetano points out that permissive norms and the drinking patterns that result appear to stem from attitudes and standards prevalent in Mexico. There, drinking among men is not as frequent as in the U.S. general population, but even among infrequent or occasional drinkers, intoxication level drinking is quite common (Caetano, 1984a, b; Caetano and Medina-Mora, 1988). Gilbert and Gonsalves (1985) discuss the historical context, humor and folklore surrounding drunkenness in Mexican culture citing one of many *dichos* (Mexican folk sayings) on the subject of intoxication: If drunkards had wings, the sky would always be cloudy!

CONCLUSION

The three most important conclusions that can be drawn from the presently available data on alcohol-related cognitions are these:

1) There are critical differences in the way Mexican American men and women *think* about alcohol consumption. These differences are

manifested in expectations about the consequences of alcohol use and the reasons for using alcohol and norms for alcohol-related behavior. Men expect more from the use of alcohol and have more and more strongly held reasons for its use. Men are subject to fewer normative restrictions on setting and amount of alcohol use than women.

2) Differences in cognitions and drinking patterns are also related to generational status, especially among women. Mexican American women born in the U.S. expect more positive benefits from alcohol consumption, have more reasons for alcohol use and endorse these reasons more strongly than immigrant women. Acculturated men and women have more permissive norms for alcohol use than the less acculturated. While gender differences in alcohol-related cognitions are visible among immigrant and U.S.-born Mexican Americans, the gender differences are much greater among immigrants.

3) There appears to be a substantive relationship between depression and heavy or problematic alcohol use among Mexican Americans. This association may be mediated by expectations that alcohol effects mood elevation or alteration. The relationship is visible in data on immigrant and native born Mexican American men and appears to be substantially stronger among men than women.

These research findings are provocative and, to the extent that they can be used to inform treatment and prevention strategies, valuable. However, research is needed to affirm and further flesh out what these data suggest. There is little information, for example, on alcohol-related cognitions among other major Hispanic groups in the United States such as Cubans and Puerto Ricans, so it is difficult to say whether or not these ideations are shared across Hispanic subcultures. Then, too, more needs to be known about possible differences in gender socialization practices which produce male/female perceptions about alcohol consumption. Information needs to be developed on the processes of social learning that accompany acculturation in order to better understand the generational differences in cognitions that have been uncovered. Finally, the complex relationships between expectancies and motives for drinking as they relate to the experience of depression need to be analyzed and disentangled.

Such insights into the cognitive elements associated with decision-making and action-taking around alcohol use could inform the design of prevention programs and treatment modalities targeted to the specific needs of the Hispanic populations.

Chapter 5

INHALANT ABUSE
AMONG MEXICAN AMERICANS

ALBERTO MATA, SYLVIA RODRIGUEZ-ANDREW, AND BEATRICE A. ROUSE

INTRODUCTION

This chapter provides an overview and profile of Mexican Americans' use of inhalants, examines current trends and developments, and provides some suggestions and directions for further research. Inhalant abuse has been defined as the deliberate inhalation of toxic fumes for the purpose of intoxication (Cohen, 1973; Wyse, 1973; Mason, 1979; Greer, 1984). Studies concerned with the extent (Bass, 1970; Crites and Schuckitt, 1979; Mata, 1984; Mata & Rodriguez-Andrew, 1988; Padilla et al., 1979; Perez et al 1980; Lowenstein, 1984; Rodriguez-Andrew, 1985) and diversity (Clinger and Johnson, 1951; Prockop, 1977; Ackerly & Gibson, 1964; Brozorsky and Winkler, 1965; Pointer, 1982) of inhalant abuse among adolescents have been explored unevenly and sporadically since the 1950's (Press and Done, 1967a, 1967b; Jackson, Thornhill, Gonzales, 1967; Barnes, 1979; Sharp and Brehm, 1977). For the past two and a half decades, "paint and glue head scenes" have been key community concerns. Yet research and policies to deal with inhalant abuse have generally succumbed or have been overshadowed or minimized by attention drawn to heroin use (Carroll, 1977), and to marijuana and other so-called "soft drugs."

In many barrios throughout the U.S., various drug use scenes have emerged if not become more or less permanent fixtures. Inhalant use among youth is increasing, yet its exact parameters are not easily established or known (Johnston, et al., 1989). In Texas, the 1990 state-wide survey of students in grades 7 through 12 found that although inhalant use had declined from 30% in 1988 to 23% in 1990, the use of inhalants continues to be a problem for Texas youth. Unlike other drugs, students are more likely to report inhalant use before or during school than other substances. More than one-fourth of students report using inhalants before or during school compared to students reporting marijuana (14%) and cocaine use (11%). Efforts to contain or reduce if not prevent inhalant abuse will need data and understanding that more adequately address the etiological, epidemiological, psychosocial, developmental, behavioral and social-environmental dimensions underlying this practice.

Given the nation's ongoing concern with youth and young adults' use of alcohol and other mood altering substances, this review attempts to put into perspective inhalant abuse, a perennial concern in many Hispanic communities throughout the U.S.

Prior to 1976, "sniffing" was presumed limited to glue and occasionally gasoline (Sharp and Brehm, 1977; Sharp and Korman, 1980; Cohen, 1979). The term "inhalant abuse" was introduced in 1976 to encompass the increasing number and type of substances found to produce intoxication (Greer, 1986). Volatile substances deliberately inhaled for the purpose of intoxication fall into three categories: anesthetics, solvents, and aerosols (Nicholi, 1983; Cohen, 1979; Brehm and Sharp, 1977). Solvents include a variety of commercial products such as gasoline, transmission fluid, paint thinner, airplane cement glue, etc. Aerosol products include spray paints, shoe shine compounds, insecticides, hairspray, etc. (Nicholi, 1983). Amyl and butyl nitrites are usually inhaled for their smooth muscle relaxant effects rather than for intoxication. Therefore, the nitrites are included only when they have been combined in the general category of inhalants but are not included as a separate category in this review.

Communities are reporting inhalant abuse involving an assortment of complex chemical compounds and a wide range of industrial gases that were never intended for human consumption (Wyse, 1973; Texas Commission on Alcohol and Drug Abuse, 1990). Given the wide range of compounds, methods of inhalation vary. Inhalant users are constantly experimenting with "new" substances and techniques. The ease with which youth may obtain these substances and youths' awareness of their need to avoid detection (Cohen, 1973; 1979) compounds the problem of providing a timely, measured response.

One of the more popular methods of administering the inhalant in most barrios across the southwest has been to pour the substance onto a cloth which is then held to the nose and mouth (Cohen, 1979; Mason, 1979). Stybel, Allen and Lewis (1976) found that plastic and paper bags, tissues, cups and cotton have all been used to contain the substances.

The use of spray paint has become particularly popular in many

Southwest communities (Wilde, 1975; Korman, 1977; Mason, 1979). The most common method has been to spray the substance directly into an empty soft drink can which is then brought to the face and inhaled. This method gives the illusion that the inhalant user is merely drinking a soft drink.

Several studies have indicated that the users avoid direct contact with the lips, nose or mucous membranes because the substances have been found to be irritating and may result in inflammation of these tissues (Glasser and Massengale, 1962; Chapel and Taylor, 1968; Corliss, 1965). The effects of these substances have been difficult to assess; however, there has been consistent speculation that continued use of inhalants results in permanent brain damage, nerve damage, kidney and liver disease, heart irregularities, cancer and even death (Bass, 1970).

HEALTH CONSEQUENCES OF INHALANT ABUSE

The full extent of the health related consequences of inhalant use have been difficult to determine. Bass (1970) identified the "sudden death syndrome" in sniffers. Dyer (1984) hypothesized that permanent brain damage is a common occurrence among chronic users. Users have reported headaches, dizziness, perspiration, nausea, vomiting and even fainting during their early use. Nerve damage resulting in loss of balance, leg weakness, numbness in fingers and toes also have been reported. Hecht (1980) indicated that users have an increased risk of kidney and liver disease, heart irregularities and cancer. Since adolescents are consuming an array of chemicals that are routinely used for commercial and household use, their effects on the human organism are just now being investigated.

The primary source of data on the acute medical emergencies and deaths associated with inhalant abuse is the Drug Abuse Warning Network (DAWN). The National Institute on Drug Abuse sponsors this reporting system of drug abuse related episodes identified by emergency rooms and medical examiners in selected major metropolitan areas. In 1987, data were available from 752 emergency rooms located in 27 metropolitan areas participating in the DAWN system (NIDA, 1988). Although national estimates cannot be made because this was not a representative sample, the mention rate for inhalants was 2.5 per 100,000 emergency room (ER) visits in the participating facilities. The most inhalant mentions per 100,000 ER visits were reported by Dallas (20.3), followed by

Denver (9.3), Minneapolis (9.1), and Phoenix (8.0). While White non-Hispanics accounted for about half of the inhalant episodes in the total DAWN system, Hispanic patients accounted for 22% and Blacks for 19%. Solvents accounted for 66% of the inhalant ER mentions. Over half of the inhalant-related episodes involved other drugs; the drugs most mentioned in combination with inhalants were alcohol, cocaine, marijuana, PCP and heroin.

Although New York City did not participate in the DAWN medical examiner system in 1987, the relationships between inhalants and other drug combinations, race/ethnicity, and region were similar to those in the emergency room episodes. As with the ER episodes, a high proportion of cases occurred in the West and Southwest; however, the rate of inhalant mentions in medical examiner cases in San Antonio (2.3 per 1,000) was higher than that of Dallas (1.4).

A panel of 564 ER facilities in DAWN which reported consistently over the 10 year period from 1976 to 1985 was examined for trends in ER mentions of inhalants (NIDA, 1985). The overall rate increased from 2.18 per 100,000 total ER visits from 1976 to a high of 2.51 per 100,000 in 1979 and declined steadily to 1.81 per 100,000 in 1985. Most of the decline appeared due to a decline in the mention of solvents, especially in Phoenix. Analysis by race/ethnicity was possible for only the period of 1981 to 1985; throughout this time except for a low of 21% in 1983, Hispanics comprised about 25% of the cases.

While in some localities a particular substance is abused as an inhalant, such as shoeshine polish in Houston, Texas (Mason, 1979; Governor's Task Force on Inhalant Abuse, 1984), it is important to note that a range of substances are used. In addition to the range of inhalants that are available, there are important specific environmental influences on the nature and dynamics of inhalant abuse in various locales.

EXTENT OF THE INHALANT ABUSE PROBLEM

Although there are some national data, the bulk of the inhalant abuse research, especially regarding Mexican Americans, consists of local community or school based studies (Padilla et al., 1979; Szapocznik et al., 1977; Mason, 1979; Swaim et al., 1986; Texas Commission on Alcohol and Drug Abuse, 1990). However, a number of problems and limitations marked their efforts and contributions.

The main difficulty with national studies of drug use in general and of inhalant use in particular has been inadequate sample sizes to get reliable estimates of Hispanics and other special populations. Even when samples contain Hispanics, data are often not reported for Hispanics as a group, much less for subgroups such as Mexican Americans.

While national data concerning inhalant abuse is limited, national data concerning inhalant abuse by Hispanics in general and by Mexican Americans in particular is even more sparse. The primary source of national data on inhalant abuse in the general population is the National Household Survey of Drug Abuse of the civilian population age 12 years and older (NIDA, 1987). This survey provides national data on a variety of illicit drug use as well as inhalant abuse by Hispanics. Such data on Hispanics are available for 1985 when Hispanics and Blacks were first oversampled in this series sponsored by the National Institute on Drug Abuse and for 1988, the most recently available survey (NIDA, 1988).

Based on the 1988 National Household Survey of Drug Abuse of the civilian population age 12 years and older, an estimated 858,000 Hispanics have deliberately used an inhalant for the purpose of intoxication, "for kicks or to get high" at least once in their life. The most frequently reported inhalants ever abused by the total general population were amyl/butyl nitrites, glue/shoeshine/toluene, gasoline and nitrous oxide. Adolescents were more likely to report having ever inhaled gasoline (3.7%), glue (2.8%), correction fluids (1.6%) and nitrites (1.6%).

Since the amount of an inhalant used is difficult to measure, the respondents were asked about the effect they were trying to achieve with the amount they usually used. Most users reported that they usually used enough inhalant to feel it a little. Some reported that they used enough to get high. However, a few indicated that they usually used enough to go beyond feelings of euphoria, i.e., to stagger and drop things and to feel like they were going to pass out. Hispanics were less likely than White non-Hispanics and more likely than Blacks to report inhalant abuse.

Although inhalant abuse was reported by all four major age groups, including those over age 35, teenagers were more likely to report recent inhalant abuse. The 1988 NIDA Household Survey also indicated that "past year" inhalant abuse was reported by less than 0.5% of Hispanics age 35 years and older, 0.8% of those age 26–34 years, 1.5% of those age 18–25 years and 2.4% of those age 12–17 years. Furthermore, last month use was highest among those age 12–17 years (1.4%).

National data on inhalant abuse by students are available for eighth and tenth graders from the National Adolescent Student Health Survey conducted in 1985. The National High School Senior Survey provides data on inhalant abuse from each senior class since 1976. Neither student surveys provide information on Hispanics. The annual senior survey, however, is useful in determining trends of inhalant abuse among adolescents in general who reach the senior year of high school. The annual rate of inhalant use among seniors is lower than the rates for marijuana, cocaine, stimulants and, of course, tobacco and alcohol. Only inhalants, however, have continued to steadily increase in use since 1976 and to peak only in the last few years (Johnston, et al., 1989).

The most recent report from the national senior survey indicates that lifetime use of inhalants (unadjusted for under-reporting of nitrites) increased from 10.3% for the class of 1976 to 17.6% for the class of 1989. Use in the past year almost doubled from 3.0% of the seniors in 1976 to 5.9% in 1989. Use in the past 30 days more than doubled from 0.9% in 1976 to 2.3% in 1989 (Johnston, et al., 1990).

Most of the inhalant abuse reported by the seniors was experimental: 57% had used inhalants once or twice and only 16% had used them 10 or more times in their life. Over half of the seniors first started their inhalant abuse by the ninth grade. After junior high school the risk of adolescent inhalant abuse decreased with age, unlike the use of marijuana, cocaine and other illicit drugs.

It is interesting to note that unlike marijuana and cocaine, rates of inhalant abuse reported by the eighth and tenth graders in the National Adolescent Student Health Survey generally were the same (21% for lifetime and 10% in the past year). Eighth graders, however, were more likely to report more occasions of inhalant abuse in the past year and in the past month. This suggests that (1) either inhalant abusers, especially frequent users, are more likely to drop out of school before their senior year or that (2) seniors are likely to forget or deny their earlier use.

Among the seniors who had ever used inhalants, however, more of the class of 1988 reported inhalant use in the past year than the class of 1976 (39% vs. 29%). The noncontinuation rate of use (i.e., the percent of those ever using who did *not* use in the past year) has always been higher for inhalants than for any of the other illicit drugs used. While inhalant use rates for the last 30 days and for daily use closely approximates the rates for cocaine, hallucinogens and stimulants—there were vast differences between the discontinuation rates for inhalants compared with all other drugs. Also, as noted earlier, inhalant use steadily increased while other illicit drug use was declining over time since 1976. These trends suggest that unique factors may be influencing inhalant abuse.

A recent sub-national survey (NIDA, 1987) of Mexican American, Puerto Rican and Cuban-American health and nutrition status (HHANES) focused some attention on selected drug use among Hispanics ages 12 to 44. Inhalant data were available only on Mexican Americans and Puerto Ricans. Mexican Americans' rates for lifetime use was 6.4%, past year use 0.7%, and past month use was 0.4%. The Puerto Ricans' past year and past month rates were the same as the Mexican Americans but their lifetime rate was less (4.8%). Similar to other studies, the median onset for inhalant use was 15 years for both Puerto Rican and Mexican American males; but, Mexican American females were more likely to report younger onset (14 years) than Puerto Rican females (16 years).

The leading types of inhalants abused by Mexican Americans were gasoline or lighter fluid (reported by 35.6% of the inhalant abusers), shoe shine, glue or toluene (33.33%), spray paint (33.2%), and amyl nitrite or "poppers" (17.4%). Puerto Ricans were not as likely to have used gasoline or lighter fluid.

One should keep in mind that data from these general surveys are subject to serious limitations concerning inhalants. The surveys generally obscure variability in level of use (i.e. recreational versus chronic use), between local communities, between schools and, more importantly, among racial/ethnic minority youth. Furthermore, they do not address issues of attitudes or behavior helpful in understanding, preventing or treating inhalant abuse. In addition, student surveys generally do not address the relationship between inhalant abuse, absenteeism, dropout rates, and racial/ethnic minority status. For Hispanics and Native Americans, these limitations obviate the surveys' utility for their respective communities.

General population studies have not found Hispanics to be more likely than non-Hispanic Whites to be inhalant abusers. Among those who do abuse inhalants, however, Hispanics may start earlier. Analysis of data from the Client Oriented Data Acquisition Process (CODAP) found that Mexican Americans experiment with inhalants at least one year younger than their White non-Hispanic counterparts (Rouse, 1986). Furthermore, treatment admissions for adolescents in the CODAP system were more likely to be for inhalant abuse among Mexican Americans than other Whites: among 12–17 year olds, 33% of Mexican American admissions were for inhalants compared to 5% for Whites.

In addition to early onset, some researchers have drawn attention to inhalant users' use of other illicit substances, or their inclination to go on to using other substances. For others, their concerns draw attention to experimental-"social users" versus "regular"-chronic users.

TYPES OF INHALANT ABUSERS

Inhalant abusers have been categorized in a variety of ways in different studies. Wyse (1973) identified two kinds of sniffers: chronic and social users of inhalants. Chronic users of inhalants were defined as those who sniff on a regular basis while social users sniff occasionally or out of curiosity and eventually discard the use of inhalants. Cohen (1973) identified three types of abusers: experimenters are those who try the solvent once or a few times then discard the practice; occasional or social users are those who use infrequently; and chronic users (the "heads") are those who sniff daily. Albaugh and Albaugh's (1979) study of Cheyenne and Arapaho Indians defined a sniffer as anyone who makes habitual use of, or has a clear sense of, the need for a feeling of intoxication through the use of a volatile solvent.

Stybel et al. (1976) defined sniffers as anyone having at one time or another inhaled hydrocarbon fumes or reported behavioral activity consistent with hydrocarbon inhalation. Frequency of inhalation ranged from three times a month or less (63%) to greater than 20 times a month. Sniffers were then divided into two categories: social sniffers defined as those with a frequency level of seven times a month or less and chronic sniffers who reported sniffing eight or more times a month. Based on this classification, 75% of the respondents were social sniffers while 25% were chronic users.

DeBarona and Simpson (1984) identified four levels of use: non-users, experimental, recreational, and chronic users in their survey of 293 youth admitted to Texas drug prevention programs. Non-users were defined as those who had not used inhalants at all in the two months prior to admission. Experimental users were those who reported using inhalants only once or twice in the two months prior to program admission while recreational users were those reporting inhalant use several times a month. Chronic users reported inhalant use almost every day prior to the two months before their admission to the program. Based on this classification, 57% were non-users, 12% were experimenters, 15%

were recreational users, and 16% were chronic users in the two months prior to their participation in drug prevention services.

It is clear that distinctions in patterns of inhalant use exist. However, there is no consensus about which dimensions or factors delineate those differences. Successful intervention and prevention efforts will depend upon these delineations.

Although frequency of inhalant use provides several useful indicators of chronicity of use, systematic exploration of the consequences of use based on frequency is notably absent. Since the earliest studies, there has been considerable agreement that inhalant use may be considered a distinct pattern of substance abuse. While there is no consensus as to which qualities, properties or dynamics underlie or make for their distinctiveness, research to date generally draws attention to the following: early onset; inhalants as a gateway drug; propensity towards delinquency; poly-drug use; harmfulness to self and others; and individual, family and social pathology.

SOCIO-CULTURAL FACTORS OF INHALANT ABUSE

Gosset et al. (1971), Hecht (1980), Sharp and Korman (1980), and Dyer (1984) noted that while inhalant abuse cuts across socioeconomic lines, there is an over-involvement of low income racial and ethnic minority adolescents, particularly young Mexican Americans and Native Americans. Cohen (1973) indicates that inhalant users are more homogeneous that those involved with other classes of abusable drugs.

Existing studies report that young males are more likely to abuse inhalants than females, especially among Mexican Americans. Yet, it appears that the use of inhalants by females is increasing (NIDA, 1987; Rodriguez-Andrew, 1985; Mata, 1984). A 1967 (Press and Done) study reported a 10:1 male to female ratio and by 1980, Korman found that the gap had narrowed to a 3 to 1 ratio.

Inhalant users have been found more likely to be abusing other substances as well, notably alcohol and marijuana (DeBarona and Simpson, 1984). The combined effects of multiple drug use on the young developing adolescent remains relatively unexplored. For example, Rodriguez-Andrew's (1985) pilot study of 83 Mexican American children in housing projects found that inhalant abusers were more likely to report multiple drug use. Sixty-eight percent of chronic inhalant users and 82% of recreational users reported also using marijuana once a day. Almost half

(47%) of the chronic users and 27% of the recreational users reported drinking once a day. The multiple drug use phenomenon is especially alarming when one considers that the average age of the respondents was approximately 14 years.

According to Cohen (1973), there appears to be general agreement that the hypothesized causal factors of inhalant abuse are related to a disorganized existence, the disagreement, however, lies in the sources of that disorganization. Padilla et al.'s (1979) review of available literature indicates that the extent and trends of inhalant abuse have not been adequately investigated. Consequently, specification of causal factors are speculative and premature.

Anecdotal reports of chronic inhalant abusers suggest that they are perceived and treated like social pariahs by their family, peers, and the community. Some are reported living in deserted houses, under bridges and makeshift shelters. Chronic inhalant use has more than likely severed relationships with a key source of support—the family. Initial efforts need to focus on establishing credibility, trust and rapport.

Since the early 1960's, familial disruption among inhalant abusers has been consistently documented. Massengale, et al. (1963) found that sniffers were more likely to come from broken homes where fathers were missing or to have had alcoholic parents. Bonnheim and Korman (1985) administered the Family Environment Scale to users and non-users and found that inhalant abusers live in a more conflictual, anxious atmosphere especially in the communication area. The social conditions have been perceived as a strong etiological factor in the flight into inhalants (Cohen, 1973).

Korman et al.'s (1980) comparative study of inhalant users and non-users indicated that inhalant users had greater difficulty in the intra-personal area. Nylander (1962) described sniffers as "emotionally disturbed." Press and Done (1967a; 1967b) indicated that sniffers perceived themselves as inadequate, bashful, and at times frustrated over their inability to reach high parental standards. Meloff's comparative study of inhalant user vis-a-vis non-users found that inhalant users scored lower on poise, ascendancy, self assurance, socialization, maturity, and responsibility (1970). Several authors contend that inhalant users are more prone to engage in self-directed aggressive behavior (Korman et al., 1980; Press and Done, 1967a; 1967b).

Chronic/regular users of inhalants are also unlikely to be attending school or participating in social or recreational activities where information about the adverse consequences of inhalant abuse is likely to be disseminated or presented (Bachrach and Sandler, 1985). As with chronic users, non-users and experimenters may not be attending school. Mexican American adolescents and young adults have a higher proportion of dropping out of school (Delgado and Rodriguez-Andrew, 1990). Some communities report drop out rates as high as 50%. Thus, while schools have been seen as a traditional vehicle for teaching about substance abuse, other sources of prevention and intervention will need to be explored for Mexican American adolescents and young adults. While lower grades, suspensions, and absenteeism have been associated with inhalant use, the dilemma is whether inhalant use is the cause or effect of poor school performance. Further, there is disagreement on whether there are differences in the intellectual functioning of inhalant users and non-users (Korman et al., 1980; Press and Done, 1967a, b).

The relative availability coupled with low cost is particularly attractive to the young adolescent and may account for the fact that many report the use of inhalants as their first self induced mood altering experience. Although the use of inhalants by peers or siblings have been suggested as strong factors that influence adolescent use of inhalants, little research has been conducted in this area (Dworkin and Stephens, 1980).

PATTERNS OF INHALANT USE
AMONG MEXICAN AMERICAN YOUTH

Research on Mexican American youth in two distinct settings concerned with their respective youths' use of volatile substances, as well as other drugs follow. The first involves an old port of entry neighborhood in a major southwestern city, i.e., an urban low-income Mexican American community. The second focuses on rural communities, long perceived to be outside the major influences of "a modern high tech society". In the former, we have a pattern of inhalant use that in many ways has come to be associated with the more commonly held image and understanding of inhalant use (Ackerly and Gibson, 1964; Barker and Adams, 1963; Padilla et al., 1979; Szapocnik et al., 1977; Wilde, 1975; Korman et al., 1980; Mason, 1979; DeBarona and Simpson, 1984). In the latter we have a setting that has traditionally not been associated with drug use (Heiligman, 1973; Swaim et al., 1986; Harrell, 1981; NIDA, 1977), much less the use of volatile substances (Albaugh and Albaugh, 1979).

Rodriguez-Andrew's (1985) pilot study on the use of inhalants among Mexican American children and adolescents in two housing projects reported that frequency of inhalant use ranged from once a day (14%) to never used (63%). A chronic user was defined as one who used inhalants consistently, that is, once a day, more than once a week and/or more than once a month. A recreational user or experimenter was defined as one who either used once a month or less or had used but was no longer using. While previous surveys have included experimenters who no longer use inhalants as non-users, the experimenters were included with the recreational users because regardless of whether experimenters used inhalants once or twice, they still made the decision to use and consequently could not be viewed as a non-user. Non-users were those that indicated they never used inhalants. Based on this classification, 19 (23%) were chronic users of inhalants, 11 (13%) were either recreational users or had experimented with inhalants and 53 (64%) had never used inhalants. The use of inhalants by gender supports earlier studies that males are more likely to abuse inhalants than females. Survey results indicate a 2:1 male to female ratio among chronic users.

Adolescents in the age category of 12 to 14 had the highest percentage of chronic users (37%). These results are consistent with earlier reports that suggest 12 to 14 is the most critical and vulnerable age for adolescents to make decisions about the experimentation and perhaps continued use of substances. Seventy-one percent of the respondents indicated that they believed their friends were currently abusing inhalants. Investigation into the respondents' use of other substances supported previous findings that indicate inhalant abusers are multiple drug users. Sixty-eight percent of the chronic users of inhalants and 82% of the recreational users reported using marijuana once a day. A similar pattern was noted in the use of alcohol. Almost half (47%) of the chronic users and 27% of the recreational users reported drinking once a day.

Youth age 9 to 11 were more likely to view inhalant use as dangerous and leading to serious problems. Those age 12 to 14, however, did not perceive inhalant use as dangerous. The data suggest that 12 to 14 is the age when most of these adolescents report regular and experimental use of various substances, and if they do not perceive difficulties in school, home, or in their relationships with peers they are not likely to view their drug use as harmful or problematic. However, by the age of 15 to 17, for those adolescents who continue in their use of inhalants, it appears that they begin to experience the adverse results of several years of alcohol and other drug use and are more likely to view it as harmful.

Preliminary results of this survey suggest that inhalants are one of the three drugs of choice for most of these adolescents and their peers. One out of three respondents indicated having used inhalants at one time or another and three fourths of the respondents reported having experimented with one substance or another, notably alcohol, marijuana or inhalants.

In the Frio county drug study which is in a largely rural area, 13% reported some lifetime use of inhalants. Similar to urban youths' use of alcohol, cigarettes, and marijuana, inhalant onset was more likely to occur in early to mid-adolescence for these rural youth. The rate of inhalant abuse for males was twice the rate for females. Onset for inhalant use for males was earlier than for females. In fact, the onset for females was more likely to occur in mid-adolescence, while for males it was in early adolescence. Both lifetime and current inhalant rates were higher for Mexican Americans than for their White non-Hispanic counterparts. There was an interaction effect between gender and frequency of use. Current use among the four race/gender groups was highest among the Mexican American males while Mexican American females reported the lowest rate of inhalant use. For most recent inhalant use seven months ago or more, White males have the highest rate while White females have the lowest. The respondents as a whole ranked inhalants as the third most easily obtained illicit substance (only tobacco and alcohol rank easier to obtain). Inhalants were perceived to be only slightly more easy to obtain than "pot" or "amphetamines."

In terms of respondents' reason(s) for use, inhalant users were more likely to report "using": "to express feelings," "to feel better," "they see that the use of drugs is okay," or "usage is related to coping with personal and family problems." Inhalant users report that their friends are more likely to use and prefer other illicit substances rather than inhalants. Only friends' use of tranquilizers and LSD is reported less than friends' use of inhalants. Also, they say that their friends approve more of using most other illicit substances than inhalants.

Inhalant users most often cite "fear of the law" (66%), "medical reasons" (62%) and "hurting their parents" (58%) as their key reasons for not using or quitting any particular substance. When concerned about using or not using drugs, inhalant users say they would seek information from their minister, priest or pastor, their peers, their teacher or the radio or related media BEFORE they would turn to a medical doctor, family member, school staff or program, or parents.

In short, the data suggest that inhalant use in this rural county is similar to patterns of use in urban areas. Onset, lifetime use and regular use, their friends' approval and use of inhalants as well as other drugs, the ease with which students report getting inhalants as well as other drugs suggest that inhalants and other illicit drug use is no longer limited to Mexican American urban communities and barrios.

RECOMMENDATIONS

The need for attention to Mexican Americans' use of inhalants as well as other substances should not be minimized, trivialized or overlooked. At the same time the problem, its changing nature and consequences/impact do not need to be overstated, sensationalized or exaggerated. The present knowledge concerning inhalant use and users would suggest the need for continued, sustained study of this phenomenon. Therefore as it concerns epidemiological and behavioral studies, outreach and intervention studies, treatment and prevention, we recommend the following:

Research

The continuing use of volatile substances, the introduction of new substances and modes of use, its early onset and role as a gateway drug among young users, adequate understanding of youth's decision to experiment, to use recreationally, to becoming chronic users and assessment of its long term effects suggest the need for basic epidemiological, longitudinal and controlled case studies. The ability to develop new programs and services appropriate for Mexican Americans and other special populations rests on continuing systematic study of inhalant users. The need to focus on the more enduring factors needs to be complimented by the need to account for an understanding of "new" developments or emerging characteristics of inhalant use.

Outreach and Intervention Services

It is recommended that outreach and intervention services focus their efforts on Mexican American adolescents and young adults based on their level of involvement with inhalant abuse. Specific strategies need to target (1) youth who have not experimented with inhalants but because of environmental, social and/or other conditions are considered at risk for inhalant abuse, (2) youth who are currently in the experimental stages of inhalant use, and (3) youth who regularly use inhalants. While the goal of outreach and intervention services is to forestall or deter inhalant abuse, strategies for the non-user, recreational and chronic/regular user need to be developed and to target each of these populations. After intensive casefinding and intervention efforts, it is important that follow-up and aftercare services be provided. It is imperative to train culturally sensitive professionals and indigenous specialists to develop a systematic method for "reaching out" to adolescents and young adults with a history of chronic inhalant abuse. It is important that didactic and experiential activities incorporate the role of the peer group and present credible and reliable information. Mata and Rodriguez-Andrew's (1988) survey reported that although adolescents are more likely to learn about alcohol and drug use from the media, ultimate sources of knowledge remain their peers, parents, and siblings.

Prevention

Historically, prevention efforts have primarily focused on changing the behavior that places adolescents and youth at risk for subsequent substance abuse involvement. Unfortunately, early prevention programs failed to document their efficacy in decreasing or eliminating substance use. Gilbert (1986) reported that only a handful of primary prevention programs have been designed for Mexican American youth. Most of these programs have not been evaluated and descriptive information about these programs has not been published. However, an emerging theme in each of these programs is the role of the family. While much more is known about the consequences of inhalant abuse, relatively less is known about factors that encourage and maintain the use of inhalants. Although not developed specifically for Hispanic youth, the Texas Commission on Alcohol and Drug Abuse have recently developed a series of posters and other educational materials that can be used in a variety of settings to inform youth about the dangers associated with the use of inhalants. Specific recommendations in the area of prevention include:

(a) The development and inclusion of culturally sensitive educational materials on inhalant abuse. These materials need to focus on special target groups such as nonusers, recreational and chronic users. Similarly, they would need to include appropriate and relevant information for young adults.

(b) The development and evaluation of specially designed programs for the prevention of inhalant abuse among Mexican American adolescents and young adults. Relatively little is known about the effectiveness of prevention and early intervention services with inhalant users. Even less is known about the treatment of inhalant abusers.

(c) Systematic research and evaluation of existing prevention programs that focus on Mexican American children. These results would be critical in developing clearly defined hypotheses for further research.

Treatment

The presenting problems of inhalant users in hospital emergency rooms need to be addressed. While it has been generally stated that there is an absence of a specific treatment regime for inhalant abusers, there is little disagreement that they do represent a special case for juvenile, mental health, health and related social services. Across the Southwest and to a lesser degree the Midwest, youth have availed themselves of community based youth programs (De Barona & Simpson, 1984; Szapocnik et al., 1977). Although Mason (1979) found that inhalant users did not respond well in treatment, there are no definitive studies to date that contrast different intensive intervention and treatment modalities as it concerns inhalant abusers.

Chapter 6

THE DRUG USE AND
CRIME CONNECTION AMONG HISPANICS:
AN OVERVIEW OF RESEARCH FINDINGS*

Mario R. De La Rosa and Luis H. Caris

INTRODUCTION

Much has been written in the social and behavioral sciences in the past 15 years about the relationship between drug use and crime (Nurco, in press). The findings from this research have yielded valuable information on the extent and nature of this relationship and have shown that drug use, deviancy, and crime are inextricably linked to each other (Gropper, 1985; Gandossy et al., 1980; McBride and McCoy, 1981).

Despite the advances made in understanding the drug/crime connection in recent years, research on this topic among Hispanics is lacking. With Hispanic communities throughout the United States experiencing high levels of drug-related violence and property crimes (Newsweek, November 28, 1988; New York Times, September 8, 1989), the need to conduct research that could provide information on how to effectively address the drug problem and drug-related criminality among Hispanics has become critical. The need for such research is compounded by the fact that the Hispanic population is expected to become the largest minority group in this country by the year 2010 (McKay, 1987).

It should be pointed out that the term Hispanic has been utilized in this chapter to describe all research conducted on the drug use and crime connection that includes Mexican Americans, Puerto Ricans living in the mainland, Cuban Americans, and/or South or Central Americans in their studies. Whenever possible in the context of the text where information exists on the composition of the Hispanic sample by specific

---

*Opinions expressed in this manuscript are those of the authors and do not necessarily reflect the opinions or official policy of the National Institute on Drug Abuse or any other part of the U.S. Department of Health and Human Services.

subgroup, it will be mentioned. This is in keeping with the fact that Hispanics in the United States are a rather heterogeneous ethnic group with significant cultural, geographic, and socioeconomic differences between each of the major Hispanic subgroups. Thus, the findings reported from a study which includes Hispanics of Puerto Rican extraction are probably not generalizable to a sample of Mexican Americans.

It is the purpose of this chapter to provide an overview and analysis of research conducted on the drug/crime connection that pertains to Hispanics. This overview and analysis will concentrate on reporting and discussing the contributions, limitations, and lack of research in the following four areas of research in the study of the drug use/crime relationship: (1) the criminal behavior of narcotic and cocaine addicts/users; (2) the drug use/violence connection; (3) the gang, drug use, and crime connection among Hispanics; (4) and the relationship between drug use, crime, and drug treatment. A secondary objective of this chapter is to make recommendations on future directions for research on the drug/crime connection among Hispanics.

THE CRIMINAL BEHAVIOR OF NARCOTIC AND COCAINE ADDICTS/USERS

Numerous studies and analyses documenting the prevalence of criminal activities among narcotic addicts have been conducted (Nurco et al., 1985). The findings from this research have established unequivocally that contemporary narcotic addiction in the United States is associated with high crime rates. It is known that narcotic addicts are involved in criminal activities on a daily basis and often commit hundreds and, in some cases, thousands of criminal offenses during their addiction careers (Ball et al., 1983). While many of these offenses involve "victimless" crimes, many narcotic addicts commit or are victims of serious and violent crimes (i.e., armed robbery, aggravated assault, homicide, etc.).

Despite the voluminous literature on this specific aspect of research on the drug/crime connection, little research has been conducted on the criminal careers of Hispanic narcotic addicts over their addiction careers. There are only two studies in the drug/crime literature which have analyzed the criminal activities of Hispanic narcotic addicts while not in jail and compared them against their White and Black non-Hispanic counterparts.

The Nurco et al. (1986) study on the criminal careers of narcotic addicts collected comparable information on the criminal activities of 150 male narcotic addicts (50 White addicts, 50 Black addicts, and 50 Hispanic addicts—mostly Puerto Ricans) admitted to a single large-capacity methadone maintenance/detoxification center in New York City. Results from this study indicate that Hispanic and Black narcotic addicts were more likely than White addicts to be involved in drug-dealing activities during periods of heavy narcotic use. The Hispanic and Black addicts were involved in an average of 200+ drug-dealing offenses per year compared to 100+ drug-dealing offenses reported by the White addicts.

Other results from the Nurco study suggest that Hispanic narcotic addicts were likely to be involved in more violent crimes during periods of heavy narcotic use, with 14 reported offenses per year, compared with the approximately 6 violent offenses per year reported by the Black addicts, and the average of 8 violent offenses indicated by the White addicts. However, Black addicts were more likely to be involved in criminal activities than their Hispanic or White counterparts. According to Nurco et al. (1986), Black addicts were involved in an average of 458 criminal offenses per year during periods of narcotic addiction, compared to 370 offenses for the Hispanic addicts and 346 offenses for the White addicts.

Furthermore, while not using narcotics or during periods of low narcotic use, Black addicts were involved in more criminal offenses per year than either the Hispanic or White addicts. In particular, Black addicts reported committing more violent crimes than their White and Hispanic counterparts during periods of no or low narcotic use. The Nurco study reported that Black addicts were involved in more than six offenses per year compared to less than one offense per year reported by both the Hispanic and White addicts. These results indicate that a reduction in narcotic use did not alter significantly the violent criminal activities of Black addicts as much as it did among Hispanic and White addicts.

Additional analysis of data on the criminal behavior of the narcotic addicts interviewed by Nurco and his colleagues in 1983 suggests that, during periods of non-narcotic addiction or low use, cocaine abuse was significantly related to the drug-dealing activities of the Hispanic addicts and to a lesser extent than that of Black addicts. On the other hand, cocaine abuse did not significantly alter the drug-dealing of White addicts.

Patterns of drug use by Hispanic narcotic addicts and drug-related criminality were also explored by Anglin et al. (1988). Data collected from 1964 through 1986 on a group of 1,781 White and Mexican-American male and female narcotic addicts admitted to a number of methadone maintenance programs and 581 male narcotic addicts admitted to the California Civil Addict Program (CAP) revealed that the Mexican American women subjects appeared to be more deviant than their White counterparts. The results from this study suggested that Mexican American women addicts were more likely than the White female addicts to be involved in criminal behavior and renewed heroin use after discharge from treatment.

Why Mexican American female addicts in the Anglin study reported high rates of criminal activities and heroin use after treatment discharge is unknown. One possible explanation for these results may be related to the Hispanic culture and its strong negative attitudes and stigmatization toward Hispanic females who use drugs (Jorquez, 1984; Moore, 1978). Ostracized by their families, friends, and community, and thus unable to receive emotional and financial support from their informal social support systems, it can be conjectured that many of these Mexican American females turn to crime for survival.

Overall, the criminal behavior of Mexican American male narcotic addicts did not differ significantly from that of the White and Black addicts in the sample during periods of narcotic addiction. However, Anglin et al. (1988) found that the Mexican American male addicts had significantly higher pre-addiction rates of arrest for property crimes; while Whites had significantly higher rates of arrest for drug-related crimes, burglary, and forgery.

Findings based on data collected from narcotic addicts participating in the Federal Drug Forecasting Reporting Program (DARP) in the mid 1970's suggest that in comparison to White, Black, and Puerto Rican addicts, Mexican American heroin addicts were more likely to be arrested and spend time in jail for illegal activities (Long and Demares, 1975). Whether the findings reported by Anglin et al. (1988) and Long and Demares (1975) on the high rate of arrest of Mexican American narcotic addicts is due more to the vigorous and intense police surveillance of individuals of Mexican American background in the Southwest or other individual and/or environmental forces present in the lives of Mexican Americans remains to be explored.

Other research conducted on the criminal behavior of Hispanic narcotic addicts has mostly involved jail and/or prison populations. One of the first studies of this type was that conducted by White et al. (no date given). Data from interviews conducted by White et al. on a group of male and female Mexican American felons in a metropolitan Texas jail revealed a number of interesting findings. He found that heroin use among the interviewed Mexican-Americans was not related to their marital or educational status. White also reported that the incarcerated women were more likely than their male counterparts to be heroin users (79% vs. 56%). These results are disheartening, given the central role that the Hispanic female plays in the well-being of their families and communities, particularly among Puerto Ricans in the mainland United States where close to half of the Puerto Rican families are headed by a single female (U.S. Census Bureau, 1985).

A second study, one conducted by Weissman et al. (1976), investigated the crime/drug connection among a group of Mexican-American, White, and Black narcotic addicts. The results from data collected on a racially/ethnically mixed sample of individuals incarcerated in the Denver city jail in 1973 and 1974 found, as in previous studies, that crime involvement was strongly associated with the onset of addiction. The results also suggested that Mexican American addicts incurred a disproportionately higher number of arrests for burglary compared to White and Black addicts, regardless of the age when they first became involved in heroin use.

On the other hand, there is a dearth of research in the drug and crime literature on the criminal behavior of cocaine addicts regardless of ethnic/racial background (Fagan and Chin, 1990). Data collected by Fagan and his colleagues on a group of 350, mostly White and Black, crack sellers (the majority of whom were also crack users) is one of the most recent studies which has investigated the criminal careers of cocaine users.

The findings from the study of Fagan and Chin revealed that the majority of the subjects were involved in a highly violent lifestyle. Fagan and Chin (1990) reported that crack sellers who were also users were more likely than other drug sellers/users to be involved in drug-related and non-drug related violent criminal acts. He attributes these results to the violent nature of the crack/cocaine market and an increasing pattern of violence and deviancy in the communities where many of these individuals lived, which was not present during the late 1960's and the 1970's. Because there were few Hispanic subjects in the study sample,

Fagan and Chin were not able to determine whether Hispanic cocaine/crack users were more or less likely to be involved in criminal activities than the Black and/or White addicts.

The drug-related activities of cocaine/crack users has also been explored by Soriano and De La Rosa (1990). Interviews conducted on a group of 391 seriously delinquent male youth (26% Hispanic, mostly of Cuban extraction, 38% Black, and 36% White) living in Miami, Florida, has shed additional light on the cocaine/crack/crime connection existing among high at-risk minority youth.

Preliminary results from this study suggest that of the Hispanic juvenile delinquents who were drug users, the crack users were more likely than their White and Black counterparts to be involved in drug-dealing activities. On the other hand, the Hispanic youth were less likely than Blacks or Whites to have been involved in drug-related major felonies, but were as likely as the other ethnic/racial groups to have been involved in petty property crimes (Soriano and De La Rosa, 1990). On the average, each subject was involved in over 700+ criminal offenses per year with no discernible difference among the three ethnic/racial groups. A disheartening finding in this study was the steadfast involvement of Hispanic youth in drug usage. Almost all Hispanics (97%) preferred the use of cocaine and marijuana over other types of illicit drugs compared to 83% of Blacks and 56% of Whites.

Overall, the findings from this research seem to indicate that Hispanic and Black narcotic addicts were more likely than White addicts to be involved in criminal activities either during periods of high or low heroin use. The results also suggest that Hispanic female narcotic addicts were as likely, or more likely, to be involved in criminal activities as their male counterparts. In regard to research on cocaine addicts, the existing literature seems to suggest that Hispanic cocaine addicts were more likely than the White or Black addicts to be involved in drug-dealing activities. It should be noted that research on the criminal activities of cocaine addicts is currently lacking.

THE DRUG USE/VIOLENCE CONNECTION

The drug use/violence connection is another topic that has been the subject of much attention in the drug abuse research literature. Researchers, driven by countless stories appearing in American's major newspapers, magazines, and television programs expounding on the violent behavior of drug users and the dangers they pose to society, have sought to explore the extent and nature of this relationship (De La Rosa et al., 1990a). The results from research conducted on this issue during the 1960's and 1970's concluded that alcohol, not illicit drug use (mainly heroin and marijuana), was the drug most often associated with drug-related violence (De La Rosa et al., 1990a). In general, this research found that heroin addicts were more likely to be involved in non-violent crimes than violent crimes (Kozel and Dupont, 1972).

With the rise of amphetamine use in the 1970's and the development of cocaine distribution networks in the 1980's, research issues tended to increasingly explore the psychopharmacological effects of drug use upon violent behavior and the violence associated with drug-dealing lifestyles (Asnis and Smith, 1978; Beezley et al., 1987; Goldstein, 1986). The findings from these studies seem to suggest that while certain types of illicit drugs (i.e., stimulants, hallucinogens) may be associated with violent behavior, most drug-related violent crimes continue to be alcohol-related. Most violent crimes involving illicit drugs, particularly crack cocaine, were found to be associated with purchasing and selling transactions taking place between drug dealers and drug users.

Again, while much epidemiological research has been conducted over the years to investigate the drug/violence connection, little information exists on the nature and extent of this relationship among Hispanics living in the continental United States. We do know, however, that recent data reported by law enforcement officials from some of America's largest cities seem to indicate that Hispanic and Black non-Hispanic individuals were more likely than White individuals to be either the victim or the perpetrator of a drug-related violent crime.

For example, data from the Crime Analysis Unit of the New York Police Department found that in 1982, 42% of the 1,663 drug-related homicides in the city involved an Hispanic victim and 27% involved both an Hispanic victim and an Hispanic perpetrator (New York City Police Department, 1982). Yet, according to the 1980 U.S. Census Bureau, 19.9% of the population in New York City was of Hispanic heritage. These results, which cannot be generalized to other areas in the United States, suggest that Hispanics are overrepresented in drug-related homicides in New York City. News media reports also seem to suggest that drug-related homicides among Hispanics are on the rise in other large urban centers and rural areas with large Hispanic populations (Laredo Times, July 3, 1989).

On the other hand, data from a number of recent epidemiological research studies on the drug/violence connection suggests Hispanic drug users are less or equally as likely as Black and White addicts to be involved in drug-related violent crimes. Results from a study conducted by Goldstein and Browstein (1987), which collected data on a sample of 283 male and female active street addicts (17% Hispanic, 51% White, and 32% Black) living in New York City, suggest that Hispanic men and women drug addicts reported less involvement in drug-related violent crimes such as aggravated assaults than their Black counterparts. However, they were equally as likely as the White addicts to be involved in violent crimes. Overall, Hispanic male and female addicts were more likely than White non-Hispanic male and female addicts to be involved in non-violent, drug-related crimes emanating from their drug dealing activities.

The findings from the Chavez (1989) and Soriano and De La Rosa (1990) studies (which also collected data on the drug/violence connection among Hispanics) seem to support some of the results reported by Goldstein and Brownstein (1987). While the Chavez et al. (1989) research project was intended to investigate the relationship between school failure and drug abuse among a group of Mexican-American and White non-Hispanic dropouts or at-risk of dropping out, it also collected data on the violent behavior of these youth. The violence data suggests that many of the subjects in the study, particularly the dropout group, live in a very dangerous world. While the data was not analyzed to determine the association between violence and drug abuse, it is apparent that the drug use behavior of the study subjects (80% and higher among the female and male dropout groups for both the Mexican American and White sample) contributed to their violent behavior.

In keeping with past findings on violent behavior, the females in the sample were less likely to be perpetrators of violence. They were, however, as likely as the males to be victims of violence, particularly the White female dropouts, 42% of whom reported having been raped or sexually assaulted at least once in their lifetime. The Mexican American females, while also living in a rather violent world, reported lower levels of victimization, with about 20% of the dropouts indicating physical and/or sexual abuse (Chavez et al., 1989).

Why Mexican American females reported lower levels of victimization is not known. One possible reason may be related to the long ascribed value of "marianismo" found within the Hispanic culture which regards the female in the family as a weak and virginal figure to be protected by the male (i.e., macho) of the family against any possible abuse. Another possible reason for such a result may be due to under-reporting of family-related violence by Hispanics. This is often due to fear that if the proper authorities knew of such problems in the family there would be negative reprisals against all its members and/or denial by the family that such a problem exists.

Among the male dropouts, the White non-Hispanic youth also reported experiencing higher levels of violence than their Mexican American counterparts. A higher percentage of the White, non-Hispanic male dropouts reported being beaten by their parents, a brother, sister, stranger, or being robbed and/or shot at than the Mexican American male dropouts. Further analysis of these results is needed to determine their accuracy and/or reasons responsible for them.

Soriano and De La Rosa (1990), mentioned elsewhere in this chapter, also explored the violent criminal behavior of a cohort of seriously addicted juvenile delinquents. They reported that White, non-Hispanic male youth were more likely to be involved in major felonies such as armed robberies and assaults at a higher rate than the Hispanic youth who were mostly of Cuban extraction. Watts and Wright (1990) are two other researchers who have also recently explored the violent behavior of Hispanic juveniles. A correlation analysis of factors with regard to violent delinquency among a cohort of 446 Mexican American youth (203 males and 243 females) revealed that illegal drug use contributed the greatest amount of variance, followed by friends' drug use, lack of parental supervision, and family drug use. The interview results also suggested that acculturation-related stress between parent and child may contribute to both drug use and violent behavior of some of the Mexican-American youth.

Other researchers who are exploring the drug use and criminal behavior including violence and its underlying factors among Hispanics are Rodriguez (1990), Thornberry (1990), and Vega (1990). Preliminary analysis of data from interviews conducted by Rodriguez and his colleagues on a randomly selected sample of 1,077 Puerto Rican male adolescents living in New York City indicates that there is a strong correlation between illicit drug use and violent crimes. Other correlational analyses of the data suggest that there were some differences in the strength of the relationship with regard to factors responsible both for drug use and violent delinquent behavior. For example, Rodriguez found that such factors as family involvement and attitudes toward deviance and association with delinquent peers were more highly correlated with violent delinquency, but only minimally correlated with drug use. Data from the Thornberry and Vega research projects are not currently available.

As can be seen, the research conducted on the drug/violence connections has not been successful in clarifying the nature and the extent of this relationship among Hispanics. The data available suggest that while a correlation exists between the drug use behavior of Hispanics and their involvement in violent crimes, the extent of this relationship remains undetermined. The results available from law enforcement data suggest that drug-related violence is more of a problem for Hispanics than the findings reported by epidemiologic research conducted on this topic.

THE GANG, DRUG USE, AND CRIME CONNECTION AMONG HISPANICS

A third substantive topic which has received much attention in the drug abuse research literature over the years has been the gang, drug use, and crime connection. Among Hispanics, much research has been conducted by a number of sociologists and anthropologists on the deviant lifestyles of Mexican American gangs in California (Borgadus, 1943; Frias, 1982; Moore, 1978, 1990; Moore et al., 1983; Morales, 1982; Vigil, 1983, 1988). Much of this research has concentrated on exploring the dynamics of the Mexican American gangs' subculture, including why and how they developed, how members are recruited and indoctrinated into a gang lifestyle, and the role gangs play in the lives of their members. Results from this research have provided extensive information on the factors responsible for the development of Mexican American gangs in Mexican American neighborhoods in Los Angeles and the significant role such gangs play in the lives of their members as well as the communities in which the gangs evolve and are formed.

For example, Vigil (1983) reported that the development of Mexican American gangs evolved from efforts by Mexican American youth in the 1920's to adapt to an urban environment where few opportunities existed for upward mobility. According to Vigil (1983), "unable to find an identity in either Mexican or Anglo culture, Mexican-American youth turned to a 'cholo' cultural lifestyle which aided in their adaptation to a rather harsh street life and impoverished social conditions". Life revolved around the "gang" for a marginal group of Mexican American youth, and many derived their self-identity from their gangs. The gang provided a natural alternative to channel their youthful energies and feelings of frustration into actions, some of them deviant, that allowed many of them to feel a sense of pride.

Research on Mexican-American gangs in California has also concentrated on exploring the criminal activities and drug use behavior of its members. The research conducted on gang-related violence is of particular attention to policymakers and law enforcement officials. The findings from this research suggest that gang violence is the result of a process which is nurtured in street socialization experiences which push the individual gang member to adopt a "locura" mindset (i.e., thinking and acting in a daring, courageous manner, and especially crazy fashion in the face of adversity) in order to manage many of the fearful and stressful situations they encounter on a daily basis (Vigil, 1988).

Other results on gang violence reported by Moore (1988) from data drawn from a study of eight male Mexican American cliques of two major East Los Angeles gangs suggest that significant variation exists in the levels of violence from one clique to another in the gang. She attributed these differences in level of violence among the cliques to the adherence in different ways to elements of the gang subculture, especially the idea of "locura." According to Moore, while one clique may define "locura" almost in terms of drugs, another clique may associate it more with non-drug-related violent behavior. Finally, Moore (1988) also reported that violence among gangs changes over time. Often, these changes appear to be a direct response to changing economics (i.e., unemployment, poverty), and social (i.e., the restructuring of the Mexican American extended family system) circumstances and the emergence of the drug trade in the "barrios" (neighborhoods) during the 1970's and early 1980's.

The emergence of the drug trade in Mexican American communities and the apparent increasing involvement of Chicano gangs in the drug distribution network has led to additional research on the criminal activities of gang members, particularly drug-related violent crimes (Moore, 1978; Moore and Mata, 1981). In her analysis on the patterns of drug use/dealing and related consequences of Mexican American prison and community gangs, Moore (1990) noted that while drug use/dealing increased among gang members, there was no statistically significant relationship between the number of members in the clique dealing/using drugs and the number of deaths in gang warfare.

Moore also argues that drug-related criminal behavior, including violent criminal activities (i.e., aggravated assaults, armed robbery, homicide) thought to be gang-related, is in most cases due to the drug-dealing activities of individual gang members or former gang members without the active participation in most instances of their gangs in these activities. In fact, Moore (1990) and Morales (1982) suggest that tradi-tional community-based Chicano gangs are only peripherally involved in the drug trade and drug-related criminal activities. Moore (1990) states that most of the youthful Mexican American and Black gangs identified by law enforcement officials as heavily involved in drug-related criminal activities did not grow out of youth gangs which were already established in Black and Hispanic communities before the onset of the cocaine/crack problem in inner-city neighborhoods. These youth-ful groups are, in fact, criminal organizations that have formed for the purpose of trafficking in the cocaine/crack and newly emerging heroin drug trade. They have few of the characteristics found in the traditional gangs.

In summary, the research on the gang, drug use, and crime connec-tions among Hispanic seems to suggest that the emergence of gangs in Mexican American communities and related criminal activities has been due largely to impoverished social conditions (i.e., poor housing, unemployment, health services, educational services, etc.). Drug-related criminal activities were found to be more due to individual gang mem-ber involvement in the drug trade than gang-sponsored activities. As a matter of fact, some of the researchers argue that while traditional Chicano gangs have become more involved in the emerging cocaine/crack trade and its related criminal activities, this involvement is peripheral.

THE RELATIONSHIP BETWEEN
DRUG USE, CRIME, AND DRUG TREATMENT

Research on the effectiveness of drug treatment in reducing the crimi-nal activities and drug use behavior of Hispanic drug users is also lacking. Most research on this topic has concentrated almost exclusively on investigating the role of methadone treatment programs in addressing the drug use behavior and criminal activities of adult opiate and heroin addicts (Booth, Castro, and Anglin, 1990). This is the case, despite the fact that data from the National Drug and Alcoholism Treatment Utiliza-tion Survey (NDATUS) and the Client Oriented Data Acquisition Process (CODAP) have indicated that an increasing number of Hispanics admitted to drug treatment facilities reported a primary problem with a drug other than heroin (i.e., PCP, cocaine, amphetamines, etc.) (De La Rosa et al., 1990b). Similar results have been reported by the Bureau of Justice statistics on the percentage of Hispanic prison inmates who reported using a drug other than heroin (U.S. Department of Justice, 1986). Data from this report indicates that 44% of the Hispanic prison inmates in 1986 reported using cocaine while 35% reported using heroin.

Nevertheless, the research conducted on drug-offending opiate addicts has provided significant information to policymakers and the drug treatment community on the effectiveness of methadone programs in reducing the criminal and drug-using behavior of Hispanics and non-Hispanic opiate addicts. It also revealed some differences in the characteristics and utilization of methadone treatment between the Hispanic heroin addicts and their Black and White counterparts. For example, results from studies conducted by Anglin et al. (1988), Knielser and Heller (1974), and Maddux and McDonald (1973), indicate that certain types of drug treatment such as methadone maintenance have short-term effects in reducing the criminal activities and drug use of narcotic users regardless of gender and ethnic group.

On the other hand, the research conducted by Anglin and his colleagues (1988) found that male and female Hispanic heroin addicts, mostly of Mexican American extraction, were more likely to relapse into heroin use than their White, non-Hispanic counterparts and consequently to increase their criminal activities. Hser et al. (1987) also reported that Hispanic opiate addicts were less likely than their White, non-Hispanic addicts to enter detoxification treatment. Overall, Hispanic women were found to be less likely to successfully complete their methadone treatment than Hispanic males. Part of the reason for this treatment outcome result may be due to the fact that Hispanic female heroin addicts, unlike their male counterparts, received little support and encouragement from their family to enter and stay in treatment. Maddux and McDonald (1973) also found that Hispanic heroin addicts who entered treatment were often older, less educated, and more likely to have tried heroin at an earlier age than other heroin addicts regardless of country of origin.

Other research conducted on the effectiveness of drug treatment programs by investigators participating in the Treatment Outcome Prospective Study (TOPS) also have suggested that under certain circumstances, drug treatment, particularly methadone maintenance, can have lasting long-term effects in reducing the criminal activities and drug use behavior of Hispanic and non-Hispanic narcotic addicts (Tims and Ludford, 1984). The researchers for the TOPS reported that court-ordered drug treatment programs (out-patient or in-patient) accompanied by supervision, including random urine testing and weekly visits to a parole officer, were associated with long-term reduced criminal activity and drug use for Hispanic and non-Hispanic addicts alike (Tims and Ludford, 1984).

In summary, research on this topic has shown the effectiveness of methadone maintenance programs in reducing the criminal activities of narcotic addicts regardless of ethnicity when appropriately supervised. However, the effectiveness of inpatient or outpatient drug treatment programs in reducing the criminal behavior of non-opiate addicts (i.e., cocaine addicts, inhalant addicts, PCP addicts, etc.,) remains unexplored. Similarly, research on the factors responsible for the poor success rate among Hispanic women who enter methadone maintenance programs is lacking.

LIMITATIONS OF CURRENT RESEARCH AND RECOMMENDATIONS

While significant progress has been made in recent years to understand the drug/crime connection among Hispanics, limitations in the current research or lack of research altogether on this topic has prevented us from more fully understanding the extent and nature of this relationship. In particular, the relationship between drug use and violent criminal behavior among Hispanics remains largely undetermined. Similarly, little is known about the effectiveness of drug treatment in reducing the criminal behavior of Hispanic addicts and the impact that the drug problem has had upon the well-being of Hispanic communities.

Previous research, when available, has been based upon studies of small non-random samples of narcotic addicts, most of whom have been incarcerated or in drug treatment or gang members before the onset of the cocaine epidemic. Moreover, often this research has been based upon data collected from Mexican American addicts and in some cases Puerto Ricans and Cuban American subjects. These weaknesses limit the generalizability of the collected data to the larger population of Mexican American narcotic addicts. It also seriously undermines the utility of the results to explain the criminal behavior of Hispanic narcotic addicts who are not of Mexican extraction as well as that of Hispanic cocaine and inhalant addicts.

Another weakness of most of the research conducted on the drug/crime connection among Hispanics, and for that matter other at-risk population groups, is its failure to explore in detail some of the underlying factors responsible for these deviant behaviors. In the past, most research on the drug/crime connection has concentrated on investigating the criminal careers of drug users according to specific types of illicit drugs. This research has generally ignored, with some exceptions, the role that factors such as negative early childhood experiences (i.e., sexual and/ or physical abuse), family dysfunction (parental drug use, lack of communication, etc.,), poor community environment (i.e., poverty conditions, availability of drugs, high crime rates), poor school conditions, acculturation-related stress, and larger societal conditions, such as racism, play in the development of drug use and criminal behavior among high at-risk populations such as Hispanics.

Furthermore, this research has failed to investigate the role that the Hispanic family and other natural support systems, such as that of non-drug using peers, may have upon the effective delivery of drug-treatment services to drug-offending individuals.** Little evidence exists whether Hispanic drug-offending individuals who have few or no contacts with the criminal justice system utilize drug treatment facilities to treat their drug problems. Preliminary results from a study which has been exploring the drug using behaviors of Hispanic and non-Hispanic juvenile delinquents not in detention centers suggest that the Hispanic subjects were less likely to seek drug treatment for their drug problem than their White and Black non-Hispanic counterparts (Soriano and De La Rosa, 1990).

Yet, a fourth serious limitation found in previous research on the drug/crime connection relates to the validity of the data collected from interviews conducted on samples of incarcerated, treatment and/or community-based populations. Several prominent researchers (Collins and Mardsen, 1990) have argued that data collected from self reports on the criminal and drug using behaviors of jail/prison, street, and treatment populations are highly suspect unless cross-checking measurements such as urinalysis and/or corroborating information is gathered from police records and/or other valid sources. Similarly, utilizing sec-

---

**Note: See Chapter 8 on Support Systems.

ondary data sources such as police records without subjects' interviews may lead to erroneous conclusions on the relationship existing between drug use crime by researchers analyzing such information. Rouse et al. (1985), in a 1985 National Institute on Drug Abuse (NIDA) publication, addressed some of the inherent problems related to the collection of data on deviant behaviors using self-reports and suggested ways in which researchers could improve on the quality of data collected via self-reports.

Finally, researchers who seek to investigate the criminal behavior of Hispanic drug users should be more sensitive to the accuracy of self-reported data in light of the fact that, because of illegal immigration status and previous negative experiences with social institutions, Hispanic individuals may be more likely to underreport their illegal activities (personal communication, Averlado Valdez, Hispanic Research Center, University of Texas at San Antonio, October 31, 1990).

As can be seen, research on the drug/crime connection among Hispanics is growing, but continues to experience serious gaps. There is a need to conduct additional research on this topic in order to more fully understand this relationship as it pertains to Hispanics. Specifically, the following types of studies are suggested:

Ethnographic Studies to Investigate

a. The criminal careers of Hispanic cocaine, PCP, inhalant users/ abusers by Hispanic subgroups (i.e., Mexican American, Puerto Rican, Cuban, and South and Central American);

b. Drug-related violent behavior, including spousal and child abuse among drug-offending Hispanic addicts;

c. The drug use, gang, crime connection, particularly that related to the emergent crack trade in Hispanic communities; and

d. The drug/crime connection among Hispanic females.

Ethnographic and cross-sectional surveys: to determine how and why emerging drug trade is affecting Hispanic neighborhoods (i.e., economic economic, social, cultural life-style).

Longitudinal studies: to explore the role that:

a. The Hispanic family, as well as other cultural factors, such as "machismo," "fatalism," "respeto," "verguenza," "orgullo," "confianza," play in determining the drug use behavior and related criminal activities among Hispanic subgroups;

b. Economic conditions and availability of illicit drugs in Hispanic neighborhoods have upon the drug use behavior and related criminal activities of drug-offending Hispanic individuals and

c. Acculturation-related stress plays in the drug use behavior and criminal activities of Hispanic youth.

Cross-sectional surveys and/or longitudinal studies: to determine:

a. The accessibility and availability of drug treatment services to drug-offending Hispanic addicts by subgroups, particularly cocaine and inhalant abusers;

b. The effectiveness of the drug treatment services available to drug offending individuals in reducing their criminal and drug using behaviors.

Methodological studies: that will determine whether or not Hispanic drug offending individuals are more likely than their White or Black non-Hispanic counterparts to underreport their illegal activities.

CONCLUSION

In summary, drug-related criminal activities are a serious social problem confronting our nation. In inner city Hispanic communities throughout the United States, drug-related crimes have been felt severely. In spite of this impact, little or no information exists on the nature and extent of this problem among Hispanics. In the past, this lack of information has prevented the development of effective strategies and programs to address the problem of drug-related activities in Hispanic communities. With Hispanics expected to become the largest minority group in this country by the year 2010, more information is needed on this topic.

PART III
PREVENTION AND TREATMENT

Chapter 7

THE HISPANIC FAMILY INTERVENTION PROGRAM: AN EMPIRICAL APPROACH TO SUBSTANCE ABUSE PREVENTION

Richard C. Cervantes

INTRODUCTION

A variety of demographic indicators all suggest that the Hispanic population will soon become the largest of all U.S. ethnic minority groups (U.S. Bureau of the Census, 1988). When one examines specific age trends in the U.S. Hispanic population, it becomes evident that this is a very youthful population, with nearly one-half of all Hispanics being under the age of 20. The implications of these age trends are many, and perhaps one can begin to sense that the social and political strength within the Hispanic community lies in its youth. Of course this is very much a function of the health, mental health and educational status of Hispanic youth. In another paper, this author and others (Padilla, Salgado de Snyder, Cervantes & Baezconde-Garbanati, in press) suggested that a variety of community level stressors, including poverty-like living conditions, high rates of unemployment, crowded housing and the stresses associated with cultural change, all combine to predispose certain segments of the Hispanic community to engage in "high risk" behavior including substance abuse. Other authors in this book have described in detail the extent to which substance abuse has become a major problem within various Hispanic communities.

In a report published by the National Institute on Drug Abuse (NIDA, 1987), it was recommended that substance abuse prevention programs for high risk communities be developed in concert with specific research which examines and identifies antecedent factors that inhibit or contribute to the risk of drug abuse. For example, in a recent longitudinal study of frequent, infrequent and experimental drug users among the general population, Shedler and Block (1990) found that in fact problem drug use is a symptom, not a cause, of personal and social maladjustment.

101

Frequent users were found to have rather disruptive family relationship histories, where caretakers of these children were described as hostile, not spontaneous or supportive of their children. These caretakers were further described as lacking pride and being ashamed of their children. As a result of this form of parenting, Shedler and Block found frequent users to be maladjusted at quite an early age. The childhood personality of frequent users was described as insecure, lacking in coping abilities and becoming "immobilized under stress" (Shedler & Block, 1990, p. 618).

While saying little about the precursors of substance abuse in Hispanic children or adolescents specifically, the above study points to the importance of fostering quality family relationships in the implementation of any preventive effort. Given the strong value placed on family relationships in many Hispanic communities, drug abuse prevention programs must consider the nuances of cultural factors and culturally specific stressors as these impact on family functioning. The importance of considering cultural factors in secondary and tertiary interventions has been recently highlighted by several clinical investigators (Sue & Zane, 1987; Acosta, Yamamoto & Evans, 1982).

Unfortunately, little is known with respect to those "antecedent" factors that lead to substance abuse within the Hispanic community. This chapter will begin to outline some of those antecedent factors which have been identified through a rigorous program of research on mental health among Southwest Hispanics (primarily of Mexican origin), and how these research findings have been tailored into a family oriented prevention program for high risk Hispanic youth. Prior to a description of the *Hispanic Family Intervention Program* this author will provide the reader with an overview of psychosocial stress theory as related to the Hispanic community, with special emphasis on the Mexican American family.

THE CONCEPT OF FAMILY AND STRESS

Mexican American family "systems" have been the focus of considerable investigation, both empirical and impressionistic, over the past three decades. Much of this investigation has been limited to a description of modal family characteristics including role-related behavior, childbearing practices, and decision-making patterns. Reviews of Mexican American family research (Ramirez & Arce, 1981; Staples & Mirande, 1980; Zapata & Jaramillo, 1981) have all pointed to emerging patterns in this body of research. These reviewers generally suggest that early studies conducted prior to 1960 were methodologically unsound and aimed at identifying "pathological" components of Mexican American family life. It is from this early body of research that many stereotypic descriptions of the Mexican American family evolved.

A second wave of family research conducted roughly between 1960 and 1970 attempted to refute these early stereotypic descriptions but tended to over-romanticize the Mexican American family, thus leading to positive, yet continued stereotypic descriptions (Ramirez & Arce, 1981). A third and current wave of Mexican American family research is more data-based with greater appreciation for the differences found within the Mexican American population, as well as for the differences found between Mexican American families and other Hispanic families.

Cultural Characteristics of Mexican Family Systems

Several investigators have identified a cluster of Mexican culture normative rules endorsed by "the traditional Mexican family" (Montiel, 1973; Murillo, 1971). Several generations ago, these rules appear to have been functional in securing the survival of large, traditional, lower class, agrarian Mexican family systems. Such family systems emphasized family unity and a cooperative division of labor. A traditional family system offered protection in exchange for family loyalty. It emphasized family harmony and cooperation while discouraging individualism, competition, confrontation and the open expression of anger. In this hierarchical system, family tasks and roles were divided by age and gender, with elders holding positions of authority and influence while children were obligated to obey elders under all circumstances. Males were encouraged to be *machos,* to express family pride, dominance, authoritarianism and discipline whereas females were encouraged to be *señoritas/señoras,* to serve family needs, show deference towards males while also expecting protection from them (Carrillo, 1982).

While these generalized descriptions tend to capture the "flavor" of traditional Mexican family values and normative rules, one must remember that *the* traditional Mexican family is an abstraction, an exaggerated and therefore inaccurate version of what various Mexican American families actually believe and practice today. Carillo (1982) has noted in this regard, that broad generalizations such as these do not do justice to regional, generational, social class and other variations in family lifestyles observable across Mexican American families today.

Even within a given Mexican American family system, striking contrasts are often evident. One family member may identify strongly with these traditional family values, thus being highly motivated to comply with these cultural normative rules. By contrast, another family member who disagrees strongly with these values may be highly motivated to actively oppose compliance with many of these cultural normative rules. On a given family issue, such opposing viewpoints may develop within a family system. Consequently, sibling or generational family coalitions may emerge, partitioning the family unit into opposing factional groups (Goldenberg & Goldenberg, 1980). Traditional Mexican culture rules have helped Mexican family systems maintain their identity and integrity and to survive across several generations. Yet today when a family member expresses a strict adherence to rules which are out of context with modern demands, this strict adherence is likely to create stress for other family members.

Currently, many Mexican American family systems function as sources of identity, self-worth and social support for their members by emphasizing *familism,* a family orientation which encourages family unity, the fostering of strong emotional ties between family members and strong reciprocal kinship obligation, *"obligacion,"* and *"deber,"* (Bengston, 1976; Grebler et al., 1970; Nall & Speilberg, 1967; Sotomayor, 1982; Vega et al., 1983). Strong familism may help individual family members cope with social pressures which originate outside of the family (Hoppe & Heller, 1975), although some investigators have argued that overly strong family bonds may discourage the individual from seeking medical and mental health care from outside resources when this becomes necessary (Grebler et al., 1970; Nall & Speilberg, 1967).

Studies of the help seeking behavior of Mexican Americans both within and outside of the extended family system report a process of differential help seeking by generational level. First generation Mexican immigrants tend to have smaller extended family networks, which the immigrant consults sparingly. By contrast, second and third generation Mexican Americans tend to have larger extended family networks (Keefe & Padilla, 1987). While having larger, more diverse family networks, second and third generation Mexican Americans also have other support resources.

Based upon both historic and current trends in Mexican American family-based research, important issues remain to be addressed and will be the focus of this article. For example, how can this rather contradictory body of research and impressionistic findings be utilized or translated into effective clinical and community applications? Further, are past research approaches adequate for investigating the impact of the family on individual mental health processes and the development of substance abuse in Hispanic youth?

Overview of Recent Approaches
to the Study of Family Stress

Stress is a pervasive life experience, particularly among individuals living in urban regions of industrialized societies. A person usually experiences stress when environmental *demands* outweigh his or her perceived ability to *respond* effectively to these demands (Cox, 1978). This occurs when demands become too many or too complex, or when the person's skills are insufficient to cope with these demands. Such demands involve the occurrence of an event or stimulus condition to which a person must respond within a certain time period or else suffer the negative consequences of not doing so (McGrath, 1978).

Many investigators now assert that the experience of stress and efforts to relieve it precede the onset of various psychophysiological disorders, such as high blood pressure (Shapiro & Goldstein, 1982), and gastrointestinal disorders (Whitehead & Bosmajian, 1982). The stress experience has also been identified as an antecedent factor of various psychosocial problems, including generalized anxiety, post-traumatic stress disorder, (Foy, Sipprelle, Rueger, & Carroll, 1984); depression, (Roberts & Vernon, 1984; Mirowski & Ross, 1984); cigarette smoking and other addictive disorders (Brownell, 1984; Hatch, Bierner, & Fisher, 1983). Among children, stressful experiences may induce childhood anxiety disorders, conduct disorders or eating disorders (American Psychiatric Association, 1983).

The stress-illness paradigm has recently gained wide acceptance in the behavioral sciences. This paradigm has been developed and utilized in investigating individual mental health processes (Fleming, Baum & Singer, 1984; Lazarus & Folkman, 1984; Pearlin & Schooler, 1978), and more recently has been applied to the study of family stress processes (Hansen & Johnson, 1979; Green, 1982; McCubbin & Figley, 1983). Further, the paradigm proves to serve as an important framework for identifying *risk factors* for future substance abuse. Substance abuse prevention efforts seem best guided by knowledge of these antecedent or risk factors.

Despite the apparent utility of this conceptual framework in describing stress-illness relationships in the general population, it has failed to gain acceptance among those investigating Mexican American mental health issues (Perez, 1983). This is particularly true in the case of investigating Mexican American family stress processes (Cervantes & Castro, 1985).

As a small, yet emerging, area of investigation, family stress theory has attempted to identify those aspects of both the environment and the family which produce negative mental health outcomes, including substance abuse among one or more family members. The classic "ABCX" model (Hill, 1949) suggested that the variable A (stressor event) interacting with B (the family's crisis-meeting resources) interacting with C (the definition which the family makes of the event) produces X (the mental health outcome). The ABCX model has been elaborated more recently by Burr (1973) as well as by Hansen and Johnson (1979). Burr (1973) elaborated a lengthy propositional form of Hill's original family stress model. Hansen and Johnson have heuristically reformulated Burr's propositions and contend that four key concepts exist which hold promise for assessing family stress processes. They suggest that a family's "vulnerability" to stress and its "regenerative power" are a function of: (a) personal influence, (b) positional influence, (c) family integration, and (d) the family's adaptability. These investigators further suggest that a key to understanding the family's overall stress experience is in identification of their "definition" or *appraisal* of a potentially stressful situation.

Santisteban and Szapocznik (1982) have identified acculturative stress and family disorganization as two major factors associated with the development of drug abuse among Cuban youths. In many Hispanic families, particularly where parents are born outside of the U.S., children acculturate to U.S. American values and lifestyles much faster than do their parents, thus setting the stage for intergenerational conflicts regarding the acceptance and rejection of cultural and family normative rules.

Santisteban and Szapocznik (1982) have found that Cuban families at greatest risk for drug abuse consist of a son who is ashamed of and rejects his culture of origin, thus striving to over-acculturate, while the mother is under-acculturated and shows neurotic patterns of behavior including the abuse of sedatives or tranquilizers. Such families become fragmented by many family conflicts, both cultural and non-cultural, and tend to consist of an overly involved mother and a father who is distant, absent, and who provides inconsistent punishment. These investigators have concluded that the most adaptive survival strategy for various Hispanic families faced with intergenerational acculturative stressors involves adjusting to the prevailing environmental milieu. Members of families needing to survive in a monocultural environment could avoid maladjustment by developing monocultural skills congruent with that environment, whereas those families living in bicultural environments would do well to develop bicultural skills congruent with their culture of origin and with the demands of the host environment. In other words, according to Santisteban and Szapocznik (1982), individuals living in bicultural environments tend to become maladjusted when they remain monocultural, although the relationship between acculturation and psychological impairment is admittedly a complex one (Griffith, 1983).

Stress Research with Children and Adolescents

If appraisal lies at the core of the stress experience, then infants and children, based upon having less developed information processing capacities, should have stress experiences differing in intensity, duration, and quality from those of adults (Hernandez, 1984; Santostefano & Rieder, 1984). However, few studies have examined the stress experiences of children, particularly in terms of the process of appraisal. In noting that exposure to noxious living conditions does not necessarily produce maladjustment, Garmezy (1981, 1983) has indicated that some children raised in such conditions of poverty and discrimination still manage to develop effective coping skills and good social adjustment. Further process-oriented research is needed to understand how such children manage to develop adequate coping skills, despite being raised in such adverse environments.

Studies which have examined stress in children have followed the stressful life events conceptual paradigm. Coddington (1972) developed a life stress inventory for children, which consisted of a modified version of the adult Social Readjustment Rating Scale. This investigator, however, did not obtain child ratings of the perceived stress value of these events but rather, relied upon adult ratings. Other similar scales have been developed by Yamamoto (1974) and by Yeaworth, York, Hussey, Ingel and Goodwin (1980).

In an effort to obtain the child's view of life events which are potential stressors, Metcalfe, Dobson, Cook, and Michaud (1982) developed a 40 item stressful events scale. A noteworthy pattern along these lines was that children identified as potential stressors chronic, daily hassles rather than discrete, catastrophic life events as are listed on the Social Readjustment Rating Scale (Holmes & Rahe, 1967). Such potential stressors included: teachers being too strict, being ridiculed for doing poor work, having personal problems and being concerned over letting down parents.

In a similar manner using child interviews, Lewis, Siegel and Lewis (1986) generated a set of items which children considered stressful. These investigators found, as did Metcalfe et al. (1982), that most of the stress items consisted of daily hassles rather than major life events. The three major sources of stress identified by such children were: (1) conflict between parents, (2) self-esteem issues (e.g. being excluded from peer activities, being too small), and (3) disrupted living arrangements such as having to change schools.

Clearly there is limited stress research which has been conducted with child populations. This, unfortunately is most profound in research conducted with Hispanic children and adolescents.

Recent Developments in Hispanic Stress Research

In order to systematically guide future prevention and clinical intervention efforts, this author and others at the UCLA Spanish Speaking Mental Health Research Center* developed a research strategy that could answer important questions related to risk factors and consequent mental health status among Southwest Hispanics. Using a stressful life events approach, the UCLA research team was first able to identify culturally specific stress events and coping responses to those events in a normal community sample of recent immigrants from Mexico and Central America (Padilla, Cervantes, Maldonado & Garcia, 1988). Using an open-ended interview schedule, these investigators found that family members were most concerned about the tasks involved in adapting to their new lives in the United States. Respondents were not only concerned about their lack of English language skills, and lack of marketable job skills, but also reported concern over the liberal family values and beliefs held by members of the dominant culture.

Using a similar research methodology, Padilla, Cervantes, and Maldonado (1988) found a number of culturally specific stressors among Mexican immigrant adolescents. Events involving family disruption were rated much more stressful among these adolescents when compared

*The Spanish Speaking Mental Health Research Center was a federally funded research center. Funding was provided by the National Institute of Mental Health, Division of Biometry and Applied Sciences (Grant No. MH 24854) to Amado M. Padilla.

with peer stressors or school-related stressors. Among those items reflecting stressful conditions for these adolescents were the following five items which were ranked as the most stressful: 1) parents getting sick and going to the hospital; 2) having a family member arrested; 3) living in a poor neighborhood where there is crime; 4) father or mother drinking; 5) leaving relatives and friends behind when moving. Four of the five most stressful situations for these adolescents involved disruptions to family unity. Similarly, those adolescents who experienced high levels of psychological stress were found to have very low self-esteem and high levels of anxiety. These results further point to the deleterious effects of family-related stressors on the psychological well-being and development of Hispanic children. Most importantly, these results strongly suggest that some Mexican American children who are prone to being at risk for substance abuse, violence and school failure, may be responding to family-level stressors. Prevention efforts with Hispanic children, or any form of early clinical intervention, must attend to these family-level stressors in order to reduce risk in these children. This notion is quite consistent with similar concepts related to Family Systems Theory and Structural Family Therapy which emanates from this theory (Minuchin, 1974).

In a more recent series of investigations by this author and others, specific stress clusters or stress factors were identified in a community sample of 493 Hispanic adults, both recent immigrants from Mexico and Central America and U.S. born Hispanics (Cervantes, Padilla & Salgado de Snyder, 1990). Following factor analytic procedures, each domain of stress was found to be associated with increased levels of depression, anxiety and somatization for both U.S. born and immigrant Hispanics in the large sample. However, the area of psychosocial stress most strongly related to emotional problems and distress was that of "family conflict." Individuals who reported high levels of family-related conflict and stress were much more likely to experience emotional distress, particularly depression. This again highlights the fact that family disruption within the Hispanic community may well, in fact, set the stage for dysfunctional family interaction, substance abuse and increased "risk" for a variety of emotional and educational difficulties in children. Further research on the impact of family-related conflict and stress across different cultural groups is sorely needed.

THE HISPANIC FAMILY INTERVENTION PROGRAM

Research on adolescent substance abuse consistently cites school-related problems as a risk factor for substance abuse (Jessor & Jessor, 1977; Kandel et al., 1978). These problems include poor academic performance and conduct problems. In addition, researchers have focused on the attitudes and peer associations of adolescents in relation to substance abuse. Many of these studies show that school performance, conduct and student attitudes are correlates of substance abuse. This Social Control Perspective suggests that youths engage in deviant behaviors, including alcohol and other substance abuse, when ties to normal social institutions such as family, school and religion become weakened (Hirschi, 1969).

The relationship between peer influence and deviant behavior has been widely documented (Elliot et al., 1985; Simons et al., 1988). Oetting, Edwards, and Beavis (1988) for example, found that problems in school led to substance abuse due to the increased associations with deviant peers, such as in remedial classes. The poor overall school performance and high dropout rates among Hispanic youth strongly points to the increased risk among these youth by virtue of their poor academic performance and subsequent exposure to deviant peers (Brown, 1980; Gibson, 1988; Matute-Bianchi, 1986). In a recent study of Mexican American youths, problems in school performance and school conduct were significantly related to substance use (Mennon et al., 1990). In addition, the study found that those youth who had an association with a "conventional" peer group in school had significantly decreased odds of being a substance user, again pointing to the critical role of peer relations and the potential for substance abuse. It must also be added that in this study, *parental substance abuse* was found to be a significant predictor of children's substance abuse in this sample of Mexican Americans.

This bridge between clinically-oriented research and actual clinical intervention is a complex one, at best. Translation of research findings into effective prevention programs or other clinical interventions for Hispanics must take into account cultural factors regarding health beliefs and family values as well as the role of the acculturation process. Following research which identifies a set of risk factors, prevention programs must be able to target these factors in a fashion that is culturally and linguistically meaningful for those participating in the intervention.

From the existing research literature on Hispanic youth, prevention efforts must address multiple risk factors. In line with the work of Hirschi (1969), the Hispanic Family Intervention Program (HFIP) is aimed at the strengthening of ties to family, school, peers and culture. Through the use of a *psychoeducational* approach, participating youths and their families are provided new techniques for identifying stressors in each of the areas listed in Table 7-1. By enhancing individual and family coping skills, the strengthening of ties to important social institution can occur among high risk youths.

In addition to the above, the Hispanic Family Intervention Program (HFIP) has been developed to improve the overall functioning of Hispanic families. This is done in a culturally relevant fashion where specific strategies for coping with stress are encouraged among participating family members, including children. Through coping skill enhancement, substance abuse education and academic skill building, the HFIP aims at: 1) reducing overall levels of family stress; 2) enhancing psychosocial coping skills in both children and adults; 3) enhancing academic achievement; and, 4) decreasing the risk for later substance abuse in Hispanic children.

The HFIP builds upon the previously cited research data base relating to culturally relevant "stress clusters." The HFIP is also more structured than traditional prevention/intervention programs and is limited to an eight week period. This eight week curricula is provided for two hours per week in a group format. Concurrent groups of 10–12 parents and 10–12 children participate in the program at any one time. Specific topical areas of the prevention program are as follows:

A weekly curricula has been developed for HFIP prevention specialists and allows replicability of the HFIP across school or community settings. A pilot test of the HFIP, conducted in conjunction with the Glendale Unified School District and the Glen Roberts Child Study Center utilized school-based referrals of elementary aged children and their primary caretaker(s). Recruitment of "high risk" children is typically coordinated through announcements which are made available to teachers, school counselors and the "resource specialist" who maintains ongoing contact with problem families. Children included in the HFIP are then screened for appropriate age level (10–12; 13–15) and specific problems. These problem criteria have included:

1) The child is currently experiencing some degree of behavioral problems in the classroom (e.g., disruptive behavior, does not

Table 7-1 Hispanic Family Intervention Program Curriculum

Week	Children	Parents
1	Concept Building (e.g., "Stress", "Substance Abuse", "Culture")	Concept Building (e.g., "Stress", "Substance Abuse", "Culture")
2	Stress Overview	Stress Overview
3	Substance Abuse Prevention	Substance Abuse Prevention
4	Acculturation Stress Awareness and Coping Skill Building	Acculturation Stress Awareness and Coping Skill Building
5	School Stress Awareness and Coping Skill Building	Occupation/Economic Awareness and Coping Skill Building
6	Peer Stress Awareness and Coping Skill Building	Parental Stress Awareness and Coping Skill Building
7	Family Stress Awareness and Coping Skill Building	Family Stress Awareness and Coping Skill Building
8	Family Stress Awareness and Coping Skill Building	Family Stress Awareness and Coping Skill Building

complete assignments in class, excessive talking, poor impulse control (1) not due to diagnosed hyperactivity);

2) The child is currently experiencing some degree of emotional problems (e.g., extremely shy, withdrawn, isolated or extremely tense, anxious or nervous); or,

3) The child is currently experiencing some degree of academic difficulty not due to a learning disorder or lack of English language proficiency.

Because children included in the HFIP are considered to be "pre-clinical," this author has found it best to recruit HFIP prevention specialists from those who have had some minimal level of training in one of the mental health professions, and from those who have had experience in providing clinical interventions with Hispanic families or children. These requirements for HFIP prevention specialists may vary, and are dependent on the availability of direct clinical supervision.

Perhaps one of the more difficult aspects of conducting prevention efforts involves an evaluation of the program's effectiveness, both in the short term, as well as over the course of children's development. The HFIP–Glendale pilot project included pre- and post-HFIP testing consisting of a variety of psychosocial questionnaires for parents and children. Parents also completed the Achenbach Child Behavior Checklist as a method of evaluating changes in children's "behavior" following the prevention program. In addition to outcome measures, some process variables have been examined, including premature termination rates. To date, the HFIP research program experiences an attrition rate of approximately 8–10% for the eight week prevention program. Further, of those families participating in the HFIP, the average attendance rate ranges from 6–7 sessions; HFIP families typically complete the program with few missed sessions. This is in sharp contrast to the high rates of premature drop out and lowered utilization rates of Hispanics in need of traditional mental health care (Yamamoto & Silva, 1987). Evaluation of the HFIP to date reflects the following:

1) Screening of high risk youth through a collaborative effort between project staff and school-based personnel (Glendale Unified School District) is possible.
2) Program content which is provided in Spanish for parents, and which is culturally-responsive appears to be an acceptable form of prevention/intervention for these high risk families.
3) The use of bilingual outreach personnel allows for tracking and retention of high risk families. Over 75% of participating families completed the eight week prevention program.
4) Participating youth were noted to improve in terms of self-esteem, school performance, and overall conduct as reported by parents.

CONCLUSION

Southwest Hispanic children pose a challenge for policy makers as well as health, education and mental health professionals. In large urban areas of the Southwest, many of these Hispanic children appear to be at risk for the development of a variety of social and personal difficulties including substance abuse. Children who develop substance abuse disorders in their early adult years may indeed have considerable difficulty integrating into a society which seems to have ever-increasing demands. The loss of human resources due to substance abuse within the Hispanic community not only takes its toll on individuals and their families, but may promulgate the lack of economic progress which we now see among Hispanics in many urban areas. In short, prevention of early drug use onset within the Hispanic community must now be made a health policy priority at the federal, state and local levels.

This chapter has provided an overview of psychosocial stress theory and recent results from several studies which have focused on Southwest Hispanics. To date, most of this information suggests that patterns of stressor events are identifiable and that family stressors are most strongly associated with negative mental health consequences in both children and adults. Events which have a disruptive effect on family unity and closeness take a serious toll on individual family members, particularly children.

The research which has been highlighted in this chapter has served as an important context and framework for the development of the Hispanic Family Intervention Program. Unlike other prevention efforts which are solely substance abuse education, the HFIP aims at enhancing individual and family coping. It is felt that this approach addresses the underlying etiology of substance use in high risk youth. To date, this program has proven successful (at least in short-term evaluation) as a prevention strategy for families with troubled, at risk children. Improvements in parenting skills, stress event identification, and coping skills have been observed and long-term follow up studies with the HFIP families will ascertain the impact of the program on reducing rates of substance abuse and related problems. By using a family-oriented approach which is culturally sensitive we anticipate success in the reduction of such problems.

Chapter 8

NATURAL SOCIAL SUPPORT SYSTEMS AND HISPANIC SUBSTANCE ABUSE*

Manuel Barrera, Jr. and Finetta Reese

INTRODUCTION

This chapter explores the influences that social support networks might have on the substance use of Hispanic Americans. It is a topic that is conceptually tied to two global questions. The first is concerned with how social relationships contribute to health and emotional well-being. Particularly over the past two decades, interest in the positive influence of social relationships has centered on the overlapping constructs of social support, social networks, and natural social support systems. These concepts convey that individuals are embedded within systems of social relationships that provide human attachment, socialization, and resources that are valuable for adaptation to the stresses and strains of living. The second question asks how social relationships lead to negative consequences such as when conflict in social ties results in distress or when affiliations with others contribute to deviant behavior. These questions have direct implications for the study of substance abuse by Hispanics. In short, how can natural social support systems be positive factors that protect Hispanics from substance abuse as well as influences that can increase their risk for abusing drugs?

The chapter begins with a brief overview of ideas from the social support literature that have implications for understanding substance use. This leads to a discussion of some theoretical models and relevant data that explain the paths through which social relationships influence the use of drugs. As suggested in some of these models, culture is a factor that shapes the structure and function of social relationships. Accordingly,

*The writing of this chapter was supported by Grant DA05227 from the National Institute on Drug Abuse to Dr. Laurie Chassin (Principal Investigator) and the first author, and by Research Training Grant MH18387 to the second author while she was a postdoctoral fellow with the Program for Prevention Research, Arizona State University.

special considerations in understanding Hispanics' social support are offered. In the final portion of the chapter, we present ways that interventions could make use of social support and social network constructs.

SOCIAL SUPPORT SYSTEMS: AN OVERVIEW

An in-depth discussion of the literature on social support and social networks is beyond the scope of the present chapter. There are numerous books (Belle, 1989; Cohen & Syme, 1985; Gottlieb, 1981, 1983, 1988; House, 1981; Sarason & Sarason, 1985; Vaux, 1988), special issues of journals (e.g., *Journal of Consulting and Clinical Psychology, Journal of Social Issues, Journal of Social and Personal Relationships*), and reviews (Barrera, 1986; Cohen & Wills, 1985; House, Umberson, & Landis, 1988; Kessler, Price, & Wortman, 1985) which can provide the interested reader with a comprehensive overview of this complex topic. Nevertheless, several general assertions are relevant to the present chapter.

The provision of tangible (e.g., goods and services) and intangible (e.g., love, advice, empathy) assistance from aid donors to recipients are at the core of most definitions of social support (see Vaux, 1988 for review of definitions). But beyond this common core, it can be asserted that *social support is a meta-construct that encompasses several relatively distinct concepts such as perceived social support, social support networks, and informal aid transactions* (Barrera, 1981; Vaux, 1985). These more distinct concepts involve different mechanisms of action on health and psychological well-being outcomes (Barrera, 1986). For example, in some models of substance use initiation, social support network concepts are useful for distinguishing peer support networks from networks of parents and other family members (Jessor & Jessor, 1977). In contrast, Cohen and Wills (1985) argued that social support moderates the effects of stress (i.e., acts as a stress-buffer) when support is defined and measured as functional features of aid transactions. This suggests that functional aspects of social support might be more appropriate than support system structure for tests of stress-reduction models of drug and alcohol use. Despite our sensitivity to these distinctions, the term social support systems is used in this chapter for making generic statements about supportive social relationships. More specific terms are used to capture the precise social support system constructs in descriptions of individual studies.

A second assertion is that *social support networks are capable of exerting positive and negative influences.* In much of the literature on social support systems there is an implicit assumption that social support has positive or, in a worst case, benign consequences (cf., Finch, Okun, Barrera, Zautra, & Reich, 1989). However, there has been some attention to the ways that support systems detract from health and well-being by providing conflict (Barrera, 1981), emotional overinvolvement (Coyne, Wortman, & Lehman, 1988), and misguided helping gestures (Wortman & Lehman, 1985). Even more specific to substance abuse is the process of drug initiation which often involves supportive peers. Other ways social support systems encourage or maintain substance abuse might be more insidious such as those processes by which family members, even those who do not use drugs or alcohol, are suspected of maintaining ("enabling") their use.

Social support systems are thought to operate through a variety of mechanisms that include (but are not limited to) stress buffering effects, socialization and social influence, self-esteem enhancement, and others (Barrera, 1986; Cohen & Wills, 1985). The first models of social support were popularized by epidemiologists who emphasized stress-buffer models (see Vaux, 1988 for a review). However, in more recent years other models that propose different mechanisms have been explored (Barrera, 1986). The number of viable pathways that lead from social support systems to substance use are discussed in the chapter.

Although they have not been researched thoroughly, there are many possible determinants of social support. These determinants might include gender (Vaux, 1985), personality predispositions (Sarason, Levine, Basham, & Sarason, 1983), community characteristics (Oxley, Barrera, & Sadalla, 1981), or cultural background (Valle & Bensussen, 1985). Because culture shapes experiences in the family that influence socialization, rules for social interaction, and the value placed on social relationships (McClintock, Bayard, & McClintock, 1983), it is conceivable that there would be cultural variations in the structure and functioning of social support systems. Whether these cultural variations exist and how they are related to substance use are questions that have not been subjected to empirical tests.

These assertions have implications that should guide our application of theories concerning social influences on substance use and our formation of conceptual frameworks that are specific to Hispanics. Such a framework should acknowledge that social support networks can promote as well as discourage substance use. It also should show that support networks can influence substance use through multiple pathways that represent distinct features of support and diverse mechanisms. Finally, the framework should suggest how culture could potentially affect social processes that are linked to the use of drugs.

A FRAMEWORK FOR LINKING SOCIAL SUPPORT SYSTEMS TO SUBSTANCE ABUSE

Figure 8-1 is a heuristic framework for depicting the gross communalities between those portions of theoretical models that concern culture, the social environment, stress, and substance use. This framework is only intended to provide a context for understanding the thrust of our review and analysis. Clearly, it is not a comprehensive model of drug use. A multitude of factors such as genetic vulnerabilities, personality predispositions, economic resources, legal structures, and others are missing from this framework. Furthermore, only four of the linkages between culture, stress, social relations, and drug use—those connections labeled 1 through 4—are discussed in this chapter. Issues represented by arrows 5, 6 and 7 are not presented. Our emphasis is on Hispanics' social support systems and how they might be related to substance use. Finally, at least three of the arrows—2, 4, and 6—could be bi-directional. To maintain this chapter's focus on social support's effect on substance use and how it could be manipulated in interventions to change substance use, only one direction of causal influence is discussed here.

Social Influences on Substance Use

Of the numerous theories that have been proposed to explain substance abuse, several include social relationships as factors that decrease or increase the probability that individuals will abuse substances (Chassin, 1984). These theories are concerned with linkage 4 in Figure 8-1 which should be understood as containing both positive and negative influences on substance use. Many of these models were developed for research with adolescents and young adults to account for the initiation of substance use as well as progressions into problematic use.**

**It is difficult to present a conceptual model that is relevant to the initiation of substance use, its progression into heavy use, and the maintenance of addiction. Similarly, general models often do not provide an equally good fit to all types of chemical use. Figure 8-1 is our attempt to present a general heuristic framework for understanding the broad factors of sociocultural influences, social support systems, stress, and substance use. Obviously, much more detailed models are needed to account for mechanisms that are specific to certain substances in certain stages of use.

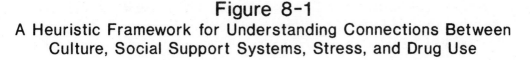

Figure 8-1
A Heuristic Framework for Understanding Connections Between Culture, Social Support Systems, Stress, and Drug Use

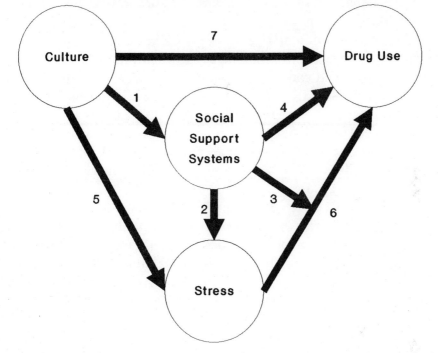

Huba, Wingard, and Bentler (1980) described a framework in which the intimate social support system exerts an influence on substance use. A prominent feature of this model is the role of sociocultural domains which exert their influences on the intimate support system (mechanisms that would be represented by linkage 1 in Figure 8-1). The expectations, values, and images that intimate social support systems communicate to individuals about drug use are derived at least in part from the sociocultural domain. For example, ethnographic studies provide some information regarding the cultural values associated with alcohol use (Bennett & Ames, 1986). Unfortunately, as Gilbert and Cervantes (1986) noted in their review of Hispanic alcohol abuse, there are virtually no data on Hispanics' parental attitudes/practices and their children's socialization of alcohol use.

The positive and negative influences of social relationships on drug use are apparent in Jessor and Jessor's (1980) Social-Psychological Model as well as a Social Learning model proposed by Simons, Conger, and

Whitbeck (1988). Jessor and Jessor's model includes personality characteristics as prominent determinants of deviant behavior, but the perceived social environment, particularly relationships with parents and peers, has equal importance. Approval or disapproval by parents and friends are thought to be closely linked to substance use. Modeling of substance use by influential people in the adolescent's social support network also is a factor proximal to drug use. More distal influences are general support and control that parents and peers provide. Consistent with this model's focus on adolescents, a positive orientation toward family and parents that comes from parental support and control is viewed as protecting adolescents from problem-prone behavior. Conversely, poor support and control from parents run the risk of providing for greater peer influence and, therefore, a greater likelihood of problematic behavior including substance use.

Several studies conducted with ethnic minority youth found results consistent with theories that feature the negative influence of adolescent peer support networks on substance abuse (Hansen, Graham, Sobel, Shelton, Flay, & Johnson, 1987; Hansen, Malotte, Collings, & Fielding, 1987; Newcomb & Bentler, 1986; Oetting, Edwards, & Beauvais, 1988; Perez, Padilla, Ramirez, Ramirez, & Rodrigues, 1979). For example, Mata and Andrew (1988) studied peer influences on the substance use of 6th to 12th grade Mexican American and Anglo adolescents in a rural South Texas community. They found that compared to Mexican American non-users of inhalants, Mexican American inhalant users were more likely to report that their friends approved of a variety of substances (such as inhalants, amphetamines, tranquilizers, cigarettes, and LSD).

Although adolescents' affiliations with drug-using peers are often related to drug and alcohol use, some peer affiliations can serve to decrease the risk of substance use. Intuitively, social participation with non-using peers provides socialization that is incompatible with substance use. Selnow and Crano (1986) drew a distinction between formal (i.e., affiliations in clubs and organizations) and informal peer affiliations. In a cross-sectional study of 760 students aged 13–17, they found that participation in formal and informal peer groups were relatively orthogonal and that they were differentially related to substance use. Whereas affiliation in informal peer groups was positively related to substance use, affiliation in formal groups was negatively related. Interpretation of these relationships is ambiguous. It is possible, for example, that more conventional youth are drawn to formal group affiliations and that it is this predisposition for conventionality that is responsible for the negative correlation of formal group participation with substance use. Nevertheless, it is possible that (a) formal groups socialize adolescents into values that are incompatible with early use of drugs and alcohol and/or (b) the competencies that are developed in formal groups serve as deterrents to substance use.

Stress and Social Support Networks

The models presented by Jessor and Jessor (1980) and by Huba et al. (1980) did not contain pathways that would be predicted by diathesis-stress or tension reduction theories of substance use, perhaps because their models were developed for understanding adolescent use and the initiation of drug use rather than the maintenance or escalation of use. Within some theoretical frameworks, stress is thought to interact with predispositions such as genetic vulnerabilities to result in drug use, or stress is viewed as contributing directly to negative affective states which individuals then try to alleviate through the use of substances (see path 6 in Figure 8-1). In either case, reducing the negative impact of stress should decrease the risk of substance use. Although they were not developed specifically for substance use, numerous models have been proposed to describe how social support and stress are connected to each other (see linkages 2 & 3), and how ultimately they are connected to negative psychological states. For example, there is research literature (see Barrera, 1986 and Cohen & Wills, 1985 for reviews) on how social support systems moderate the effect of stress on mental health outcomes (linkage 3), how stress deteriorates social support (linkage 2), and how stress results in increased affiliation or mobilization of supporters (linkage 2).

In a review of stress and distress of Mexican Americans, Barrera, Zautra, and Baca (1984) discussed how culture influences exposure to stressful life conditions (linkage 5) as well as stress moderating conditions such as social support (linkage 1). Accordingly, researchers who study Hispanic substance use within diathesis-stress and tension reduction models should be sensitive to sociocultural effects on the experience of stress (e.g., differential exposure to certain types of stress events) as well as social processes that could influence vulnerability to stress (e.g., attitudes toward helpseeking or barriers to the mobilization of social support).

From the perspective of stress reduction models, social support systems could influence substance use by decreasing the negative affective states that some individuals might attempt to relieve through the use of drugs. Understanding how social support alters negative affective states such as depression and anxiety has central importance for this model. For example, Vega, Kolody, Valle and Hough (1986) found that confidant support was related to depression in Mexican immigrant women such that those without confidant support were twice as likely to show symptoms that approximated diagnostic levels as those who reported a confidant.

In a separate report of 635 Anglos and 533 Mexican Americans from the Santa Clara County epidemiological survey, Vega and Kolody (1985) found additional evidence for the association between social support and psychological distress. A series of causal models which included various contrasts between Anglos, U.S.-born Mexican Americans, and immigrant Mexican Americans showed that satisfaction with support from friends and relatives was negatively related to psychological distress independent of the effects of ethnicity, gender, education, and disrupted marital status. If negative psychological states increase Hispanics' risk of abusing drugs, then intimate support that comes from confidants and satisfying supportive relationships can reduce drug abuse indirectly by decreasing psychological distress.

These general theoretical considerations suggest numerous ways Hispanics' natural social support systems could contribute to substance abuse or deter its use. As systems of influence, "supportive" peers can introduce individuals to substance use and support the maintenance of its use. Deterioration of supportive relationships with parents increases the influence of deviant peers. In contrast, support systems provide models for healthy lifestyles, they lessen stressful conditions, and they create affiliative bonds with parents and other socialization agents who could deter drug use. In considering their applicability to Hispanics, these theoretical mechanisms lead directly to additional questions. What is the nature of Hispanic social support systems? What are Hispanics' orientations toward helpseeking and the use of social support?

HISPANICS AND THEIR SOCIAL SUPPORT SYSTEMS

There have been several efforts to summarize what we know about Hispanic social support systems and to outline considerations for understanding their functions. The most notable discussions are provided by

Valle and Bensussen (1985) and others that appeared in an edited volume by Valle and Vega (1980). The literature identifies the importance of the family as a system of support, cultural practices that define certain social support providers (e.g., compadrazgo), and indigenous systems of helping (e.g., curanderismo). Valle and Bensussen (1985) organized Hispanic network types into three categories: (a) aggregate networks which consist of non-kinship affiliations, some of which develop from participation in Hispanic community groups, (b) kinship networks, and (c) linksperson networks which include friends and neighbors as well as the wide array of more formal helpers such as consejeras (informal advisors), curanderos (folk healers), espiritualistas (spiritual advisors), servidores (community leader/helper), sobadores (masseuses), and yerberos (herbalists). Valle and Bensussen also identified some dynamics of supportive exchanges and relationship characteristics (e.g., confianza, personalismo, "la platica") that add some distinctiveness to Hispanic social relationships and some utility for understanding their social support processes. Beyond these descriptions of Hispanics' natural social support, some literature has examined factors that influence its availability and use.

Immigration and Acculturation

Even though many Hispanics have lived within the geographic boundaries of the United States for generations, Hispanics from Mexico and other Latin American countries continue to immigrate in sizable numbers. Immigration is relevant for the study of Hispanic social support systems in light of the separations and social losses that can occur as a result of leaving one's country of origin. Several studies examined the relationship between immigration and social support, but often times immigration or generational status is conceptualized as part of an acculturation construct.

Because of the hypothesized importance of the Hispanic family as a source of social support, some research has examined the factors that influence the availability and functioning of family support (Keefe, Padilla, & Carlos, 1978). A study of three southern California communities which compared the family support systems of Mexican American and Anglo adults partially confirmed the special significance of the family for Mexican Americans. A composite index of family integration was formed from questions that asked about mutual aid between family members, frequency of visiting relatives, and number of local households of relatives. Family integration was much higher among Mexican Americans than Anglos. Among the Mexican Americans, generational status was related to family integration such that the most recent immigrants (first generation) were less likely to report high levels of family integration than second or third generation Mexican Americans. Furthermore, the authors found that unlike Anglos who utilized emotional support from a variety of sources such as friends, co-workers, as well as family members, Mexican Americans reported a more exclusive reliance on family members for emotional support.

Griffith and Villavicencio (1985) reported results that were consistent with Keefe et al.'s findings concerning acculturation and the availability of social support. A sample of 259 Mexican Americans living in a catchment area in southern California was selected through random-digit dialing. Two measures of acculturation—generational status and language used to complete the interview—were related to several measures of social support. In general, greater acculturation was positively related to involvement with network members. However, these relationships with acculturation were no longer significant when several socio-demographic characteristics (such as education, income, and age) were considered as statistical controls. Vega and Kolody (1985) also found that immigrant Mexican Americans had less *available* support compared to Anglos and U.S.-born Mexican Americans. However, group differences were non-significant for support that was *actually* provided by friends and relatives, and for a measure of support satisfaction.

These studies consistently found that immigrant Mexican Americans reported less support available than non-immigrants. Controlling for sociodemographic factors eliminated group differences in one study; results for social support variables other than available support are less clear. It would not be surprising to learn that the immigration process leads to the deterioration of socially supportive ties. Leaving one's country of origin invariably results in the severing of supportive relationships with family members and friends. Residing in a new country where one becomes part of a cultural and linguistic minority group presents obvious barriers to the formation of social support networks. Because of the important consequences of immigration on social support systems, it is misleading to include immigration status as an "acculturation" indicator in studies of Hispanic social support systems. If immigration status is included in composite acculturation measures, the disruptive effects of immigration on social support systems might be misinterpreted as an effect of the culture-of-origin's values and social practices.

Szapocznik and Kurtines (1980) went beyond the usual analyses of acculturation effects on substance use in their research with Cuban Americans in Florida. Not only did they predict that the acculturation level of Cuban adolescents would be positively related to their use of substances, but they also predicted that the discrepancy between child and parental acculturation would be predictive of adolescents' involvement in substance use. They observed that age of immigration was related to the rate of acculturation such that those who immigrated at an early age would acculturate faster than those who immigrated later in life. Consequently, children would be expected to be more acculturated than their parents, even though parents and children would have resided in the United States for identical periods of time. Szapocznik and Kurtines found that families with drug abusing adolescents had larger intergenerational acculturation differences than families with nonabusing adolescents.

Although the authors did not explicitly offer this explanation, social support between parents and adolescents could mediate the relationship between acculturative gaps and substance use. If acculturation gaps between parents and their adolescent children lead to the deterioration of supportive bonds, then acculturation would contribute to substance abuse through the mechanisms described by Jessor and Jessor (1980) and Simons et al. (1988). Extrapolating from these models, acculturation gaps between parents and adolescents would diminish parental influence as a deterrent to substance use and would contribute to greater peer influence which is associated with increased risk of substance use. The effects of parent-child acculturation differences are seldom tested. We are unaware of any research that has evaluated the potential mediational role of parental social support and influence in the relationship between parent-child acculturation gaps and adolescent substance use.

Availability of Social Networks and Help Seeking

The availability of social networks does not guarantee that they will be used in times of stress or personal need. Working with a multi-ethnic group sample of elderly adults living in the San Diego metropolitan area, Weeks and Cuellar (1981) studied individual's help-seeking strategies in response to several hypothetical situations. In addition to non-minorities, the sample included sizable numbers of Hispanic, Black,

American Indian, Filipinos, Samoans, Guamanians, Japanese, Chinese, and Korean elders. Even after controlling for factors such as age, gender, number of family members living in the metropolitan area, and immigration status, Hispanics (as well as non-minorities, Blacks, and American Indians) were less likely to rely on family members for social support than were those from Asian heritages. Through a variety of analyses, a rather consistent picture emerged: Hispanics had family members and other supporters available, but they expressed a preference for self-reliance relative to the other ethnic groups. Weeks and Cuellar (1981) commented that even though Hispanics who lived alone had an average of four times more extended kin in the area than non-minority elders, Hispanics were more likely than other ethnic groups to turn to no one — to "suffer in silence." There also was evidence in this study that Hispanics expressed great reluctance to seek professional help, a result that Weeks and Cuellar found consonant with Valle and Mendoza's (1978) research on Hispanics' helping networks. Although these findings were based on samples of elderly adults, they signal a disconcerting possibility: Hispanics might have support available, but relative to other ethnic groups, they might have greater reluctance to utilize supportive resources.

ROLE OF SOCIAL SUPPORT NETWORKS IN PREVENTION AND TREATMENT

The theme that has been developed in this chapter is that natural social support networks contain the potential for deterring substance abuse as well as the potential for elevating its risk. It follows then that interventions directed at social support networks should center on harnessing their beneficial powers and/or diminishing their harmful influences. What are some ways that interventions could involve existing support networks or build new ones that would assist in treating or preventing Hispanic substance abuse?

Although they are not specific to Hispanics, there are several discussions of interventions that utilize socially supportive relationships. Gottlieb (1988) outlined three basic support interventions: (a) support of a partner, (b) network-centered interventions, and (c) support groups. Support of a partner actually includes two different strategies — using an existing support provider (such as a spouse) or adding a new partner. Partners who are spouses or members of existing networks have been used as adjuncts to interventions for a variety of disorders, particularly behavior excesses such as smoking and overeating (Cohen, 1988; Cohen, Lichtenstein, Mermelstein, Kingsolver, Baer, & Kamarck, 1988). Similarly, there are well-known community-based interventions such as Big Brother-Big Sister organizations and Silverman's Widow-to-Widow program that make use of new, non-family supporters who receive some training to perform their roles.

Network-centered interventions include steps to mobilize existing supporters or improve the quality of support obtained from one's network. Mobilizing a network to support a caregiver who is attending a chronically ill spouse would be an example of a network intervention. These treatment or consultation programs are directed at the natural social support system rather than newly created networks.

Support groups, on the other hand, are artificially created social units that compensate for the lack of natural supporters or that constitute a peer group with special sensitivities and resources for supporting a member. Some of the best examples of peer-directed self-help groups were developed to address drug and alcohol abuse (Alcoholics Anonymous, Narcotics Anonymous) and have served as models for self-help groups designed to treat other problems (Overeaters Anonymous, Gamblers Anonymous, Parents Anonymous).

Vaux's (1988) description of social support interventions overlapped somewhat with Gottlieb's. From Vaux's perspective, clinical interventions such as network therapy, family therapy, and couples therapy might be regarded as social support interventions because the extended family, nuclear family, and marital relationship are primary sources of social support. Similar to Gottlieb, he also discussed companionship therapy (linking a support recipient with a specific helper such as a Big Brother or peer advisor) and mutual aid groups. Vaux also reviewed indirect social support interventions such as (a) consultation to support groups for improving their provision of social support, (b) enhancing support resources in the community such as training cadres of community helpers (e.g., the Community Helpers Project by D'Augelli, Vallance, Danish, Young, & Gerdes, 1981) or (c) improving the helping skills of professionals who find themselves in support-donor roles, but who are not professional counselors (e.g., hairdressers, bartenders, classroom teachers).

There are two approaches for translating these general strategies for use with Hispanics. The first is to adapt existing modalities that have been used with non-Hispanics to increase their applicability for Hispanics.

Here the emphasis is on features of the intervention that would make it more convenient, comfortable, and accessible. For example, AA or NA chapters that are sponsored by Hispanic community organizations and that conduct their meetings in Spanish are illustrations of modifying existing social support interventions. Other support strategies such as the use of partners, marital, or family therapy modalities could be adapted with similar sensitivities to ethnicity of partners and therapists, language used during meetings, and physical setting characteristics.

A second approach for developing social support interventions is to identify characteristics of social support exchanges or providers that are unique or relatively more prominent for Hispanics. Recognition that Hispanics have a more exclusive reliance on family support (Keefe et al., 1978) gives family-based interventions special significance for Hispanics and elevates the need for strategies that overcome Hispanics' reluctance to utilize even family help-giving (Weeks & Cuellar, 1981). Other strategies might incorporate natural helpers (e.g., consejeras, espiritualistas) that are indigenous to many Hispanic communities.

A rare social support intervention with Hispanic natural helpers illustrated a preventive intervention for depression in middle-aged Hispanic women that made use of servidoras and meriendas educativas (Vega, Valle, Kolody, and Hough, 1987). Their preventive intervention was designed to improve social competence and self-efficacy through the assistance of natural (nonprofessional) social support. They argued that self-efficacy could be altered by modeling, conjoint problem solving, and linking women to community resources. All of these activities could occur in semistructured contacts with Hispanic natural helpers. Two interventions were developed. In one, servidoras met individually with participants over the course of the 12-month intervention. *Servidoras* were natural (non-professional) helpers who were known in Hispanic neighborhoods for their leadership, knowledge of the community, and ability to help others. The second intervention also used *servidoras,* but in this modality they conducted informal group sessions called *meriendas educativas.*

Although the outcome of these preventive interventions is still being evaluated, they illustrate innovative ways program developers could involve supportive resources that exist in Hispanic communities. The feasibility of strategies that use indigenous helpers hinges on their prevalence as well as Hispanics' appraisal of them as effective agents of support. Research on curanderos, for example, contains conflicting reports on how extensively they are used—some reports indicating that they are used by an extremely small and narrow segment of Hispanics (Ramirez, 1980).

DEVELOPMENT OF SOCIAL SUPPORT INTERVENTIONS FOR HISPANIC SUBSTANCE USE

The National Institute of Mental Health brought together an interdisciplinary group of social support researchers who drafted guidelines for the development and evaluation of social support interventions (Gottlieb, 1988). From the 12 specific recommendations that emerged from the conference, three basic principles have special prominence: (a) researchers should have a sense from theory and data why the manipulation of social support should make a difference in the outcome of interest; (b) they should have replicable methods for manipulating social support components; and (c) they should have a valid strategy for evaluating the effectiveness of the intervention. These principles should guide the planning and empirical testing of interventions that are developed for Hispanics.

If we attended to the first of these guidelines we would conclude that there are theories to guide the design of social support interventions, but there are few data that provide convincing links between social support factors and Hispanic substance abuse. One possible exception is the empirical support for the adverse effects of substance-using peers on Hispanic adolescents' initiation of substance use. Research should examine the special life experiences of Hispanics that might determine peer group influences and their role in drug use initiation. As suggested earlier, it is possible that gaps in acculturation between parent and child might contribute to the deterioration of parental influence and the increased vulnerability to the influence of deviant peers (Szapocznik & Kurtines, 1980). This hypothesis has not been studied adequately. Are there special classes of stress events that occur to Hispanics or cultural practices that increase their affiliation with substance using peers? In general, an understanding of support system interactions that increase the risk of substance abuse would lead to interventions that disrupt, redirect, or replace these systems.

Research has not produced good evidence that social support systems reduce Hispanics' risk of substance abuse. As a result, much research is needed to determine if there are mechanisms that link Hispanic social support systems with substance abuse. In contrast, there is a sizable literature on the beneficial effects of social support when psychological distress and physical health are treated as outcomes. Nevertheless, it would be dangerous to extrapolate from this vast literature to the problem of substance use and abuse. If social support is to avoid its characterization as a panacea, there should be some differentiation between the conditions that are modified by social support systems and those that are not. Intuitively, it seems that the role of the social environment in preventing the *initiation* of certain substances would be quite different from its role in the modification of chemical *addiction.* In addition to their addictive qualities, the other physiological effects of drugs and the illegal nature of some substances also distinguish them from psychological distress and health outcomes that have been used in previous social support research.

Beyond establishing empirical connections between the functions of Hispanic social support systems and drug abuse, research could address the characteristics of Hispanics that influence help seeking both inside and outside natural support systems (cf., Litwak, 1985). We have models for building social support interventions that are derived from data and theory on specific stress conditions (e.g., Sandler, Gersten, Reynolds, Kallgren, & Ramirez, 1988). These interventions are sensitive to the special conditions that give rise to psychological dysfunction and how the social environment might alter these processes. Social support interventions that are built on special sensitivities to Hispanics should consider their helpseeking styles in addition to the structural and functional characteristics of their natural support systems.

Chapter 9

AIDS AND INTRAVENOUS DRUG USE AMONG HISPANICS IN THE U.S.: CONSIDERATIONS FOR PREVENTION EFFORTS*

FERNANDO I. SORIANO

INTRODUCTION

Two of the most challenging contemporary social problems facing Hispanics are drug abuse and the acquired immunodeficiency syndrome, more commonly known as AIDS. Although there is a significant amount of literature on each of these subjects alone, there is a growing body of literature treating these two topics together. The reason for this is tragically simple. Intravenous drug use (IVDU) is currently implicated in about a third or 32% of all adult and adolescent AIDS cases in the U.S. The rates are even more alarming when considering Hispanic rates. Intravenous drug use is implicated in over half (52.8%) of all Hispanic adult and adolescent AIDS cases. The rate for pediatric AIDS cases is even more startling, with over two-thirds (71.7%) contracting AIDS as a result of IV drug use by either the mother or her sex partner (Centers for Disease Control (CDC), 1991a).

These rates suggest that a consideration of drug use is vital to an understanding of the incidence of AIDS among Hispanics. Addressing the problems of drug abuse and AIDS among Hispanics is an essential step necessary for improving the health and well-being of Hispanics in the U.S. The purpose of this chapter is to more fully describe the AIDS epidemic among Hispanics, to point to its association with IV drug use and to discuss the role of cultural values in developing promising prevention efforts directed at Hispanic populations.

*The assistance of Ms. Felicia Fernandez is gratefully acknowledged in the preparation of this chapter. Her efficient skills at retrieving and reviewing of some of the literature used in this chapter made the writing of this chapter possible within the time allowed for its preparation.

131

BACKGROUND

AIDS Among Hispanics

As a single population, Hispanics share the unfortunate distinction of being disproportionately represented among AIDS cases in the U.S. Currently, the number of Hispanic AIDS cases is nearly twice their representation in the U.S. Although they make up 8.4% of the total U.S. population, Hispanics currently represent about 15.9% of all AIDS cases in the U.S. (CDC, 1991a). Furthermore, Hispanic women, men and children with AIDS are likewise overrepresented within their respective gender and young age classification (Amaro, 1987). Forty-six percent of male adult and adolescent Hispanics with AIDS contracted the disease through homosexual or bisexual contact, but an increasing 6% contracted it from heterosexual contact (CDC, 1991a). These rates compare with 76 and 2% for White non-Hispanics, respectively.

As of May 1991, there were 28,051 Hispanic AIDS cases in the U.S. (CDC, 1991a). This represents a 47% increase from only February 1989 when there were only 13,300 Hispanic cases (Fimbres & McKay, 1989). It is clear from Hispanic prevalence rates that AIDS is not a problem of solely individuals, but of entire families because it is affecting all family members, such as fathers, mothers, and in ever increasing numbers, children (Soriano, 1991). Furthermore, in times of crisis Hispanics are more likely to rely on family members for assistance and support (Sabogal, et al., 1987; Soriano & De La Rosa, 1990). In general, AIDS impacts Hispanic families—emotionally, financially, and otherwise.

Males and AIDS

Even with the increase in the number of females with AIDS, males are still more likely to be challenged by AIDS compared to females. Eighty-seven percent of adult Hispanics with AIDS are male and 13% are female. Among Hispanic male adults, 46% contracted AIDS through homosexual or bisexual contact compared to 80% of White males with AIDS (as of May 1991). However, a large and growing number of Hispanics are becoming infected through the use of injectable drugs. It is not the sharing of syringes that is in itself responsible for the spread of the HIV virus, but rather the sharing of syringes among individuals who are infected with the HIV virus.

Altogether, almost half or 46% of Hispanic adult and adolescent males may have contracted AIDS through the sharing of infected IV needles, compared to only 14% of White non-Hispanics. In contrast to Hispanic adult and adolescent females, Hispanic males are rarely infected through heterosexual contact. Heterosexual contact with persons infected with the HIV accounted for only 2% of Hispanic males with AIDS, while the comparable percent for Hispanic females infected thru sex with males was 38% (CDC, 1991a).

Females and AIDS

Hispanic adult and adolescent females are overrepresented among AIDS cases in comparison to their proportion in the general population. Hispanic adult and adolescent females are twice as likely to have AIDS compared to White non-Hispanic females. Among Hispanic adult and adolescent AIDS cases, 13% are female, while among White non-Hispanic cases 4.5% are female. As of May 1991, contracting AIDS through IV drug use accounted for half (50%) of Hispanic females with AIDS compared to 40% of White females with AIDS. Having sex with an infected IV drug user accounted for additional 30% among Hispanic females with AIDS, compared to only 15% of White females. Drug use is much more likely to be linked to contracting AIDS among Hispanic female AIDS cases compared to Hispanic male cases. Altogether, IV drug use was implicated in four out of five or 80.6% of Hispanic female AIDS cases compared to 46.9% of Hispanic male cases and 56.3% of White non-Hispanic female AIDS cases (CDC, 1991a).

Since 1989, the number of IV implicated AIDS cases have about doubled for most ethnic and racial groups. Compared to CDC figures in June 1989, there has been a 52% increase in the number of Hispanic female IV related AIDS cases and a 50.8% increase in comparable White female AIDS cases. These increases compare with a 46.5% increase among Hispanic adult and adolescent male IV related AIDS cases and a 43.7% increase in White males. These figures point to the serious role of IV drug use in the spread of AIDS.

Children and AIDS

While there has been a significant increase in the total number of Hispanics with AIDS, females and children with AIDS (less than 13 years of age), children showed the greatest increase over the past year. For example, from December 1989 to October 1990 the number of Hispanic children and women with AIDS increased by 42 and 42.6%, respectively.

This compares with 29% for either White or African American children over this same short period of time.

Overall, Hispanic children comprise 26% of all infected children, yet they make up less than 11% of the total population of children of that age. Of all non-Hispanic Whites with AIDS, less than 1% are children with AIDS compared to Hispanic children who make up 2.8 percent of all Hispanic AIDS cases (CDC, 1990).

Like adult and adolescent Hispanic females, drug use is heavily implicated in the spread of AIDS among Hispanic children. Contraction through mothers using infected needles for drugs accounted for the majority of Hispanic pediatric AIDS cases (44%) and another 27% resulted from mothers having sex with intravenous drug users (IVDUs). In all, 71% of all Hispanic pediatric AIDS cases resulted from IV drug use.

Adolescents and AIDS

An assessment of information about AIDS transmission and prevention among adolescents revealed that Hispanic teens knew less than other groups (DiClemente, Boyer & Morales, 1988). Yet, adolescent sexual experimentation and behavior place them at risk for exposure to HIV infection (Nader, et al., 1989). Currently only 1% of people with AIDS are younger than 20 years of age, but seropositivity in adolescents is likely to become higher because 21 percent of current AIDS cases are between the ages of 20 and 29. Since the HIV virus has a long incubation period (roughly five to seven years), many of the current adult AIDS cases in this age range were adolescents at the time of infection.

Nader et al. (1989) reported the findings of three recent surveys that showed adolescents are becoming more knowledgeable about AIDS (11 to 14 years of age). They indicated that 51% learned about AIDS and HIV infection from listening to TV and radio, while 16% became informed through magazines or newspapers. However, these studies still showed there were several knowledge gaps. In a 1986 phone survey only 15% of sexually active adolescents changed their behavior due to educational campaigns and only 10% used a condom when engaging in sex. Even less is known about Hispanic adolescents. Clearly, more research is needed on the attitudes, beliefs and practices of Hispanic adolescents.

In general, these figures on AIDS among gender and age groups show AIDS is indeed affecting Hispanics to a greater extent than it is White non-Hispanics. Also, the data show that for Hispanics AIDS is a disease affecting homosexuals and heterosexuals about equally, which stands in contrast to the White non-Hispanic population. Finally, these figures point to the devastating role of IV drug use in the spread of AIDS among all Hispanic age and gender groups.

ACCURACY OF AIDS PREVALENCE RATES

Unfortunately, due to current criteria for AIDS counts, official prevalence rates seriously undercount actual HIV related deaths among IVDUs. For example, it has been estimated that in New York more HIV infected IVDUs die prematurely from illnesses related to a weak immune system, such as from bacterial pneumonias and endocarditis, than from such illnesses associated with full-blown AIDS as Kaposi's sarcoma (Des Jarlais, Friedman, & Stoneburner, 1988). This has resulted in a serious undercount of AIDS cases and of HIV infection prevalence rates in regions with high IVDU rates (Stoneburner, et al., 1988).

Another factor resulting in an undercount of AIDS cases is the CDC's surveillance definition of AIDS, which excludes many women. The current definition of AIDS is based on mainly symptoms common to male AIDS patients. However, physical symptoms, such as a swollen pelvis, chronic vaginitis, yeast infections, vaginal warts, and/or cervical cancer are all common only to women with early symptoms of AIDS. In later stages of AIDS, however, both men and women commonly experience similar life-threatening conditions, such as Pneumocystis carinii pneumonia, wasting syndrome and esophageal candidiasis. The only exception is Kaposi's sarcoma, which is infrequently found in either women or heterosexual men (Centers for Disease Control [CDC], 1991b). Public pressure on CDC to alter the current definition to accommodate women's unique symptoms has resulted in the CDC undertaking projects charged with providing recommendations for adjusting the current definition. Broader criteria will undoubtedly result in higher numbers of AIDS cases among women. A more inclusive definition will also allow more women to qualify for medical and social security benefits, which are currently denied to them due to restricted nature of the current definition. A broader definition would also increase the participation of women in clinical trials, which normally require a positive diagnosis (U.S. Public Health Service, 1988). Participation in clinical trials will allow women more fair access to new promising experimental vaccines and therapeutic agents, such as dideoxyinosine (DDI).

PREVENTION AND INTERVENTION APPROACHES

The serious impact of AIDS and HIV infection on the U.S. population suggests both prevention and intervention efforts are essential to curtail the increasing numbers of affected people. Initiatives are particularly needed that target ethnic minority populations, such as Hispanics. Much of the literature on prevention and intervention efforts directed at Hispanic communities have focused on three main types of activities: (1) increasing the awareness and knowledge related to drug use and the spread of AIDS; (2) facilitative efforts to change risky behavior, (3) and initiatives that promote or facilitate positive outcomes or incentives for maintaining behavior change.

Awareness of IV Drug Use and AIDS

According to social learning theory, awareness is a critical precursor of behavior change (Bandura, 1986). Awareness here refers to knowledge about AIDS and HIV infection, particularly concerning its spread through IVDU. Unfortunately, studies have consistently shown Hispanics are less knowledgeable and maintain more misconceptions about AIDS and HIV infection than non-Hispanics (Dawson & Hardy, 1989; Friedman, Sufian & Des Jarlais, 1990; DiClemente, Boyer & Morales, 1988). Several factors, such as isolation, lack of access to full range of media, education, acculturation and benign neglect by health agencies have all been thought to contribute to a general lack of AIDS awareness among Hispanics. Education and acculturation, in particular, have been found to be related to knowledge and awareness. Data from the National Health Interview Survey has shown that education is a significant predictor of knowledge and attitudes related to AIDS across ethnic groups (Dawson & Hardy, 1989). That is, the lower the education attainment, the lower the awareness of AIDS issues. This makes intuitive sense, since education levels largely determine access to information. These findings suggest that awareness campaigns need to be targeted to lower educated Hispanics. Also, these findings suggest the development of awareness materials need to be written at lower grade levels. B. Marin (1990) suggests awareness material should be written at no more than a fifth or 6th grade level.

Acculturation has also been shown to be a predictor of AIDS knowledge and awareness. In a telephone survey in San Francisco, B. Marin and G. Marin (1990) found acculturation was strongly associated with knowledge—with less acculturated having many more erroneous beliefs about "casual" transmission and about being able to visually tell when a person has AIDS. These findings continued to hold even after controlling for education levels. These results suggest that awareness efforts should be targeted to less acculturated Hispanics, and emphasize the many ways that the HIV virus is not transmitted.

The spread of AIDS through IV use is not solely tied to injecting mind altering drugs. For Hispanics, injecting vitamins and medicines available over the counter outside of the U.S. is not uncommon. A study by Fairbank, Bregman and Maullin, as reported by B. Marin (1989), has indicated that approximately 13% of Hispanic respondents in San Francisco occasionally injected medicines or vitamins in the home. This suggests that efforts to increase the awareness of the spread of AIDS through the sharing of needles with HIV infected individuals need to include non-drug abusing Hispanics, as well.

Although several social scientists point to the importance of increasing awareness of AIDS among Hispanics (Friedman, Sufian & Des Jarlais, 1990; Mays & Cochran, 1988), its efficacy in affecting seropositive rates has not been established. Moreover, it is recognized that awareness in itself is not sufficient to change behavior (Des Jarlais & Friedman, 1988; Schilling, et al., 1989). IVDUs need to be presented with concrete steps that they need to take to prevent contracting HIV infection (Solomon & DeLong, 1986).

Changing Risky Behavior

Once increasing the knowledge and awareness of AIDS and its spread through IV drug use, it is important to promote changes in behavior that put individuals at risk of contracting HIV infection. Preventative efforts that attempt to do so have focused mainly on reducing IV drug use and/or on promoting responsible sexual relations. Studies have shown that there has been more success changing risky drug use behavior (e.g., disinfecting needles with bleach) than in changing risky sexual behavior (Des Jarlais & Friedman, 1988). According to Des Jarlais and Friedman (1988), relative stabilization of seroprevalence rates and lower rates of new HIV infections in specific areas of New York, San Francisco and Stockholm can be reasonably linked to both drug abuse treatment programs and/or to safer methods of injecting drugs due to promotion efforts.

Promoting changes in compromising sexual behavior has been shown to be more difficult to change in most ethnic groups (Des Jarlais &

Friedman, 1988). However, a few studies do suggest promising or at least point to ineffective preventative efforts directed at Hispanics. For example, promoting condom use among Hispanics is reportedly more difficult among Hispanic men who often associate condom use with prostitution (Marin, B., 1989). B. Marin (1989) cited a study in Bogota that found men using condoms more often for sex outside of marriage than for marital sex. Interestingly, Hispanics have been found to be as likely as other ethnic groups to use birth control methods, despite organized religion's objections to it (National Center for Health Statistics, 1986). Even so, married Hispanic women report lower usage of condoms for contraception (14%) compared to non-Hispanics (25%) (Marin, B., 1989). Furthermore, Sabagh (1980) suggests that promoting condom use among married Hispanics may be impeded by Hispanic desire for large families.

Promoting the Maintenance of Behavior Change

After increasing awareness of the relationship of drug use and AIDS is established, and promoting of changes in risky behavior is undertaken, there is the need to foster positive behavioral patterns. This entails supporting, reinforcing and/or instilling attitudes and beliefs that are in line with appropriate behavioral patterns. Furthermore, social mechanisms need to be in place to reward or reinforce these positive attitudes and beliefs (Des Jarlais & Friedman, 1988).

Studies are lacking that examine the efficacy of establishing reward systems for behavior change among IVDUs. However, studies have suggested the importance of social support networks in the treatment of drug abuser (Fraser & Hawkins, 1984; Schilling, 1989). Social support networks that reinforce abstinence from engaging in high-risk behavior can serve as the reward system necessary for maintaining behavior change. On the other hand, a support network reinforcing recidivism will serve as a strong force countering programmatic efforts aimed at positive behavioral changes (Hawkins & Frazer, 1983).

Efforts to reinforce behavior change among Hispanic IVDUs need to utilize natural support systems, such as the family. Moreover, prevention efforts would do well to convey culturally specific messages that also act as powerful reinforcing agents. For example, messages to particularly Hispanic male IVDUs can stress the benefit to the health and well being to immediate family resulting from not engaging in high-risk behavior (B. Marin, 1990).

Cultural Considerations in Prevention Efforts

According to G. Marin (1989), Hispanic cultural values, such as simpatia, familism, personalismo and power distance need to be taken into consideration in developing effective AIDS prevention efforts for Hispanics. Care needs to be taken in selecting appropriate wording and communication channels to transmit messages to Hispanics that take cultural values into account. A review of dominant cultural values follows, which can be used effectively in AIDS related prevention efforts.

Familism. Although Hispanics are heterogeneous, social scientists have been pointing to a number of cultural values which are shared by most Hispanics. One very strong cultural value is familism. Familism refers to the strong identification and attachment of individuals with their nuclear and extended families and it involves strong feelings of loyalty, reciprocity and solidarity among family members (Triandis, Marin, Betancourt, Lisanski & Chang, 1982). According to social scientists, the family is the single most important institution for Chicanos (Alvirez & Bean, 1976), Puerto Ricans (Glazer & Moynihan, 1963), Cuban Americans (Szapocznik & Kurtines, 1980) and for Central and South Americans (Cohen, 1979).

In addressing AIDS and IVDU topics with Hispanics, familism can be found to be a potential hindrance or an asset when initiating preventative efforts to stop the disease. For example, loyalty to the family is a strong value for the majority of Hispanics. Personal issues and problems including problems with substance abuse are considered private family matters (Brown, et al., 1985).

In one study on differences between talking to a relative at risk for HIV infection, involving 218 Hispanics and 201 non-Hispanics from San Francisco, Marin, Marin and Juarez (1990) found that Hispanics were more willing than non-Hispanics to talk to a relative about methods of preventing HIV transmission. Hispanics also indicated that the most appropriate person to talk to a relative would be an older person, preferably a family member. The authors of this study concluded that the family is a useful source for disseminating AIDS prevention information, especially in Hispanic communities.

According to B. Marin (1989), the strong family orientation of the Hispanic culture creates a number of obligations, but is a source of support in times of trouble. Hispanics commonly feel a strong need to consult with other family members before making important decisions.

There is a strong sense of obligation to help others in the family, both economically and emotionally. Also, there is a strong sense of love and nurturing towards children (Sabagh, 1980). All of these characteristics are also found among non-Hispanics, but are not as strong as they are among Hispanics.

The strong family ties of Hispanics can be used as a motivator to change high-risk or detrimental behavior. For example, it has been suggested that familism can be used to help Hispanics stop the use of drugs through the use of messages pointing to the bad example that drug use gives to one's children or siblings or by suggesting the failure of a drug-using father to protect and to provide for his family (B. Marin, 1987). The same type of message can be used in AIDS prevention efforts, by similarly emphasizing the implications of AIDS to the family and children.

On the other hand, loyalty of family members to one another and the need for the family to present a good image to the outside world, can dictate that problems, such as drug abuse, will be hidden (Smith-Peterson, 1983). Similarly, the risk of contracting AIDS through unprotected sex or other high-risk behavior can be also be held hidden or ignored in order to preserve a positive image of the family.

The importance of children to Hispanics also has implications for Hispanics faced with AIDS. For example, the importance placed on children may increase the willingness of HIV positive women to carry a pregnancy to term (Gross, 1987). While familism may create special problems for AIDS prevention, the powerful influence of familism, as mentioned earlier, can also be used in the fight against AIDS (B. Marin, 1990). The impact of AIDS on the family and children can be used effectively to motivate a change in high risk behavior among Hispanics. Furthermore, research suggests that Hispanics may be more motivated to talk to family members about prevention than previously believed (B. Marin, 1989).

National data reported by Dawson and Hardy (1988), indicated that almost half of Hispanic adults in the sample used reported having discussed AIDS with their children age 10–17 years, and another 60% stated that their children in that age range had received instruction about AIDS in school. Although discussion of AIDS may not be uncommon in Hispanic families, gender and ethnic group origin differences seem to be common. Hispanic men were found to be less likely than Hispanic women to have discussed AIDS with their children (39% versus

56%). Moreover, persons of Mexican ancestry were less likely to discuss AIDS with children than were other Hispanics, 42% and 57%, respectively. In general, Hispanic persons were less likely to have discussed AIDS with their children than non-Hispanics, 48% and 62%, respectively (Dawson, 1988).

Other cultural values. According to some researchers, another important Hispanic cultural value of Hispanics is *collectivism* (Marin, 1988). This cultural value places great emphasis on the concerns and needs of others (Hofstede, 1980; Marin & Triandis, 1985). Collectivism expresses itself in Hispanic culture as a strong orientation toward the family (Sabogal, et al., 1987). This includes the extended family and fictive kin. It places great importance on respect in social relationships. *"Simpatia"* or being nice to others is another manifestation of collectivism. Simpatia has important implication for those designing health intervention methods, since confrontation and assertiveness are incompatible with being "simpatico" (B. Marin, 1987). These cultural values are important in that they influence and shape health attitudes of Hispanics (B. Marin, 1988).

B. Marin (1990) suggests other AIDS prevention efforts should also consider another Hispanic cultural value called "personalismo," which gives high importance to interpersonal relationships and dictates "respeto" or respect to particularly authority figures. In the context of prevention efforts, B. Marin (1990) suggests, " . . . personalismo means Hispanics may be more likely to trust and cooperate with health care workers whom they know personally, and with whom they have had pleasant conversations, often referred to as 'la platica' by Mexican Americans". A lack of respeto is said to result in dismissing prevention information conveyed, since Hispanics will not feel respected or appreciated. By the same token respeto can also result in Hispanics convey understanding information given in order to show respect to health care workers, even when they fail to truly understand or accept messages.

Finally, B. Marin (1990) suggests "machismo" can be used in prevention efforts aimed at IVDUs. According to B. Marin, "Machismo incorporates the idea that the male has a serious responsibility to provide for and protect his family . . . ". Like familism, machismo can be used to convey the message that adhering to preventative methods will protest family members from acquiring HIV infection and AIDS.

CONCLUSION

It is recognized that reducing the spread of AIDS through IV drug use among Hispanics is a very complex undertaking that requires considering cultural as well as psychosocial and economic factors (De La Cancela, 1989). According to Amsel (1990), preventing the AIDS epidemic associated with IV drug abuse, " . . . requires a broad program that includes multiple strategies . . . designed to alter high-risk behaviors among IV drug users and their sexual partners . . . and [entails efforts] to educate the public about the infection . . . " (p. viii). Hence, prevention and intervention efforts need to be cognizant of the several population groups that need to be targeted, which include IVDUs, their sex partners and the community at large.

Amsel (1990) offers specific suggestions regarding prevention efforts directed at IVDUs that are relevant to developing initiatives aimed at Hispanics. AIDS prevention programs should separate information disseminating initiatives that provide general information about the spread of AIDS through IV drug use from those that specifically attempt to alter behavioral patterns. Although both complement each other, they have different objectives.

Information programs aimed at attempting to change behavioral patterns of IVDUs need to target specific subgroups, e.g., ethnic and age groups, etc. (Amsel, 1990). For example, prevention initiatives directed at Hispanic IVDUs need to consider such cultural values as familism, simpatia, personalismo, and acculturation levels in the design and implementation of such programs (B. Marin, 1989). The same applies for efforts to reach sex partners of IVDUs.

According to Amsel (1990) prevention or intervention efforts are more likely to succeed if they address multiple objectives, are coordinated with other initiatives and are community based. She suggests such interventions should: "(a) prepare various members of the community for forthcoming AIDS prevention efforts, (b) overcome barriers to high-risk-behavior change, and (c) bring about high-risk-behavior change among those in the community" (p. xi). Moreover, messages to the community need to be clear, simple, be to the point, and be repeated. Finally, Amsel (1990) suggests emphasizing human-interest stories to help individuals better understand and identify with those at risk. Among Hispanics, both radio and television dramatizations, like soap operas, have been extremely successful in gaining the attention and educating Hispanics.

More of such initiatives need to be developed that are targeted at specific Hispanic subgroups, e.g., spouses, adolescents, and IVDUs.

Following a social learning framework, prevention efforts have higher likelihood of success if they increase awareness, suggest alternative behavioral patterns and promote norms that reward or reinforce positive behavioral patterns (Des Jarlais & Friedman, 1988). However, as mentioned earlier effective efforts to curtail the spread of AIDS among Hispanic IV drug users need to take into account sociocultural perspectives, such as family roles, familism, simpatia, personalismo, acculturation levels (Marin, B., 1989; Marin, B., 1990), as well as sociopolitical status of Hispanics (De La Cancela, 1989).

Continued research on AIDS and IV drug use among Hispanics is clearly needed to more clearly identify successful culturally relevant and sensitive prevention efforts. As the Hispanic population is heterogeneous, studies are needed that suggest successful prevention strategies that take heterogeneity into account, as well as take gender, age group, and acculturation differences into consideration. Epidemiological studies on specific Hispanic populations are vital for gaining a better understanding of the extent to which IV drug use is responsible for the spread of HIV infection among this fast growing segment of the U.S. population (Schilling, et al., 1989).

The purpose of this chapter was not so much to present a comprehensive review of the extant literature on prevention efforts directed at U.S. Hispanics, but rather to call attention to critical factors relevant to developing successful prevention initiatives. Addressing such health issues as the spread of AIDS among Hispanics is essential for insuring the well-being of Hispanics who will be increasingly relied on to provide a viable and well-trained labor force in the U.S. Substance abuse and AIDS represent true threats to the well-being of Hispanics. There is a need for public policy makers to be sensitive to the needs and challenges that are specific to minority groups, such as Hispanics, particularly when initiating funding priorities for research and community prevention projects or programs.

Finally, relevant and available Hispanic researchers need to be encouraged to conduct research on Hispanic populations. This encouragement can be represented in any of several forms, such as through the development of specific Hispanic research training grant programs, graduate and postgraduate fellowships, research grants and community demonstration grant programs. In particular, there is a need for Hispanic researchers to be mentored by those with a longstanding research grant funding track record.

Attempting to stop the spread of AIDS through IV drug use among Hispanics is a challenging and complex task, which requires sociocultural sensitivity in the design of prevention and intervention efforts. Research will undoubtedly continue to play a critical role in pointing to effective and ineffective methods of reaching Hispanics. Public policy makers need to understand that investments in addressing such critical problems as substance abuse and AIDS among Hispanics will result in positive dividends to U.S. population as a whole, due to the increasing dominant role that Hispanics are expected to play in the U.S. economy in the future. However, it is likewise important to recognize that substance abuse and AIDS are symptoms of other serious problems facing many Hispanics, such as poor education, unemployment, discrimination, poor access to health care, and low economic resources. Addressing these more basic problems will have an even broader beneficial impact on this population, which will encompass the prevalence rates of IVDU and AIDS among Hispanics.

Chapter 10

CHEMICAL DEPENDENCE, SELF-HELP GROUPS, AND THE HISPANIC COMMUNITY

Melvin Delgado and Denise Humm–Delgado

INTRODUCTION

The impact of chemical dependence is felt throughout the Hispanic community and is not restricted to any one socioeconomic class, age group, gender, or other sector. This impact has been addressed in the professional literature in the last five years (Delgado & Rodriguez-Andrew, forthcoming; Singer, Davison, & Yalin, 1987; Szapocnik & Kurtines, 1989). Yet, the use of self-help, or mutual support, groups to meet the growing needs of Hispanics has not received much attention in the professional literature. This may be the result of factors such as bias on the part of professionals against this form of assistance; the inaccessibility of this form of help to Hispanics, or people's reluctance to speak about their involvement because of the stigma associated with drugs. Nevertheless, the topic deserves exploration because of the momentum of the self-help movement in addressing chemical dependence in other groups, the need for additional, culturally relevant programming for Hispanics, and the inadequacy of current public funding to initiate and maintain sufficient formal agency services.

In order to examine the realities and possibilities regarding this use of self-help or mutual aid groups within the Hispanic community, this chapter will explore the relationship of Hispanic culture to chemical dependence and help seeking and discuss experiences and issues Hispanics have encountered in self-help and other groups. Implications for the use of self-help groups with Hispanics will then be drawn. Before focusing on Hispanics, however, the self-help concept will be reviewed briefly.

145

THE CONCEPT OF SELF-HELP

Self-help or mutual-aid groups have been used for centuries to help people in need in both the United States and abroad (Katz & Bender, 1976; Lieberman, Borman & Associates, 1979; Kahn & Bender, 1985; Weber, 1982). Examples of self-help organizations in United States history include voluntary societies that were begun in the seventeenth and eighteenth centuries by white colonists from Europe who belonged to the same ethnic, religious, or artisan groups (Axinn & Levin, 1982), Black beneficial societies, usually associated with Black churches, that were started in the eighteenth and nineteenth centuries (Hershberg, 1989), and the twentieth century Alcoholics Anonymous movement. Examples of other twentieth century self-help movements that have attracted large numbers of Hispanics include the United Farm Workers for Chicanos and the Pentecostal Church for Puerto Ricans. Especially in a society like the United States, with an historical reluctance to develop a "welfare state," self-help and mutual aid groups have provided needed privately sponsored social supports.

Self-help groups are still flourishing (Nash, 1989; Chesney, Rounds & Chesler, 1989). The definition of self-help groups we will use was developed by Katz and Bender (1976, p. 9):

> Self-help groups are voluntary, small group structures for mutual aid and the accomplishment of a special purpose. They are usually formed by peers who have come together for mutual assistance in satisfying a common need, overcoming a common handicap or life-disrupting problem, and bringing about desired social and personal change. The initiators and members of such groups perceive that their needs are not, or cannot be, met through existing social institutions. Self-help groups emphasize face-to-face social interactions and the assumption of personal responsibility by members. They often provide material assistance, as well as emotional support; they are frequently "cause" oriented, and promulgate an ideology or values through which members may attain an enhanced sense of personal identity.

In short, self-help groups are important in meeting the instrumental and expressive needs of vulnerable individuals. The need for the groups may result from an inadequate or culturally irrelevant social service system; a preference for a peer or collegial approach to problem-solving rather than a professionally led approach; or a lack of professional interest or effective "technology" regarding the problem.

Charles Zastrow (1989) does an excellent job of summarizing the classification work done by Katz and Bender (1976). The classification looks at self-help groups in five categories: (1) groups that focus on personal growth or self-fulfillment (e.g., Alcoholics Anonymous); (2) groups that focus on social advocacy (e.g., Mothers Against Drunk Driving); (3) groups that focus on creating alternative patterns for living (e.g., gay rights groups); (4) groups that attract individuals who have elected to withdraw from society and have as a common bond past affiliations (e.g., people in various forms of recovery); and (5) groups that incorporate mixed types (e.g., personal growth and advocacy).

Shulman (1985/1986) notes nine processes that enhance the effectiveness of self-help groups: (1) sharing data about methods and processes that have served to aid in difficult times; (2) the dialectical process of group development of an idea or solution; (3) exploration of taboo subjects through group members taking a risk in discussing them; (4) the "all in the same boat" phenomenon because of similar experiences, problem resolutions, and concerns; (5) emotional support; (6) mutual demand (a willingness to put aside defenses and listen to others' perceptions); (7) mutual expectations (a willingness to take action and share with the group the process and outcome); (8) rehearsal through role play; (9) the strength in numbers phenomenon since many share similar experiences.

Kahn and Bender (1985, p. 9) cite Borman's five "curative factors" that account for much of self-help groups' success: (1) universality (a recognition by group members that they are not alone; the others with whom they meet have the same problem); (2) acceptance (members neither condone nor disapprove of the problem but accept the person and the problem); (3) hope (the element of hope is instilled by these groups, especially as members see they are helping others with similar problems); (4) altruism (feeling better about oneself through the experience of giving help, support, or guidance to others); and (5) cognitive restructuring (the acquisition of an alternate "culture" of language, ritual, symbols, which set the stage for new knowledge imparted to group members about the causes and effects of their problem).

Self-help groups also serve to reverse a process of disempowerment by aiding individuals to take control over significant events in their lives and community; empowerment allows individuals to contribute and encourages action (Kahn & Bender, 1985; Maguire, 1981; Nash, 1989). Yet, while self-help groups often empower members and encourage social action, it is important to remember that their very existence is indeed often a response to a lack of publicly supported services. Exclusive reliance on referral to self-help groups, when other services are also necessary, can represent a capitulation by human service agencies and advocates to a conservative political ideology that seeks to withdraw funding from public sector human services and rely on the private sector (Schilling, Schinke & Weatherly, 1988).

ATTITUDES OF HISPANICS TOWARDS CHEMICAL DEPENDENCE

For Hispanics, there is a stigma attached to admitting that one has a problem with alcohol or other drugs. Generally, there is greater tolerance of alcohol dependence than other chemicals such as "crack-cocaine" or heroin. This tolerance has been traced back to the important role alcohol has played in celebrating important life events such as births, weddings, and baptisms (Singer, Davison, & Yalin, 1987; Eden & Aguilar, 1989). In the last decade, Hispanics who use intravenous drugs have been especially hard hit by Acquired Immune Deficiency Syndrome (AIDS) and all the stigma society associates with it (Honey, 1988; Kosterlitz, 1988), so some chemically dependent persons carry a double stigma. Additionally, one could speculate that chemically dependent Hispanic women who give birth to chemically dependent babies would carry the stigma of not fulfilling the culturally sanctioned maternal, caretaking role, and so have stigma about this in addition to their chemical dependence.

Chemical dependence is seen as an essentially moral issue rather than a disease for both men and women, making help-seeking difficult (McGough & Hindman, undated). Yet, the chemically dependent woman is especially seen as having poor impulse control and "weak" character, since it is comparatively more acceptable for men to be chemically dependent than women. Regarding alcohol, for example, popular Hispanic folklore ("machismo") measures men's strength, in part, by how much alcohol they can consume.

Hispanics sometimes believe that chemical dependence is the result of some supernatural cause such as a hex (Singer, 1984, 1984a). As a result, only intervention involving the supernatural can be effective in those cases; sometimes the client and his or her family will utilize both mainstream social services and traditional folk healers, both "earthly" and "metaphysical" healers (Delgado, 1988; Delgado & Humm-Delgado, 1982).

There also may be a passive acceptance of chemical dependence, part of a larger fatalistic attitude of Hispanics that results in their accepting situations seen as outside their control; this can block efforts by both the chemically dependent person and family members to make active efforts toward recovery (Eden & Aguilar, 1989).

VALUES THAT INFLUENCE
HELP-SEEKING BY HISPANICS

Several values influence Hispanics' help-seeking preferences, and must be considered in terms of their impact on the use of self-help groups (Lusero, 1977; Padilla, 1985). Four important ones are "simpatia," cooperation, family loyalty, and an action orientation to problem solving.

"Simpatia"

"Simpatia" does not have a literal English translation, but roughly indicates an importance attached to graciousness, manners, and courtesy by Hispanics that cannot be overestimated. This is manifested in an avoidance of interpersonal conflict (e.g., not disagreeing, criticizing, contradicting, or losing one's temper) and a striving to be pleasant and likeable in social situations (Triandis, Lisansky, Marin & Betancourt, 1984). People are to be treated with honor, dignity, and respect and are not be made to "lose face" in front of a group (Delgado, 1983).

Cooperation

Cooperation is very different from the values of independence and competition that are stressed in the larger American society; for Hispanics, it is important that interactions not result in "winners" and "losers." By seeing people as interdependent rather than as competitive, there is an emphasis placed on reciprocity and mutual aid within families, social networks, and communities. The natural support systems to which Hispanics traditionally turn in times of stress are ones with which the individual either already has a reciprocal, cooperative relationship, or which will take a personalized, cooperative approach to problem solving (De La Rosa, 1988; Valle & Bensussen, 1985). These natural support systems can be classified as follows (Delgado & Humm-Delgado, 1982): (1) family and friends; (2) religion (i.e., Catholic, Pentecostal, Seventh Day Adventists, and Jehovah's Witnesses); (3) folk healers (curanderos, herbalists, santeros, and mediums); and (4) merchants and social clubs (grocery stores, market places, and home-town clubs).

Family Loyalty

The family is highly valued and members are expected to be available to help in crises and, in turn, can turn to the family in times of personal crises. There are both opportunities to give help and to receive help over time, which enhances the self-esteem of the person seeking help. In general, Hispanics are expected to pay attention to the needs, goals, values, and points of view of others to a greater extent than their own (Triandis, Lisansky, Marin, & Betancourt, 1984), and this holds true for their relationship with their families. It is also important to recognize that Hispanics define "family" in a broad context that involves individuals who may not be related by blood or marriage but rather are "adopted" as family ("como familia"). This broad definition, with open boundaries, combined with a propensity to want to include people, very often provides Hispanics with a number of people, indeed a cohesive group, on whom they can depend in crisis and for whom they must be responsible in crisis.

Action Orientation to Problem Solving

Hispanics tend to stress problem solving by actions rather than by a lengthy process of historical insight into one's personal development. Delgado (1983, p. 86) explains why an action-orientation is so important: "The preference for an action-oriented focus can derive from any one or combination of the following aspects: (1) environmental demands (poverty, unresponsive institutions, crisis); (2) locus of control may be perceived to exist outside of the individual (environment may be perceived to be uncontrollable, unpredictable, and hostile); and (3) cultural value orientation focuses on concrete solutions to present problems." The focus on a action-orientation does not mean that verbal interactions are not important. However, actions provide a basis from which to discuss emotions, beliefs, concerns, and hopes.

EXPERIENCES AND ISSUES IN
SELF-HELP AND OTHER GROUPS

While most literature on Hispanics and group work focuses on leader-led therapeutic, socialization, or task oriented groups, there is a small, but increasing body of literature on Hispanics and self-help groups. Gutierrez, Ortega and Suarez (1990) give evidence that self-help is congruent with Hispanic culture and provide guidance for forming groups. Leon, Mazur, Montalvo, and Rodriguez (1984) note the effectiveness of self-help groups with Hispanic mothers in helping them address conflicts between Hispanic and Anglo cultural systems and values. Schaefer and Pozzaglia (1986) discuss this form of aid for Hispanic parents with children with cancer within a hospital setting; self-help served to minimize isolation and provided information and materials about cancer and children. Farber and Rogler (1981) report on their work with Hispanic and Black children in the Bronx, New York, in which teenage leaders played a critical role in the functioning of support groups for youth with a wide range of problems (e.g., with school and the courts). Eden & Aguilar (1989, p. 215) speculate that Alcoholics Anonymous may have drawbacks that need to be addressed: The need for admission of loss of control and dependency before treatment can progress may cause many Hispanic male clients to reject AA as a form of therapy. If and when necessary, Hispanic clients should be referred to Spanish speaking AA organizations to help reduce the effects of cultural differences during treatment.

While there are concerns about self-help for Hispanics in the literature, there are also instances documented in which the intervention has been successful. Leader-led groups for Hispanics have been discussed in the literature far more frequently than self-help groups. They have been shown to be a highly effective and economical means of addressing needs of Hispanics (Delgado & Humm-Delgado, 1984), but certain barriers to their use have been identified. Therefore, it is wise to avoid similar pitfalls in self-help groups. Barriers can be categorized into four areas: (1) organizational; (2) group process; (3) acculturation levels of group members; and (4) group leadership.

Organizational Barriers

Historically, community mental health and drug treatment centers were the primary sites for Hispanic groups. These settings, however, were stigmatizing and experienced great difficulties in being accepted by the community. Settings, as a result, must be non-stigmatizing and have a history of positive relationships with the community. In addition, they must be staffed by bilingual and bicultural staff, be geographically accessible, and have a highly personalized approach to the recruitment of group members (Cooper & Cento, 1977; Delgado, 1983; Mizio, 1979). Because of the "grassroots" approach of self-help groups, one would expect that organizational barriers would be at least as easy to surmount in these as in leader-led groups. For example, Alcoholics Anonymous and Narcotics Anonymous are often held in non-stigmatized settings such as churches.

Group Process

Failure to accurately assess member expectations of what constitutes a group experience is a very common occurrence. Member expectations of what constitutes a group experience must be actively addressed prior to and during the initial meetings. For example, self-disclosure of "bad actions" may be seen as exposure for judgement rather than for under-standing (Olarte & Masnick, 1985). Group meetings should be scheduled on days and times that are most conducive to group participation (e.g., take in to account transportation and child care constraints) and allow sufficient time for socializing before and after meetings. Groups may even decide to celebrate birthdays and holidays and bring traditional food or musical instruments (Olarte & Masnick, 1985). Group process is greatly facilitated when members and leaders can speak Spanish and English and focus on group themes that have a particular relevance to Hispanics (Delgado & Siff, 1980; Hynes & Werbin, 1977; Martinez, 1977; Normand, Iglesias & Payn, 1974). The process of self-help groups may be flexible to some extent, but they still do reflect the dominant culture's expectations for appropriate process in that setting, as well as the norms of the self-help movement per se.

Acculturation Levels of Group Members

It is not sufficient to balance a group according to Hispanic origins, gender, and socioeconomic class; acculturation levels also must be taken into account, to facilitate member communication and degree of comfort in the group (Rogler, Cortes & Malgady, 1991). Acculturation levels can influence the language used to describe highly emotional content (English versus Spanish), issues to be discussed within the group (cultural con-flicts between Puerto Rican and Anglo values), extent to which family is defined (extended, with open boundaries, to nuclear, with very fixed and closed boundaries), and degree of comfort with other Puerto Ricans in the group (very acculturated Puerto Ricans may not feel very comfort-able with low-acculturated Puerto Ricans). The level of acculturation can have an influence on the use of external resources such as social agencies and natural support systems, sophistication in obtaining information and services, stress related to conflicts about traditional values, and the ability to discuss personal issues in a mixed gender environment (Kraidman, 1980; Menikoff, 1979; Olarte & Masnick, 1985; Szapocznik & Kurtines, 1980). Self-help groups often can accommodate individual differences by offering a selection of groups which potential members can "try out" until they find one with a personal "goodness of fit," so the concept of somewhat specialized groups is not alien to the self-help movement. Yet, grouping by acculturation level may be a somewhat new approach.

Group Leadership

Group leaders must have a keen understanding of how they fulfill their role within groups. Disparity between expectations and reality will result in dissatisfaction on the part of the leader and members. Expectations and roles of group members and leader will vary according to the function and nature of the group and the acculturation levels of the members. Nevertheless, in leader led groups, leaders are expected to take an active part, including role modeling, leading didactic discussion, sharing of their personal background, providing information and brokering group needs, and being flexible by acting out a variety of roles (Delgado, 1981; Delgado, 1983; Kraidman, 1980; Olarte & Masnick, 1985). It may be difficult for some Hispanics to adjust to self-help groups without a designated leader or with a revolving leader, so care must be taken to address this at referral or in the group. Also, since self-help groups can be used in combination with individual treatment, the counselor the group member sees individually may need to provide guidance and support in using the group.

IMPLICATIONS FOR THE USE OF
SELF-HELP GROUPS WITH HISPANICS

Because of the historical use of natural support systems by Hispanics within their own communities, self-help or mutual aid can be seen to be well ingrained in their experience. Yet, this mutual aid has been culture-specific and so is not totally consonant with Anglo conceptions of self-help or mutual-aid. It is important to appreciate where there are similarities and where there are differences in the two forms of aid, as well as where there are larger cultural or social differences between Hispanic and Anglo societies, in order to develop a model for culturally relevant self-help groups for Hispanics who are chemically dependent.

Since chemical dependence is not restricted to any one socioeconomic class or acculturation level, comfort in any particular group will vary according to these factors. For well acculturated Hispanics, goodness of fit with existing Alcoholics Anonymous groups, for example, may exist. For less acculturated Hispanics, referral to a Spanish speaking Alcoholics Anonymous group may be the only reasonable referral.

For Hispanics who are not acculturated, and have not been socialized into the medical model of chemical dependence, stigma will be an especially difficult issue to address. For any person who is chemically dependent, denial is a serious impediment to acknowledgement and recovery, but for the Hispanic person, culturally negative perceptions of dependence will, no doubt, compound the denial and shame. While this may be less so for men than women, it should be understood that the medical model is not available to Hispanics as an explanation of chemical dependence to the extent that it is available to Anglos.

The referral process for Hispanics then becomes especially sensitive and crucial. While a Anglo American may have several role models of people who have benefitted from self-help groups in recovering from chemical dependence, an Hispanic may not. It may prove helpful to introduce the person for whom one is encouraging a referral to someone who is already in a Spanish speaking group, to provide a role model, ease the transition, explain the expectations of the group, and personalize the group experience. The professional doing the referral, or the self-help group doing outreach, may do well to draw parallels in the experience of problem solving of the new person to the experiences they will likely have in the group. It should be expected that this may take some time, and reticence need not necessarily be interpreted as denial of the problem of chemical dependence.

The group itself may have different norms from other self-help groups, and these culturally specific norms will be strengths that will make the group comfortable for the Hispanic. It may have more of a social feeling at times than others, and this should not be seen as a avoidance of issues. Rather, Hispanics expect group experiences to allow for the graciousness, manners, and courtesy that "simpatia" connotes. Hispanics will move slowly towards self-disclosure, may be more willing to give of one's self and listen to others' problems rather than revealing their own at first, and may be unwilling to confront or contradict others' points of view. Listening rather than being very active in verbal interactions may not mean that the person is resistant to learning and sharing with the group. They may, however, need encouragement and a very nonjudgmental response in order to feel free to share what are perceived by them as stigmatizing experiences resulting from their own or a family member's chemical dependence. Their desire to problem solve present day problems will be a strength on which to draw, and a quality very compatible with self-help group goals. Additionally, their experience with being expected to help others, their cultural value of cooperation, will help to draw them into the group. The group itself, being non-bureaucratized, will also help them to feel comfortable, since natural support systems are very personalized in their approach.

Participation would most likely be enhanced by referral to single-sex groups, since there will be a reticence to confront what are seen as women's or men's issues in a mixed sex group. Both sexes may need to be helped with reconciling their own needs for recovery or assistance with the needs of others in their family, since there is such a strong family loyalty, and with traditional values, such as the expectation that one put one's own needs in second place to those of others. Women may also have a greater sense of stigma than men for their chemical dependence, while men may have a greater need to see their drinking, for example, as of not much significance. These are, in fact, issues that may need to be surfaced and addressed before a person even considers joining a self-help group.

Self-help sponsorship and referral may be enhanced if already existing natural support systems are involved. For example, professionals may be able to work along with traditional healers who are already involved in the person's treatment to help the person to become involved in a self-help group. Also, self-help groups may be able to be sponsored and housed by local agencies, clubs, or churches. Additionally, because of the strong family, efforts should be made to help the whole family, not just the identified chemically dependent person, through Spanish speaking self-help groups for family members and the provision of concrete services that professional agencies can provide, such as economic, housing, and health care assistance.

With a group that is largely economically deprived, it is doubtful that self-help alone will address all the individual or family's needs. Consequently, it is important to explore how social agencies can work more effectively with Hispanic self-help groups as a means of addressing the needs of Hispanics. The very nature of the work undertaken by self-help groups, and the context and circumstances that lead to their development, make it very difficult to develop a working relationship between an agency and a self-help group. Nevertheless, Maguire (1981) maintains that development and enhancement of self-help groups can be facilitated by agencies in a variety of ways.

Applying Maguire's concepts to Hispanic self-help groups suggests that agencies that already have a good working relationship with the Hispanic community, and that wish to help, can doing the following: (1) provide meeting space for the group (if the setting is stigmatizing, such as a drug treatment center or a mental health center, then one can help arrange space in a non-stigmatizing area, such as a church, health center, hospital, or school); (2) help locate funds to be used in carrying out group activities, purchase of food, provision of transportation, and other purchases the group may need to make; (3) act as a referral agent for the group by either referring directly or helping with publicity to obtain referrals from other settings; (4) provide education, training, or consultation for group facilitators or organizers; (5) accept referrals from the group since a formal agency service may be necessary for individuals whose needs cannot be met by the group alone; (6) provide institutional legitimacy within the Hispanic community and human service community to serve to destigmatize the presenting problem and validate the form of assistance.

SUMMARY

This chapter has explored self-help principles, the relationship of Hispanic culture to chemical dependence and help-seeking, and issues and experiences Hispanics have encountered in self-help and other groups. Further, a framework was presented to aid practitioners in the development and nurturance of self-help groups for this population. The needs of Hispanics who are chemically dependent are great, and seem to be increasing at a rapid pace. Consequently, practitioners need to consider alternative means of reaching this group, and self-help groups are an important resource. However, if self-help groups are going to be a resource, they must be made culturally relevant and accessible.

Chapter 11

FAMILY THERAPY FOR HISPANIC SUBSTANCE ABUSING YOUTH

Daniel A. Santisteban, Jose Szapocznik, and Arturo T. Rio

INTRODUCTION

There is growing concern about the increasing prevalence of alcohol and other drug (AOD) use among Hispanic adolescents (Office of Substance Abuse Prevention, 1990). This phenomenon is of particular importance from an epidemiological perspective, since Hispanic youth comprise a substantially large sector of the rapidly growing Hispanic population (U.S. Bureau of the Census, 1986, 1988). Hence, there is an urgent need to further develop effective interventions for the prevention and treatment of AOD use among Hispanic youth. This chapter presents an overview of conceptual models and practical approaches based on our own work found useful in working with Hispanic youth already identified as AOD users, as well as those considered at high risk for future AOD use.

THE BEHAVIOR PROBLEM SYNDROME

Behavior problem Hispanic youth present a formidable challenge because they generally demonstrate a constellation of coexisting and interacting behavior problems rather than a single behavior problem such as AOD use. Research has shown that for many adolescents a specific behavior problem such as AOD use is generally one symptom within a broader, more complex syndrome of acting out behaviors. Within this context, AOD use is viewed as part of a more general behavior problem syndrome.

This perspective differs from the tendency in the past to treat AOD use or other individual behavior problems in isolation, without much regard for the coexisting nature and interrelationship between these problems. The notion of the behavior problem syndrome, based on the

157

pioneer work of Jessor and Jessor (1977), and Jessor (1983), has lent support to a model in which multiple problem behaviors coexist as a syndrome. The literature on AOD use among youth serves as an example of how behavior problems in youth in general—and Hispanic in particular—tend to cluster.

The literature on youth in general has documented associations between AOD use and other problems, such as school dropout (Mensch & Kandel, 1988) and runaways (Manov & Lowther, 1983), while literature focusing specifically on Hispanics has shown similar relationships between AOD use and a number of other behavior problems such as delinquency (Inciardi, 1991) and teenage pregnancy (Moss & Hensleigh, 1988).

A research study by Inciardi with Hispanic adolescents in the Miami area helps illustrate the ramifications of the syndrome. Inciardi (1991) found that among 100 regular and heavy drug using Hispanic adolescent males (ages 14–17), 49% reported involvement in a major felony at least once per month and 87% were involved in petty property crimes at least once per week. Seventy-four percent of the total Hispanic sample had committed at least one major felony in the past 12 months. Of these, 47% had been involved in robbery, 58% had been involved in a burglary, and 52% had been involved in motor vehicle theft.

The Role of the Family in the Behavior Problem Syndrome

There has been a tendency in the past to attribute behavior problems of Hispanic and other minority group youth to social, economic, and political conditions (Canino, 1982). While these social factors can have powerful, debilitating effects, there is evidence that family functioning is an important moderating variable between stressful social conditions and behavior problems among minority youth (Kumpfer, Whiteside & Jensen, in press).

Numerous studies have focused on the important role that family functioning plays in the emergence, development, and maintenance of the behavior problem syndrome in the general adolescent population (Hendin, Pollinger, Ulman, & Carr, 1981) and among minority adolescents (Kumpfer & DeMarsh, 1985). One approach that has been fruitful considers the relationship between family functioning and the behavior problem syndrome from two perspectives (Kumpfer, in press). The first perspective is comprised of what are generally referred to as "protective" (or resiliency) factors. These are factors that promote the adjustment of children and families by moderating the damaging effects of macrosocial factors such as poverty and deprivation. The emphasis here is on adaptive family characteristics which protect children from the effects of stressors. An example of such protective factors include a close-knit, supportive family and a social/community network that helps strengthen families and insulate them from negative outside influences. Our own research and clinical experience suggests four protective family characteristics (Szapocznik & Kurtines, 1989; cf Szapocznik, Rio, Hervis, Mitrani, Kurtines & Faraci, 1991). First, parents or parent figures demonstrate good family management skills. This means that parents are able to provide effective leadership (behavior control and guidance) and are capable of supporting each other and working together vis-a-vis the child or adolescent. Second, communication between family members is characterized by directness, reciprocity and specificity. Each dyad within the family is able to communicate clearly and effectively. Third, family members demonstrate a certain level of flexibility in terms of handling intra-familial and extra-familial stressors in adaptive ways. Finally, these families allow important conflicts to surface and are able to reach some level of conflict resolution. Functional families realize that all problems cannot be resolved and so prioritize them in order to handle those problems which are most critical to adaptive family functioning.

The "high risk" perspective is a second general approach to the study of the relationship between family functioning factors and the emergence of behavior problems in children. In the past, this literature has dominated the field of study. The high risk perspective is based on studies of adolescent AOD abusers which have consistently reported high rates of family pathology, fragmentation, and conflict in their families (Austin, Macari, & Lettieri, 1978; Stanton, 1979; Green, 1979; O'Donnell, & Clayton, 1979). For example, a review of studies of antisocial and delinquent children/adolescents and their families by Kazdin (1987) revealed that parents of antisocial children demonstrated less acceptance, attachment, warmth, affection, and emotional support toward their children (Loeber & Dishion, 1984). These parents were more defensive in communication and participated less in family activities than parents of "normal" children (Alexander, 1973; Hanson et al., 1984). Parents of antisocial children tended to have poor marital relationships (Heatherington & Martin, 1979; Rutter & Guiller, 1983) and to be harsh in their attitudes and disciplinary practices with their children (Farrington, 1978). These parents have also been found to use behavior control techniques in an inappropriate and/or inconsistent fashion (Patterson, 1982). Parents of problem youth are often unable to effectively monitor and supervise the activities of their children. Our own research and clinical observations (Szapocznik & Kurtines, 1989) support the above findings and also indicate that in families of Hispanic behavior problem AOD using adolescent boys, one of the parents (typically the father) tends to be withdrawn and distanced from the entire family, whereas the other (generally the mother) tends to be overly close or enmeshed with the behavior problem youth.

THE IMPORTANCE OF CULTURAL VARIABLES IN WORKING WITH HISPANIC FAMILIES

As has been stated throughout this volume, the Hispanic population is quite heterogeneous with regard to sociodemographic variables such as geographic area of residence, number of years in the U.S., socioeconomic status, age, and education. Despite the significant variation that exists among Hispanic Americans in terms of historical, linguistic, cultural, and social variables, there are also fundamental similarities. One common thread which joins Hispanic Americans is their heritage. This serves to promote a source of identification that transcends national origins and persists even when large differences exist between individuals with regard to acculturation. The implication for mental health professionals is that those who work with Hispanic clients should have a basic understanding of the culture, history, values, and sociopolitical orientation of the Hispanic subpopulation(s) with which they work; and when working with Spanish monolingual or bilingual Hispanics, the professional should be matched linguistically with the client.

While cultural knowledge and sensitivity are necessary criteria for mental health professionals, they are not, in and of themselves, sufficient for effectively working with Hispanic families. As we have argued elsewhere (Rio, Santisteban, and Szapocznik, 1990), therapeutic interventions must be based on an integrated treatment model for which there is empirical support concerning its efficacy. Our own work, based on eighteen years of clinical research with Hispanic adolescent drug users in the Miami area, has attempted to address the many challenges that emerge in the treatment of these youth.

The first challenge encountered by our clinical program was to identify a culturally appropriate and acceptable treatment intervention. A preliminary study on cultural value orientation (Szapocznik, Scopetta, Aranalde, & Kurtines, 1978; Szapocznik, Kurtines, Santisteban, & Rio, 1990) suggested that a family oriented approach should have therapists that take an active, directive, present-oriented leadership role in order to match the cultural expectations of the population.

In addition, much of our early work focused on the effects of the process of acculturation (Szapocznik, Scopetta, Kurtines & Arnalde, 1978). Acculturation presents special problems for immigrant Hispanic families (Szapocznik, Scopetta & King, 1978). Clinical experience with adolescents and their families, as well as acculturation-related research (Szapocznik, Kurtines, & Fernandez, 1980), indicate that intergenerational conflicts between adolescents and their parents are often intermingled with culturally determined behavioral and value conflicts (Szapocznik, Santisteban, Kurtines, Rio, Perez-Vidal, Kurtines & Hervis, 1986; Szapocznik, Santisteban, Rio, Perez-Vidal, Kurtines, 1989). Youngsters acculturate more rapidly than their parents since they tend to learn English quickly and become more involved in American culture. Parents, on the other hand, continue to function within the traditional Hispanic culture. These intergenerational differences produce acculturation stress within the family. This added stress exacerbates parent-child conflicts normally associated with adolescent development, as well as other existing family problems. Thus, intergenerational differences are accentuated by acculturation differences. This exaggerated intergenerational/intercultural gap intensifies family conflict and increases the probability of acting-out behaviors on the part of the adolescent.

Acculturation related disorders in Hispanic families can be treated by focusing on their effects on family functioning and by facilitating the emergence of new and alternative forms of relating within the family (Szapocznik, Scopetta & King, 1978). Consistent with our approach to family therapy (Szapocznik & Kurtines, 1989) which is rooted in the pioneer work on Structural Family Therapy of Minuchin (1974), we focus on the way family members relate to, and interact with, each other. In families in which members are at different levels of acculturation, culturally loaded topics become the content of *what* is discussed. However, from our clinical and theoretical perspective we use culture as content, and place primary emphasis on *how* the issues are discussed (i.e., interaction patterns) (Szapocznik, Santisteban et al., 1984; Szapocznik, Santisteban, Rio, Perez-Vidal, Kurtines & Hervis, 1986; Szapocznik, Santisteban, Rio et al., 1989).

Because of our central emphasis on family interactions as the crucial aspect of family functioning that must be targeted in therapy, in the next section we present a brief overview of novel applications of structural family therapy in addressing the obstacles to engaging the adolescent AOD user and her/his family into treatment and in handling situations in which the family is not willing or able to participate. These modalities assume a knowledge of culture and a use of cultural issues as content for the family interactions that are the focus of our structural family therapy work. A full description of structural family therapy concepts is beyond the scope of this chapter. A description of Structural Family Therapy can be found in the work of Minuchin (Minuchin, 1974; Minuchin & Fishman, 1981) and its application to Hispanic AOD using adolescents and their families can be found in a recently published book by Szapocznik and Kurtines (1989).

INTERVENTION STRATEGIES

One obstacle to effective treatment is the identification of the AOD user. Identification is often a problem because adolescents tend to hide AOD use from their parents, school officials, and authorities. In addition, parents and other adults may underplay or deny the use of AOD use in youth, even when there are strong indicators of use, such as AOD using friends or physical signs of AOD use. Efforts at treatment are often hindered by the fact that youth do not generally perceive their own use as a problem. In fact, many AOD using youth perceive AOD favorably, since drug use is perceived as an effective coping strategy.

A second obstacle which emerges once drug abusing adolescents and their families are identified, is that attempts to treat these youth are often hindered by resistance to entering treatment (Davis, 1977–78; Coleman, 1976; Weidman, 1985; Wermuth and Scheidt, 1986). Despite advances in some areas of patient outreach and recruitment (e.g., Szapocznik, Lasaga, Perry & Solomon, 1979), the engagement of drug abusers into treatment remains a serious problem.

Stanton and his collaborators (Stanton, 1979; Stanton & Todd, 1981) have suggested that the problem of engaging drug abusers in treatment has been one of the most urgent obstacles to service delivery with this population. It appears that a large proportion of families who seek treatment for their AOD using youths are never engaged into treatment. Our early research (Szapocznik et al., 1983, 1986) has revealed that a substantial proportion of clients are lost prior to the first treatment session, thus confirming the difficulties inherent in engaging drug abusers and their families in treatment.

There are a number of different reasons why the challenge of actively engaging the adolescent and family for treatment is a difficult one. In our view, to be effective, handling this resistance must become an integral part of the therapist's responsibility. The next section describes a strategy which has been found effective in meeting the challenge of resistance to entering treatment.

Strategic Structural Systems Engagement

Strategic Structural Systems Engagement (SSSE) was developed as a procedure to more effectively engage adolescent AOD users and their families into treatment. SSSE (Szapocznik & Kurtines, 1989; Szapocznik, Perez-Vidal, Hervis, Brickman & Kurtines, 1988), is an extension of the Structural Family Therapy principles developed by Minuchin (Minuchin, 1974; Minuchin & Fishman, 1981) and the Brief Strategic Family Therapy approach of Szapocznik and Kurtines (1989; Szapocznik, Kurtines and Rio, 1991). One basic premise of the model is that the family is a self-regulatory system that strives to maintain its equilibrium or status quo, and thus resists attempts toward change. Thus, despite the stress of a presenting symptom such as adolescent AOD use, the family resists change by staying out of treatment. The family unit continues to behave within the established patterns of interaction which have endured over time.

The SSSE approach is a planned, purposeful way of joining, diagnosing, and restructuring a family from the initial telephone call through the first therapy session. SSSE utilizes the same structural family therapy techniques as in Brief Strategic Family Therapy (Szapocznik & Kurtines, 1989), but applies them to overcome the family's initial resistance to participating in treatment. A brief overview of the adaptations of the major components of Structural Family Therapy to Strategic Structural Systems Engagement is presented below.

Joining

Joining is a process that begins with the very first contact of a family member with the therapist. Hence, it is often necessary to "join" the family through the person who initially calls for help. The focus during this early engagement phase is on working with the initial contact person in order to bring about the changes necessary to engage the entire family into therapy. By using the contact person as a vehicle for joining with other members of the family, the therapist can eventually establish a therapeutic alliance with each member, and thereby elicit the cooperation of the entire family in the engagement effort.

Diagnosis

Diagnosis is the process through which the nature of the relationship between family patterns of interaction and undesirable symptoms is identified. In the SSSE model, the undesirable symptom is defined as the family's inability or unwillingness to come into treatment. "Diagnosis of resistance" is accomplished by first, asking questions of the contact person that allows the therapist to infer what the interactional patterns may be. Second, the therapist explores the family system for resistance to the central task of coming to therapy.

Restructuring

Restructuring is the process by which the therapist brings about changes in interactive patterns that will allow the family to come for therapy. In practice, the therapist may see only one or a few of the members of the family initially. It is through these individuals that attempts are made to promote shifts in the family's usual pattern of interactions that protect the family from treatment toward new interactions that will promote the family's coming into treatment.

Work at the Spanish Family Guidance Center has led to the identification of four basic patterns of resistance often seen in families of adolescent AOD users (Szapocznik, Perez-Vidal, Brickman, Foote, Santisteban, Hervis, & Kurtines, 1988; Szapocznik & Kurtines, 1989). These are outlined below in order of frequency of occurrence. It should be noted that *only* about one-half of our cases are intact families. However, we will present the example below for the simplest case, of the intact family, in the understanding that from a family process point of view, these interactional patterns can occur—and thus be generalized—to authority figures other than those found in intact families.

Powerful identified patient. This type of resistance is characterized by a powerful AOD using adolescent, often referred to as the Identified Patient (IP) in the family. In these families, parent(s) are hierarchically positioned at a lower level of power relative to the Identified Patient.

The Identified Patient resists therapy because: 1) it threatens his position of power by moving him/her to a "problem-person" position, and 2) it is the parent's agenda to come to therapy and thus, if followed, will enhance the parent's power at the expense of the IP's power.

The therapist must restructure or alter the existing hierarchical organization of the family in which the Identified Patient—the substance abusing adolescent—is in power. In these cases, the hierarchical organization is altered not by "demoting" the Identified Patient (that move would be totally rejected by the family system) but rather by allying the therapist to the "ruling structure." The therapist brings respect and concern for the Identified Patient, but also brings an agenda of change that will be shared by the Identified Patient. The therapist thus focuses on the adolescent's complaint(s) in order to enlist the adolescent's cooperation and make him/her feel that he has something to gain as a result of therapy. This often involves therapy benefits such as increased independence and autonomy.

In the engagement phase of treatment, it would be a tactical error to directly challenge the Identified Patient's hierarchical position. It is preferable to transfer the symptom from the Identified Patient to the family (further supporting the Identified Patient's power, to be later challenged in therapy). The therapist should initially avoid the other alternative, that of forming an alliance with the parents. When the adolescent is so powerful, initial alliances with parents are often ineffective at the early stage of the engagement process because they tend to further alienate the resistant and powerful adolescent.

Contact person protecting structure. The second most common type of resistance to entering treatment is characterized by a parent who protects the existing family structure. The caller gives a double-message to the therapist. The caller typically expresses a desire for the therapist's help while at the same time "protecting" the system by agreeing that the "excuses" for non-involvement in change are valid.

In order to bring these families into treatment, the therapist must first form an alliance with the caller by acknowledging the caller's frustration in not getting any cooperation from the "unwilling" family member(s). Through this alliance, the therapist then requests and obtains permission to contact other family members, in an effort to access other family members, and by accessing other family members directly, circumvent the ambivalent behavior of the caller. For example, in a case seen at the Center, the initial resistance was found in the caller's (mother) ambivalent behavior. The mother wanted help in dealing with her son's drug abuse but sought to maintain the current family structure (mother-son alliance, father peripheral) by attempting to exclude the father from therapy.

The first step in working with this type of family is to move beyond the ambivalent mother and reach out directly (with mother's permission) to the father. Father is usually frustrated by the strong alliance between mother and identified patient. Therapist might ally with father around his frustration. During engagement, the therapist joins the father individually by acknowledging his concerns and providing understanding of the situation. With the father, the therapist may emphasize the need for his leadership in order to mobilize the family to come to therapy. The therapist achieves this by emphasizing the important and necessary role the father must play in order to mobilize the family. The goal is to place the father in a more central role in the family system and thus overcome the caller's ambivalent resistance.

Disengaged parent. In this pattern of resistance, one parent plays a peripheral role in the family in the sense that there is little meaningful involvement between the disengaged parent and the rest of the family. These family structures are characterized by little or no cohesiveness or alliance between the parents as a subsystem. As a result, one of the parents (usually the father) refuses to go to therapy. This is typically the parent who has remained disengaged from the problematic behavior. This interactional pattern often serves to further disengage the parent from another problematic relationship: the spouse.

The therapist must form a strong alliance with the caller in order to engage these families into treatment. The therapist begins by focusing on changing the caller's interactions with the disengaged spouse. The therapist gives the caller tasks to do together with his/her spouse pertaining *only* to the issue of taking care of their adolescent's problems. This is done because it must be assumed that if the father and mother have become distanced there must be a conflict of some intensity between them. For this reason, the therapist attempts to ensure the insulation of the broader conflict until the marital couple is ready to confront it.

The case of the disengaged father is substantially different from the case of the ambivalent mother, although in the face of it they must both look similar. The disengaged father is a father who does not want to be involved, while mother wants him involved. The ambivalent mother does not want to have her husband involved in therapy.

Therapy as an exposé. Family members may refuse to seek treatment because of a fear that family secrets will be revealed. While these concerns sometimes seem unfounded, they represent real fears or potential danger to certain family members. In order to avoid arousing fear of revelation of family secrets, the therapist generally remains focused on the presenting complaint until the family is ready to deal with the emergence of issues relating to family secrets. Secrets typically involve problems such as infidelity/physical abuse/alcoholism in a parent as well as adolescent-related taboo topics such as homosexuality. With drug using adolescents it is recommended that the therapist focus initially on general parent-adolescent issues and adolescent-related complaints, letting the person with the secret know that the therapist will not reveal the secret. Typically, however, once the family feels that the therapist can be trusted, there is often an increased acceptance of the emergence of secrets or problems other than the presenting complaints. The therapist who approaches the "secret" without flexibility will arouse resistance.

In order to engage families which may hold secrets as a component of resistance, the therapist begins by informing the adolescent and family of the confidential nature of the relationship between client(s) and therapist. It should be made clear that no family member will be forced to discuss issues they are not willing or ready to confront. In summary, to achieve success in reducing the risk of exposure of secrets in therapy as a resistance, the therapist focuses on the development of trust, provides confidentiality assurances, and respects the wishes of individual family members pertaining to the sensitivity of issues to be discussed.

One Person Family Therapy

Although SSSE has been shown powerfully effective in bringing into treatment resistant family members, it is sometimes virtually impossible for either the drug abusing adolescent or other significant family members to be involved in treatment. Engagement efforts may simply fail to enlist the cooperation of a family member or a family member may be physically unavailable to attend treatment sessions. This section addresses the issue of how to handle situations in which family therapy is the treatment of choice but circumstances make seeing the whole family impractical or impossible. This approach uses the techniques of One Person Family Therapy, designed to accomplish the goals of family therapy while working primarily with one family member (Szapocznik,

Foote, Perez-Vidal, Hervis & Kurtines, 1985; Szapocznik, Kurtines, Hervis & Spencer, 1984; Szapocznik et al., 1990).

In One Person Family Therapy, the therapist aims at achieving two central goals of conjoint family therapy (therapy with the entire family present). First, the therapist works to change the way family members act toward each other so that they will not do or say things that might contribute to maintaining or promoting the adolescent's symptoms. Second, the therapist works to actually reduce the symptoms exhibited by the identified patient. To make the changes necessary to achieve these goals the therapist uses adaptations of the usual structural family therapy joining, diagnosing and restructuring techniques. These techniques are modified for carrying out family therapy through the one person, who is called the "OP."

The therapist works through the OP to change the family's maladaptive patterns of interaction. The therapist must first determine who will be involved in treatment as the OP. Sometimes there is no real choice since there is only one family member able to participate in therapy. However, more often than not there is a choice among family members in terms of choosing the OP. Our experience has been that generally the best OP is the adolescent drug user. This choice is made not because this person is the symptom carrier, but rather because in our population the adolescent AOD user usually occupies a central position in the problematic nature of interactions. We have found that we can access many of the interactional patterns affecting the symptom through the adolescent. Modification of the basic structural family therapy techniques (joining, diagnosing and restructuring) for use in One Person Family Therapy, are outlined below.

Joining

Since the entire family is not available for most or all treatment sessions, the therapist must enter the family, as well as direct change, through the OP. The first step in accomplishing this is to establish a therapeutic alliance with the OP.

Diagnosis

In conjoint family therapy it is possible to diagnose by observing the family patterns of interactions in vivo. When working only through the OP, however, there is only limited information available which can be used to diagnose those family patterns of interactions that are supporting the symptoms. In One Person Family Therapy, since just one person is present, an "enactment analogue" is often used as a diagnostic tool. The enactment analogue is a way of depicting the family's characteristic interactional patterns. When asked to represent the family, the OP will usually offer a perception of the behavior of others rather than her/his own behaviors. The therapist assumes from the systems concept of complementarity (Minuchin & Fishman, 1981) that for the system to maintain itself, the OP must behave in a fashion that complements the reported behavior of others. Complementarity refers to the principle that the behavior of each family member must coordinate with, be maintained by, and be contingent upon the behavior of other family members. In simpler terms, the principle of complementarity helps explain how the behaviors of each member fit together. The enactment analogue utilizes the concept of complementarity to infer the kinds of interactions that may characterize the family and which maintain the symptoms.

To conduct an enactment analogue, the therapist begins by asking the OP to describe or act out interactions which have taken place between family members. The therapist focuses on exploration of interactional patterns to obtain an understanding of the complementarity between the reported behaviors of the OP and those of the other family members. The therapist's goal is to get as complete a picture as possible and then fill in the missing information using her/his understanding of complementarity. An AOD abusing adolescent may, for example, complain that his parents are constantly "on his case" and that he is treated like a child. The therapist uses the concept of complementarity to explore the ways in which the OP's behavior elicits this "nagging" behavior by the parents. The OP is helped to see that within the family he acts like a child by not completing important tasks responsibly. Rather than taking the initiative he waits until his parents are annoyed and begin to nag before starting or completing a task. Complementarity also helps explain how, on the one hand, one set of parents' overinvolvement keeps an adolescent from becoming responsible and achieving the "adult" status (s)he enjoys; or in the case of another family, how the parents' abdication of leadership and behavior control in the family creates a leadership vacuum that gives an adolescent considerable power.

Another useful technique during the process of diagnosing is role playing. The therapist directs the OP to role play some of the typical interactions and situations that occur within the family. During role playing, the therapist often helps the OP recall incidents and relive them with almost the same emotional intensity as when they originally occurred. At other times the therapist may present hypothetical situations as a way of exploring how members of the family, including the OP, would handle a situation. In the example cited above the OP's child-like irresponsibility elicits and sets the stage for the parental overinvolvement and nagging which annoy the OP.

Restructuring

Although the OPFT therapist sees only one person in most therapy sessions the aim is to make significant and lasting changes in the entire family's structure. The therapist begins by helping the OP understand her/his role within the family system and second, by using the OP as an ally to make interpersonal/interactional changes in the family.

The therapist begins by facilitating changes in the OP that are likely to promote changes in family structure. The therapist engages the OP by clarifying the OP's own personal goals and how certain family interactions may be interfering with the OP's achieving what (s)he wants. Once these undesirable/maladaptive interactions are identified, the therapist points out how the OP may be contributing to maintaining these interactions. Once the OP realizes that (s)he would like to be treated as an adult at home (possibly as (s)he is in her/his gang) and realizes that her/his own child-like behaviors at home keep her/him from being treated as an adult, the necessary changes become more readily obvious. The therapist helps to expand the OP's view of the family and her/his own role within it.

Each family member tends to have somewhat distorted and rigid impressions of other family members. For example, in problem families individual members tend to be polarized so that the negative aspect of some individual is exaggerated while the positive qualities of others are also exaggerated. In these cases it is always necessary early in therapy to reframe these rigidly held perceptions. In reframing, the therapist seeks to help the OP or other family members to see each other and their situation in a new light. In promoting a different way of viewing the underlying meaning of behavior and communication, change is made possible. For example, an overinvolved/overprotective parent can be described as *overly caring* and wanting to be a *perfect* parent, a frame which sheds a more positive light on the relationship while maintaining that it may be restrictive and unnecessary.

The therapist helps the OP learn how (s)he has participated in creating the role (s)he is in. In that way, the OP takes responsibility for problem behavior that is both a reaction to, and elicits, the behavior of other family members. The OP learns to change or "reframe" her/his self-perception from "I am a problem person," to "I have taken on a role within the family which creates problems for me." In the example cited above the OP realizes that child-like behavior elicits overinvolvement from parents and that the overinvolvement of parents keeps the OP in the "bad child" role.

Once the OP sees the family and her/his role within the family in a new light, interventions can begin to modify the family interaction patterns. In One Person Family Therapy, the therapist creates changes in family interactions by changing those OP behaviors that help to maintain the problematic interactions. The OP is thus used as the vehicle for change. If the OP changes her/his behavior in interactions in which (s)he plays an important role, the concept of complementarity predicts that the others involved in the interaction must also change in order to accommodate the new behavior. The OP, as an agent of the therapist, brings about changes in the family. The therapist plans her/his strategy carefully to make the most effective use of the family members' complementary role relationships with the OP.

A typical case seen by our staff is characterized by an AOD abusing adolescent who is in conflict with parents around the issues of the adolescent's bad friends and his coming home late. In these cases the conflict is such that the adolescent begins to reject parental authority and overidentifies with his peer group. The OP (adolescent) complains of overinvolved and controlling parents particularly as concerns the OP's friends and life-style. The therapist works with the OP to help him see how irresponsible behavior with peers (loitering, trouble with police, etc.) and total rejection of parental rules, serves only to frustrate his parents even further and triggers an increase in their controlling behavior. The therapist points out the complementarity between the OP's "perceived out of control" behavior and the parental attempts at overcontrol.

The therapist directs the adolescent to initiate interactions with his parents aimed at changing this pattern of conflict and facilitating negotiation. Because of the difficulty of this task, the task must be carefully selected to increase the probability that negotiation occurs successfully. Rather than immediately attempting to handle issues as

complex as the OP's involvement with drug abusing friends, the therapist selects a less emotionally charged issue such as curfew.

Typically, families will not make significant changes without putting
up a fight. Often the response to the OP's changed behavior is family
pressure to return to its previous patterns of interactions. The confrontation between the OP trying to create change, and the family's non-
involvement in this process, will tend to produce a family crisis. At this
point, families are often accessible to the therapist and the therapist must
seize the moment. At this stage the therapist should request, and typically obtains, a family therapy session.

A family session or two provides an opportunity—albeit a limited
one—for the therapist to intervene directly in family interactional patterns.
Obviously, in one or two family sessions, it may not be possible to bring
about major structural changes. The therapist must be strategic in modifying those problematic interactions that affect the OP. This means that
in treatment, the therapist might, for example, work with the O.P.'s
mother to encourage her to set limits on the father's overly punitive
behavior towards the O.P. The therapist, however, might not address the
larger difficulty of a mother that has difficulty in being assertive with
the father. Instead, the therapist may promote, in the mother, assertiveness
in the circumscribed area of setting effective linkages between behaviors
and consequences toward the O.P.

CONCLUSION

Clinical experience and research findings have been presented that
suggest that adolescent behavior problems, including alcohol and other
drug use, tend to co-exist rather than emerge in isolation. Furthermore,
the critical role that the family can play in the emergence and treatment
of the behavior problem syndrome has been underscored. It has been
argued that the family's role has been particularly central among many
Hispanics because of the added stressors resulting from the acculturation process.

Structural family therapy has been found to be an approach well-
suited to address the treatment needs of the Hispanic families and
compatible with their values orientation. Finally, innovative approaches,
based on structural family therapy and theory concepts, were presented
for engaging and treating families that are not easily mobilized to come
to treatment. The clinical research reported here represents work with

many hundreds of troubled Hispanic families. Using a well-conceptualized theoretical framework, we have been able to stretch and modify theoretical notions to permit us to meet grave clinical needs. We present our work as an example of how the interplay between theory, practice and research has helped to find solutions for working with Hispanic AOD adolescents and their families, solutions that may also have implications for work with other populations.

Chapter 12

PREVENTION AND TREATMENT OF HISPANIC SUBSTANCE ABUSE: A WORKPLACE PERSPECTIVE

RAYMOND SANCHEZ MAYERS, FEDERICO SOUFLEE, JR.,
AND CARANN SIMPSON FEAZELL

INTRODUCTION

Substance abuse is not confined to the streets. It has invaded the workplace. Alcohol and drug abuse on the job costs employers and consumers millions of dollars a year. There are several indicators of just how pervasive substance abuse has become in the workplace. One indicator of the problem is the incidence of occupational injury and illness reported by industry, which is often related to substance abuse. The total incidence of injury and illness in 1987 was 8.3 cases per 100 full-time workers (Occupational . . . , 1988). This varied by industry, with a high of 18.9 cases per 100 for those working in the lumber and wood products trade, to a low of 2 per 100 for those working in finance, insurance, and real estate. All cases resulted in average lost workdays of 69.9 per 100 workers. Again, there are variations by industry, with a high of 176.5 lost workdays for lumber workers and a low of 14.3 lost workdays for finance employees.

Lost workdays due to occupational illness and injury, a second indicator of the cost of substance abuse, translate into millions of dollars lost by American industry. Additionally, millions are lost in days of work missed due to health problems related to substance abuse. Neither of these figures reflects the hidden cost of lowered productivity due to impaired work performance resulting from employee abuse of drugs and alcohol. Less hidden costs of substance abuse in the workplace are the escalating costs of health care coverage and federal/state regulations. The national debate on health care currently taking place in the United States is fueled by the increasing influx of substance abuse on the job. Federal regulations, such as the Drug-Free Workplace Act of 1988, require busi-

175

ness to take several measures, including prevention and rehabilitation, in order to comply. Penalties for non-compliance are severe.

Both government and business have attempted to address the problem of employee substance abuse. By the end of 1985, thirty-five states had mandated that alcohol treatment be covered or offered in insurance plans and 18 states had mandated the same for drug abuse (Morrisey & Jensen, 1988). Health insurance coverage for substance abuse problems is often covered by many employer-sponsored health insurance plans. Moreover, this coverage is now being enjoyed by the growing number of Hispanics moving from low-wage or seasonal occupations into mainstream positions which offer better benefits.

Most major corporations in the United States have also reacted to the problems engendered by substance abuse in the workplace by offering some type of Employee Assistance Program (EAP) to employees and their families. Employee Assistance Programs typically offer crisis counseling, assessment, and referral to outside providers to help employees deal with a myriad of problems, including substance abuse, family and marital problems, legal, and even educational, matters. EAP's may be internal—that is, staffed by employees of the corporation professionally trained in counseling—or external. External EAP's are independent, non-profit or for-profit entities staffed by professionals. These external EAP's establish contracts with one or several employers to provide counseling and other services to their employees, services that are paid for in-part or in-full by the employer's insurance carriers. A major goal of both types of EAP's is to provide services to employees for the purpose of helping them maintain their jobs and enhance their job performance.

Whether the EAP is internal or external, it must be able to effectively provide services to employees who come from a multitude of cultural backgrounds. However, most EAP's are not prepared, nor their personnel trained, to assist the increasing numbers of Hispanics moving into the labor force who are covered by the benefits that major companies provide. An informal survey by the authors of internal and external EAP's in a Southwestern state with a combined employee population of more than 100,000 found that not one of them had any special services for Hispanics. Yet, this state has the second largest Hispanic population in the United States. Part of the reason for this neglect is that, until recently, Hispanics did not work in the kind of industries that provided high quality benefits or even suitable working conditions. They were mostly relegated to the secondary labor market, with low wages and tenuous job security. As younger Hispanics receive more education and training, and as Hispanics increase their numbers in the working population, the special cultural needs of Hispanics are becoming increasingly important to employers who want to retain good workers.

This chapter attempts to redress the lack of EAP programming for Hispanics by introducing culturally sensitive approaches to prevention and treatment of substance abuse problems in the workplace. These approaches apply to those employers who seek to help and retain good workers by offering Employee Assistance Programs as well as those who offer adequate insurance coverage for these problems. This topic is particularly germane, as Hispanics are increasingly represented in the general population and in the workforce, as illustrated by the following overview of Hispanic participation in the labor force and projections for its increase in the future.

Overview of Hispanic Participation in the Labor Force

Hispanics are clustered in certain broad occupational categories, although there are differences by subgroups within those categories. For example, 16% of Hispanics are in service industries (excluding private households, where the number is unknown) compared with 12.1% of non-Hispanics (U.S. Bureau of the Census, 1989) (see Table 12-1). Twice as many (13.1%) are machine operators, assemblers, and inspectors, as compared with non-Hispanics (6.7%). On the other hand, non-Hispanics are more likely to be found in higher-level, better paying jobs such as executive, administrative, and managerial positions (12.8%) than are Hispanics (7.1 percent). The types of jobs that Hispanics are likely to be found in should be an important factor for EAP professionals to consider in designing prevention programs in the workplace.

While the labor force as a whole is expected to grow 1.2% between 1988 and the year 2000, Hispanics are projected to increase their participation in the labor force by 3%, from 7% in 1988 to 10% in 2000 (see Table 12-2). In 1988, there were 5.3 million Hispanics in the labor force; by the year 2000 it is anticipated their number will grow to 14.3 million (Fullerton, 1989). Not only will Hispanics increase their presence in the work force dramatically, they are projected to remain the youngest group in the labor force. For example, in 1988 the median age of white workers was 37.8; in 2000 it is projected to be 39.6 years. By contrast, Hispanic

**Table 12-1 Selected Occupational Categories of Hispanics
and Non-Hispanics, March 1988* (in percentages)**

Occupation	Spanish Origin	Non-Spanish Origin
Executive[1]	7.1	12.8
Professional	7.0	13.9
Administrative[2]	14.7	16.3
Service[3]	16.0	12.1
Precision, Craft, Repair	13.6	11.6
Machine Operators[4]	13.1	6.7

[1]includes administrative and managerial
[2]includes clerical
[3]except private household
[4]includes assemblers and inspectors

*Taken from Table 14, *Current Population Reports*, U.S. Bureau of the Census, Series P-20, No. 438.

workers in 1988 had a median age of 32.9 and are expected to have a median age of 35.2 years in 2000 (Fullerton, 1989).

**Table 12-2 Civilian Labor Force by Race and Hispanic Origin, 1976, 1988,
and Moderate Growth Projection to the Year 2000.***

Group	Percent Distribution			Growth Rate	
	1976	1988	2000	1976–88	1988–2000
White	88.2	86.1	84.3	1.8	1.1
Black	9.9	10.9	11.7	2.7	1.9
Hispanic	4.4	7.4	10.1	6.4	4.0

*Adapted from: Fullerton, H.N., Jr.: New labor force projections, spanning 1988 to 2000. *Monthly Labor Review, 112* (11):1989, Table 1, p. 4.

These two facts—that Hispanics will increase in the labor force and will continue to be the youngest group in the labor force—have implications for employers who are concerned about a drug-free workplace. One such implication is obvious: the greater the number of Hispanics in the work force, the greater the need for employers to understand and address their culture. A second implication is more conjectural: since substance abuse tends to start at a young age, irrespective of ethnic or cultural factors, employers must be prepared to implement preventive and ameliorative measures for their younger work force, Hispanic or otherwise.

PREVENTION IN THE WORKPLACE

It is difficult to generalize about all Hispanics due to the heterogeneity of the population; thus, any program that purports to offer culturally relevant substance abuse prevention and counseling programs must consider those factors that do make a difference both between and among the various Hispanic groups. Some of the differentiating factors, as discussed elsewhere in this book, include origin (e.g., foreign born vs. U.S. born), age, gender, region (Southwest vs. Northeast), level of acculturation, generation (e.g., first generation American vs. third), religion, and socioeconomic level. In addition, there are no definitive studies that we can point to and conclusively say *this* is one way to treat Hispanic substance abusers, or *this* is the way to develop programs to prevent substance abuse among Hispanics. Therefore, we can only point to significant patterns in the research literature and frame our comments within an Employee Assistance perspective.

Substance abuse prevention in the workplace is usually initiated by the company's Employee Assistance Program and becomes an ongoing part of its services. The prevention activities most often involve different types of outreach such as posters, brochures included in paycheck envelopes, and "brown-bag" seminars offered at lunchtime. At the "brown-bags" a movie may be shown, or a speaker will discuss work-related issues (for example, stress on the job). All these approaches, of course, have to be tailored to the specific employee population in a given work environment. And often, the EAP professional must go to a work site in the field or in the shop at a time convenient for the majority of workers.

Well-known marketing methods can be employed in prevention efforts to reach Hispanic workers. A common marketing technique is called "market segmentation" (Kotler & Andreasen, 1987). In market segmentation, a subpopulation with specific, identifiable traits is targeted, a profile of the group is developed, and a plan is devised for this specific "market." This is what must be done for Latino employees. "Experience with public health issues . . . has shown that, in order to be successful, prevention strategies must address a group's needs as well as reflect its culture-specific values, beliefs, norms, and attitudes" (Marin, 1989, p. 412). Johnson and Delgado (1989), and Marin (1989), have pointed to some approaches that need to be considered in developing a prevention strategy in the workplace that may be effective with a Hispanic population. These include: the importance of recognizing diversity, presenting culturally appropriate information, using the belief in the centrality of the family, addressing intrafamilial communications barriers, reinforcing norms that counter substance abuse, and using credible channels of information.

Recognizing Diversity

Hispanics are a heterogeneous group; thus such factors as national origin, level of education, gender, and socioeconomic status have to be considered in designing messages to reach a particular work force. For example, a company in the Southwest would most likely have a predominantly Mexican American workforce while a company in New York City would have a mostly Puerto Rican (and increasingly Central and South American) workforce. As has been addressed elsewhere in this book, frequency and use of various substances varies among these groups; therefore, educational materials and prevention approaches should be directed specifically to the substances most commonly abused in each population.

Presenting Culturally Appropriate Information

Messages aimed at Hispanics should be more than mere Spanish translations of information. Literature designed for Latinos has to fit the population; it should be bilingual and incorporate the dialect of the region. The literature should also be at a reading level appropriate to the employee population. Video tapes developed for Hispanic audiences would probably do well at "brown-bags," especially if they emulated the styles of the popular "telenovelas" (i.e., Spanish-language soap operas), although this has not been tested to our knowledge. Most importantly, due to the differences in cultural nuances and norms within the Latino population, the approach chosen will only be effective if it is pretested with the target population.

Using the Persistent Belief in the
Centrality and Importance of the Family

Many studies have shown that, more than anything else, strong family norms persist among Latinos (Keefe & Padilla, 1989; Sabogal et al., 1987). Johnson and Delgado say that few communication programs aimed at prevention have utilized this knowledge to target three groups: children and parents, women of childbearing age, and heavy-drinking men. For each of these groups, the message would be the disruptive and dysfunctional consequences of substance abuse to the family.

Addressing Intrafamilial Communications Barriers

Johnson and Delgado have cited studies that show limited frank discussion between parents, and parents and children, in blue-collar Mexican American families. This seemed to hold true in other Hispanic subgroups as well. While it may not be possible to change these communication patterns, encouraging more family communication may help Hispanics become more knowledgeable about substance abuse as well as problems often associated with it, such as AIDS.

Reinforcing Attitudes, Norms, and Behaviors that Counter Substance Abuse

While the data cited in this book point to heavy alcohol use by Hispanics, the data also show that large portions of the Hispanic population, including women and older males, are abstainers or light users of alcohol. There is some conjecture that light use is probably related to religious and family values, but more study needs to be done in this area.

While there may be cultural values that reinforce non-abuse, there are also organizational cultural values that must be examined by the EAP professional in consultation with management. In many organizations there is a "culture of drinking" that reinforces substance abuse (especially alcohol use) after work and during lunch hours. If an organization has tolerated such behavior in the past, new activities need to be initiated to replace them. For example, sports teams or exercise programs sponsored by the EAP or Wellness Coordinator may be effective in changing some behaviors. Noon-time programs of interest, such as issues related to parenting, stress management, or other self-help type seminars, may be helpful.

Using Credible Channels of Information

Marin (1989) has pointed to media usage surveys that show the importance of radio as a marketing medium for Hispanics. EAP professionals can work through their professional organizations to help develop and market public-service announcements regarding drug and alcohol abuse on Hispanic television and radio as well as print media. These professionally developed Spanish-language videotapes could also be shown to employees at noon-time meetings, as previously mentioned.

TREATMENT APPROACHES

One measure of an EAP's effectiveness is its ability to demonstrate utilization by all levels and types of employees. For large numbers of Hispanic employees to use an Employee Assistance Program's services, the EAP must be sensitive to their needs, culturally relevant, and an advocate when necessary. The three main stages in the EAP process— assessment, referral, after-care—will be viewed in terms of their cultural relevance for Hispanic employees.

Assessment

Many EAP's have turned to a short-term counseling model to help employees with problems. This means that usually three to eight counseling sessions are provided by the EAP provider. If the problem is assessed to be unresolvable within this time frame, the client is referred elsewhere. Of course, alcohol and drug problems on the job are usually chronic ones that have been known to co-workers and supervisors for quite a while. It is only when the substance abuse problem affects job performance markedly that a supervisor is likely to act and refer to the company's EAP. At this point, the EAP counselor must be sufficiently culturally aware to make an assessment that will produce the most favorable outcome for the client.

Obviously, the EAP counselor must ask questions of the worker to ascertain a number of things: extent of abuse, insurance available, familial and other social supports available, and acculturation level.

Extent of abuse by the worker: While Hispanic and Anglo perceptions of what constitutes abuse may differ, as may consumption patterns, there are two key concerns of the EAP professional. The first is that abuse is occurring. This is known because the worker has self-referred or been referred by a supervisor. The second concern is that the abuse is affecting job performance in a detrimental way for the employee. It is detrimental in that it may result in losing a job, with deleterious consequences for the worker and the worker's family.

Insurance available to the worker: Every company may have a different configuration of benefits for employees. These benefits are difficult for most employees to decipher. The role of the EAP counselor is to evaluate the level of benefits available to the employee and help make a match between what the employee needs and what is affordable. Another role of the EAP professional is to advocate for an equitable range of services for all employees. While this is required by law, employees often do not understand the consequences of choosing one health care plan over another. Additionally, denial is high among substance abusers; therefore, even if the worker understood differences in coverage, few (if any) workers would choose a benefit plan based on the level of substance abuse coverage provided.

Familial and other social supports available to the worker: As has been shown above, family is extremely important to Hispanics. This is one of the reasons, we believe, that they more often choose outpatient treatment over inpatient care. For example, there is much documentation that attests to Hispanics' underutilization of mental health services, but this does not seem to be true for alcohol treatment services. In this case Mexican Americans seem to be overrepresented as alcohol treatment clients, especially in outpatient programs in Texas and Colorado [data for other Hispanic groups is unavailable] (Gilbert & Cervantes, 1986).

Being away from the family is disruptive to family life, and for most women an impossible choice. But having family support and close friends (e.g., "compadres") who will encourage and assist the worker through a difficult time can be a factor in successful treatment.

Level of acculturation of the worker: Acculturation of the Hispanic client is a multi-faceted phenomenon in which culture change and ethnic persistence occur simultaneously (Keefe & Padilla, 1987). To make the referral decision, the counselor needs to assess the level of acculturation of the Hispanic client. This involves examining several factors including age, generation, educational level, preferred language, marital status, ethnic identification, as we have mentioned. Why is understanding of level of acculturation important? Because making the wrong client-counselor match may spell failure in efforts to treat the substance abuse problem. As Malgady et al. (1990, p. 711) have said:

> In the case of a Hispanic client, cultural distance intrudes on the relationship with a non-Hispanic therapist, not only because of differences in ethnicity and language usage, but also as a function of their less ostensible differences in values structure and culturally patterned orientations toward therapy.

While it is not expected that every Hispanic client be administered an acculturation questionnaire, some key questions may help the counselor ascertain appropriate referral, treatment, and aftercare services for the client. For the EAP with a large number of Hispanics, there are a number of acculturation scales available that could be useful, some especially developed for clinical populations (see Table 12-3 for a short list).

Table 12-3 Acculturation Instruments

The Acculturation Rating Scale for Mexican American Normal and Clinical Populations (ARSMA). Cuellar, Harris, & Jasso, 1980.

The Bicultural Inventory (BI). Ramirez, Cox, & Castenada, 1977.

The Behavioral Acculturation Scale (BAS). Szapocznik, Scoptta, Kurtines, & Arnalde, 1978.

Cultural Awareness and Ethnic Loyalty. Keefe & Padilla, 1987.

It is not just enough to be able to diagnose the substance abuse problems of the Hispanic client; the crucial decision is the proper referral for the client. "Consideration of a client's culture in treatment planning may not necessarily have a direct link to outcome but may enhance the process of therapy, which in turn is more proximately linked to outcome" (Malgady, Rogler, & Costantino, 1990, p. 711).

Referral

A study by Ponce and Atkinson (1989) found that Mexican American college students preferred seeing an ethnically similar counselor for personal, social, as well as academic and career problems. These respondents perceived the Mexican American counselors to be a more credible source of help. This was true no matter what the level of acculturation of the subject. These Mexican American students also preferred a directive as opposed to a non-directive or passive style of counseling. But the authors caution that there are other factors to be taken into account, such as regional and language differences.

In another study of more than 1,000 White, Black, and Hispanic clients it was found that ethnicity of counselor and client were not important for White and Black clients, but significantly important for Hispanic clients (Beck, 1988). This was true even when socioeconomic status was taken into account. Same ethnicity was found to be most helpful when the client problem was family relationships rather than some other type of problem.

Atkinson, Poston, Furlong, and Mercado, (1989) found that among Mexican American college students, same ethnicity ranked sixth as a preferred counselor characteristic after such features as more education, similar attitudes, being older, and having a similar personality. However, one could argue that some of these traits, such as having a similar attitude, could be assumed by a client to be related to same ethnicity. In this study, Mexican Americans and Whites ranked same-sex as fifth in preferred characteristics, much higher than Blacks.

Pomales and Williams (1989) found there were two important factors in Hispanic (mainly Puerto Rican) subjects' perception of counselors: acculturation and counseling style. Anglo-acculturated Hispanics in this study perceived a white female counselor to be more trustworthy than did bicultural and Hispanic-acculturated students. In this study, Hispanic subjects preferred the directive counseling style.

In order to make an appropriate referral, an EAP professional must have surveyed and evaluated community resources that are available to help the Hispanic client in a culturally sensitive manner. The development of an evaluation checklist (see Table 12-4) is helpful. At a minimum, the EAP counselor should be aware of, and be able to refer to, bilingual counselors and/or bilingual support groups in the client's community, if the client so desires. However, socioeconomic status may be a factor here. In some parts of the country, there are no identifiable Hispanic enclaves. Hispanics may be dispersed throughout an area. In other regions, clustering in barrios is a lower- and working-class phenomenon, while middle-class Hispanics may live in predominantly middle-class Anglo neighborhoods. Furthermore, Hispanic managers may be just as reluctant as blue-collar Hispanic workers to go to the company's EAP for an alcohol or substance abuse problem unless a concerted effort has been made to make them feel welcome by having bilingual materials and culturally relevant activities available to them.

Aftercare

Aftercare is that stage in the treatment process in which the client is seen far enough along in recovery to need only periodic meetings, either individual, or group, or both. These aftercare meetings, especially if they involve AA, tend to be highly structured. There is ample literature

Table 12-4 Community Resource Evaluation Checklist

Yes	No	
_____	_____	Accepts third-party insurance
_____	_____	Sliding-scale fee
_____	_____	CAC or MSW's with expertise in sub. abuse
_____	_____	Bilingual counselor(s)
_____	_____	Bilingual support groups
_____	_____	Bilingual AA groups
_____	_____	Bilingual religious leader available

that shows the importance of follow-up with aftercare. In fact, aftercare is often the most important factor in determining the success of treatment for the Hispanic substance abusing worker (Costello, 1987). The EAP professional is vital in providing a "link-up" for the recovering worker to a support system in aftercare. Thus, the EAP professional should be able to identify AA and other recovery groups that have sizeable Hispanic members. This culturally sensitive connection can be further extended to include a one-to-one pairing of long-term recovering Hispanics with newer recovering Hispanics as the EAP becomes successful in building a core base of long-term recovering workers.

CONCLUSION

As Hispanic workers move into better jobs in the primary labor market they will begin to be covered by the same types of employee benefits that others now enjoy. They will also have access to the services of employer-sponsored Employee Assistance Programs. EAP's will not be prepared to provide the most effective services to Hispanic clients unless they are aware of crucial cultural factors at the important stages of assessment, referral, and aftercare in the EAP process.

While there are wide variations between and among the Hispanic subgroups, they also share a common Hispanic language and heritage. It is for this reason that we have generalized about some of the most important characteristics for EAP providers to consider in designing culturally appropriate services for Hispanic employees.

PART V
APPENDICES

Appendix A-1

RESOURCES ON HISPANIC
SUBSTANCE ABUSE FOR PROFESSIONALS

GERTRUIDA C. DE GOEDE AND THOMAS D. WATTS

The substance abuse (S.A.) professional conducting research on this subject should remember two of its characteristics: it is multi-disciplinary, and much of the most relevant work is recent. Many older citations are general or analogous in nature and are useful chiefly for background information. This section offers some sources for consideration of what is rapidly becoming a large body of specialized literature.

INDEXES AND ABSTRACTS

If the researcher lacks personal contacts or is far away from major research institutions, the secondary indexes are a good starting point. The list below includes those available in paper; most of them are also available electronically, either online or on compact disc. S.A. professionals with access to electronic versions of the information will typically obtain it through the mediation of librarians who are conversant with online searching of the databases on such systems as BRS and Dialog. If the S.A. professional has access to the information on compact disc, he or she will usually conduct the search in person and be more likely to get the information free of charge.

AMERICAN STATISTICS INDEX (ASI). Washington, D.C.: Congressional Information Service, 1973—.

A compilation of statistics compiled by the U.S. federal government, this is an annual service with monthly supplements. Three cumulative indexes simplify research of the earlier years.

THE CHICANO INDEX. Berkeley, California: The Regents of the University of California, 1989—.

Superceding the CHICANO PERIODICAL INDEX, this index includes monographs, essays, and reports, as well as articles. It is issued quarterly with annual cumulations.

CIS ANNUAL. Washington, D.C., Congressional Information Service, 1970—.

This compilation gives access to everything issued by Congress except the Congressional Record. It is a monthly with annual and multiple year cumulations.

CURRENT INDEX TO JOURNALS IN EDUCATION (CIJE). Phoenix, Arizona: Oryx Press, 1969—.

This portion of the ERIC database, a highly interdisciplinary index to education, covers the journal literature. It provides abstracts. In paper it is issued annually with semiannual cumulations. CIJE is complemented by the Eric Documents, a body of material indexed in Resources in Education. Online ERIC is one of the least expensive databases.

DISSERTATION ABSTRACTS. Ann Arbor, Michigan: University Microfilms, 1952—.

Dissertations are an indicator of the latest trends in research. This highly interdisciplinary index is issued monthly with annual indexes and comprehensive, retrospective indexes.

EDUCATION INDEX. New York: H.W. Wilson Co., 1929—.

More closely tied to the education literature, per se, than ERIC is, this index will look familiar to anyone acquainted with the indexes published by the H. W. Wilson company. It is issued monthly, except for July and August. It cumulates annually.

EXCERPTA MEDICA: DRUG DEPENDENCE, SECTION 40. Amsterdam: The Netherlands, 1972—.

This is a major index to the literature on drugs and drug abuse. It is issued monthly.

GOVERNMENT REPORTS ANNOUNCEMENTS AND INDEX (GRA). Springfield, Virginia: U.S. Department of Commerce, National Technical Information Service, 1975—.

GRA is the index to the NTIS reports. It is issued semi-monthly with indexes by author, subject, contract number, and accession number.

HISPANIC AMERICAN PERIODICALS INDEX (HAPI). Los Angeles: UCLA Latin American Center Publications, 1974—.

This index provides comprehensive coverage of the literature on the arts, humanities, and social sciences for Latin America and for Hispanics in the United States. Access is by subject and author. It is compiled annually.

HOSPITAL LITERATURE INDEX. Chicago: American Hospital Association, 1957—.

This print index is published with the help of the National Library of Medicine and draws on the database HEALTH PLANNING AND ADMINISTRATION ABSTRACTS for its contents. Its subject headings are derived from the Medical Subject Headings, the controlled vocabulary of Index Medicus. It is issued quarterly with the last quarter being an annual cumulation. There are also quinquennial cumulations.

INDEX MEDICUS. Bethesda, Maryland: United States Department of Health, Education, and Welfare, Public Health Service, National Institutes of Health, National Library of Medicine, 1960—.

This index gives subject and author access to both domestic and international journals. It is published monthly, and provides especially good coverage of the medical literature reviews. Online it is a powerful database that is made more attractive by its modest price.

INDEX TO U.S. GOVERNMENT PERIODICALS. Chicago: Infordata International Inc., 1974–1987.

This index is now discontinued. It gave access to more than one hundred government journals with substantial articles.

MONTHLY CATALOG OF UNITED STATES GOVERNMENT PUBLICATIONS. Washington, D.C.: United States Government Printing Office, 1895–.

This index makes available only those publications released through the Government Printing Office. It gives access by author, title, and subject, and it gives reference to the Superintendent of Documents number.

PAIS INTERNATIONAL IN PRINT (PAIS). New York: Public Affairs Information Service, Inc., 1915–.

Specializing in public policy, PAIS includes domestic and international publications, government and private sector works, monographs and serials. Entry is by subject with an author index. It issues monthly updates, three of which cumulate, and an annual cumulation, in its paper form. It is available online.

PSYCHOLOGICAL ABSTRACTS. Washington, D.C.: American Psychological Association, 1927–.

This important index gives access by subject and author. It indexes dissertations online as well as duplicating the print index. It is updated monthly.

PSYCHOPHARMACOLOGY ABSTRACTS. Rockville, Maryland: U.S. Department of Health, Education, and Welfare, Public Health Service, Alcohol, Drug Abuse, and Mental Health Administration; 1961–.

This index is issued quarterly with an annual cumulation. The indexing language is derived from significant words in article titles.

READER'S GUIDE TO PERIODICAL LITERATURE. New York: H.W. Wilson Co., 1905–.

Specializing in the popular and general journals, this index can be very useful as a gauge of public awareness of and response to a subject.

SCIENCE CITATION INDEX (SCI). Philadelphia: Institute for Scientific Information, 1961–.

SCI is one of three computer generated indexes issued by the Institute. The underlying premises are that cited references are a primary indexing source, and that significant words in titles can be used to give keyword subject access. There are no abstracts. Citation indexes give access by cited and source author and they provide the bibliography and author affiliation.

SOCIAL SCIENCES CITATION INDEX. Philadelphia: Institute for Scientific Information, 1981–.

See the remarks for SCI above. Decennial cumulations provide coverage back to 1956 for this all-encompassing index to the literature of the social sciences. This index has three issues per year with an annual cumulation.

SOCIAL SCIENCES INDEX. New York: H.W. Wilson Co., 1974–.

Issued quarterly, with an annual cumulation, this index, like other indexes published by Wilson, uses a standard format: access is by author and subject in a single alphabetical sequence.

SOCIOLOGICAL ABSTRACTS. San Diego, California: Sociological Abstracts, 1953—.

This is a highly interdisciplinary index to the literature of Sociology, including applied as well as theoretical material. It indexes papers presented at meetings as well as published works. It is issued six times per year.

STANDARD PERIODICALS INDEX. New York: Oxbridge, 1964—.

This is a biennial service with information on American and Canadian serials. It is especially good for smaller, lesser known titles.

STATISTICAL REFERENCE INDEX. Washington: Congressional Information Service, 1980—.

This index gives reference, with abstracts, to statistics of all kinds published in the private sector. It also provides, on microfiche, the data themselves as they appeared when originally published.

ULRICH'S INTERNATIONAL PERIODICALS DIRECTORY. New York: Bowker, 1965—.

This biennial multi-volume set is a guide to the world's serial literature. It has indexes by title and ISSN. Among other things, it indicates where a journal is indexed, and it records title changes.

CURRENT AWARENESS.

A very effective way to stay abreast of the literature is to arrange for online searches restricted to very recent time periods on certain databases. For Hispanic alcoholism relevant databases include Psychological Abstracts, the citation indexes, and Index Medicus. Databases such as Sociological Abstracts that index papers presented at national meetings are also relevant. Lastly, Current Contents because it reprints the tables of contents of recent journal issues, can be useful. The citations are given below.

Current Contents: Clinical Practice. Philadelphia, Institute for Scientific Information, 1973—weekly.

Current Contents: Social and Behavioral Sciences. Philadelphia: Institute for Scientific Information, 1969—weekly.

BOOKS

Here below are references to selected works on the subject of Hispanic alcoholism. Many broader studies have been written, and many classic works predate this material. The compilers have included book length bibliographies in order to guide the reader to as many other sources as possible.

Abel, Ernest L. (compiler): *Alcohol and Reproduction: a Bibliography.* Westport, Connecticut, Greenwood Press, 1982.

——. *Drugs and Sex: a Bibliography.* Westport, Connecticut, Greenwood Press, 1983.

Alers, J.O.: *Puerto Ricans and Health: Findings from New York City.* New York, Fordham University, Hispanic Research Center, 1978.

Andrews, T.: *A Bibliography of Drug Abuse, Including Alcohol and Tobacco.* Littleton, Colorado, Libraries Unlimited, 1977.

——. *A Bibliography of Drug Abuse.* Supplement, 1977–1980. Littleton, Colorado, Libraries Unlimited, 1981.

Aquino, J. and Poliakoff, V. (Eds.): *Health Education, Drugs, and Alcohol: An Annotated Bibliography.* Washington, D.C., National Education Association, 1975.

Barnes, Grace M., Ernest L. Abel, and Ernst, C.A.S. (compilers): *Alcohol and the Elderly: a Comprehensive Bibliography.* Westport, Connecticut, Greenwood Press, 1980.

Barnes, Grace M. and Brown, Robert J. (compilers): *Alcohol and Youth: a Comprehensive Bibliography.* Westport, Connecticut, Greenwood Press, 1982.

Becerra, Rosina M. and Shaw, David: *The Hispanic Elderly: a Research Reference Guide.* Washington, D.C., University Press of America, 1984.

Becerra, Rosina M., M. Karno, and Escobar, J. (Eds.): *Mental Health and Hispanic Americans: Clinical Perspectives.* New York, Grune and Stratton, 1982.

Brecher, E.M.: *Licit and Illicit Drugs.* Mount Vernon, New York, Consumers Union, 1971.

Casavantes, E.M.: *El Tecato: Social and Cultural Factors Affecting Drug Use Among Chicanos,* 2nd ed. Washington, D.C., National Coalition of Spanish Speaking Mental Health Organizations, 1976.

Chalfant, H.P., B.S. Roper, and Rivera-Worley, C. (compilers): *Social and Behavioral Aspects of Female Alcoholism: an Annotated Bibliography.* Westport, Connecticut, Greenwood Press, 1980.

de la Garza, Rodolfo et al., (Eds.): *The Mexican American Experience.* Austin, The University of Texas Press, 1985.

Downard, W.L.: *Dictionary of the History of the American Brewing and Distilling Industries.* Westport, Connecticut, Greenwood Press, 1980.

Fazey, C.: *The Aetiology of Psychoactive Substance Use: a Report and Critically Annotated Bibliography on Research into the Aetiology of Alcohol, Nicotine, Opiate and Other Psychoactive Substance Use.* Paris, UNESCO, 1977.

Gilbert, M.J. and Cervantes, R.C. (Eds.): *Mexican Americans and Alcohol.* Monograph 11. Los Angeles, Spanish Speaking Mental Health Research Center.

Greeley, Andrew M, McCready, William C. and Theisen, Gary: *Ethnic Drinking Subcultures.* Brooklyn, J.F. Bergin Publishers, 1980.

Heath, D.B. and Cooper, A.M.: *Alcohol Use and World Cultures: a Comprehensive Bibliography of Anthropological Sources.* Toronto, Addiction Research Foundation, 1981.

Iiyami, P., Nishi, S.M. and Johnson, B.C.: *Drug Use and Abuse Among U.S. Minorities: an Annotated Bibliography.* New York, Praeger, 1976.

Jaffe, J., Cullen, R.M. and Boswell, T.: *The Changing Demography of Spanish Americans.* New York, Academic Press, 1980.

Kane, Geoffrey P.: *Inner-city Alcoholism: An Ecological Analysis and Cross-Cultural Study.* New York, Human Sciences Press, 1981.

Keller, M. (Ed.): *International Bibliography of Studies on Alcohol.* New Brunswick, New Jersey: Rutgers Center of Alcohol Studies, 1966—.

Lobb, Michael L. and Watts, Thomas D. (compilers): *Native American Youth and Alcohol: an Annotated Bibliography.* New York, Greenwood Press, 1989.

McKay, E.: *Hispanic Statistics Summary: a Compendium of Data on Hispanic Americans.* Washington, D.C., National Council of La Raza, 1982.

Mail, Patricia D. and McDonald, David R. (compilers): *Tulapai to Tokay: a Bibliography of Alcohol Use and Abuse Among Native Americans of North America.* New Haven, Connecticut, HRAF Press, 1980.

Marin, Gerardo and Marin, Barbara Vanoss: *Research with Hispanic Populations.* Beverly Hills, Sage Publications, 1991.

Martinez, Joe L, Jr. and Mendoza, Richard H. (Eds.): *Chicano Psychology* (2nd ed.). Orlando, Academic Press, 1984.

Menditto, J.: *Drugs of Addiction and Non-Addiction, Their Use and Abuse: a Comprehensive Bibliography, 1960–1969.* Troy, New York, Whitston Publishing Co., 1970.

Moore, Joan W., and Pachon, Harry: *Hispanics in the United States.* Englewood Cliffs, Prentice-Hall, 1985.

Newton, Frank et al.: *Hispanic Mental Health Research: a Reference Guide.* Berkeley, University of California Press, 1982.

Trotter II, Robert T. and Chavira, J.A.: *El Uso de Alcohol: a Resource Book for Spanish Speaking Communities.* Atlanta, Southern Area Alcohol Education and Training Program, 1977.

Watts, Thomas D. and Wright, Roosevelt Jr. (compilers): *Black Alcohol Abuse and Alcoholism: an Annotated Bibliography.* New York, Praeger, 1986.

GOVERNMENT PUBLICATIONS

Government, at both the federal and state level, is a major source of research and funding in the substance abuse field. It was not possible to research the efforts of all fifty state governments for this book. The S.A. professional working at the state or regional level should be aware that state agencies and private organizations active within the state can be looked to for information and assistance. The list below is restricted to federal publications.

Austin, Gregory A. et al. (Eds.): *Drugs and Minorities.* Rockville, Maryland, Department of Health, Education, and Welfare, Public Health Service, Alcohol, Drug Abuse, and Mental Health Administration, National Institute on Drug Abuse, 1977. (Research Issues—National Institute on Drug Abuse: 21)

Austin, Gregory A, Macari, Mary A. and Lettieri, Dan J.: *Guide to the Drug Research Literature.* Rockville, Maryland, Department of Health, Education, and Welfare, Public Health Service, Alcohol, Drug Abuse, and Mental Health Administration, National Institute on Drug Abuse, 1979. (Research Issues—National Institute on Drug Abuse; 27)

Bentler, Peter M., Lettieri, Dan J. and Austin, Gregory A. (Eds.). *Data Analysis Strategies and Designs for Substance Abuse Research.* Rockville, Maryland, Department of Health, Education, and Welfare, Public Health Service, Alcohol, Drug Abuse, and Mental Health Administration, National Institute on Drug Abuse. (Research Issues—National Institute on Drug Abuse: 13)

Bibliography on Multi-Cultural Drug Abuse Prevention Issues. Rockville, Maryland: U.S.

Department of Health and Human Services, National Institute on Drug Abuse, 1981.

First Special Report to the U.S. Congress on Alcohol and Health from the Secretary of Health and Human Services. Rockville, Maryland, U.S. Department of Health and Human Services, Public Health Service, Alcohol, Drug Abuse and Mental Health Administration, National Institute on Alcohol Abuse and Alcoholism, 1971. The first report was followed by a second, third, fourth, fifth, sixth and seventh. They were released by the same federal government agency as the first in 1974, 1978, 1981, 1984, 1987, and 1990 respectively.

National Directory of Drug Abuse and Alcoholism Treatment and Prevention Programs. Rockville, Maryland, U.S. Department of Health and Human Services, Public Health Service, Alcohol, Drug Abuse, and Mental Health Administration, National Institute on Drug Abuse, National Institute of Alcohol Abuse and Alcoholism, 1983.

Padilla, Amado, and Aranda, Paul (compilers): *Latino Mental Health: Bibliography and Abstracts.* Rockville, Maryland, U.S. National Institutes of Mental Health, Alcohol, Drug Abuse, and Mental Health Administration, 1974.

Padilla, Amado M. and Ruiz, Rene A.: *Latino Mental Health: a Review of the Literature.* Rockville, Maryland, U.S. Department of Health and Human Services, National Institute of Mental Health, 1974.

Report of the Secretary's Task Force on Black and Minority Health. Washington, D.C., U.S. Department of Health and Human Services, Task Force on Black and Minority Health. 1985 – .

ONLINE DATABASES WITHOUT PRINT COUNTERPARTS

Some valuable indexes do not occur in print. The list below is of indexes that exist only in electronic forms.

- NAME: AGELINE
  BRS ACRONYM: AARP
  PRODUCER: American Association of Retired Persons, National Gerontology Resource Center, 1909 K Street NW, Washington, D.C. 20049
  TIME: 1978 to date, updated every month

- NAME: ALCOHOL AND ALCOHOL PROBLEMS SCIENCE DATABASE
  BRS ACRONYM: ETOH
  PRODUCER: National Institute on Alcohol Abuse and Alcoholism (NIAAA), Alcohol, Drug Abuse, and Mental Health Administration, Public Health Service, 5600 Fishers Lane, Rockville MD 20857
  TIME: 1972 to date with monthly updates

- NAME: ALCOHOL INFORMATION FOR CLINICIANS AND EDUCATORS DATABASE
  BRS ACRONYM: CORK
  PRODUCER: Project Cork Institute, Dartmouth Medical School, Hanover NH 03756

TIME: 1978 to date with quarterly updates
- NAME: DRUGINFO AND ALCOHOL USE AND ABUSE
  BRS ACRONYMS: DRUG, DRSC, HAZE
  PRODUCER: Drug Information Services, College of Pharmacy, University of Minnesota, Minneapolis, Minn. 55455
  TIME: 1968 to the present, with quarterly updates. Since 1978 HAZE has been inactive and material on alcoholism is located in the concatenated file, DRUG.
- NAME: HEALTH PERIODICALS DATABASE
  DIALOG FILE NUMBER: 149
  PRODUCER: Information Access Company, 362 Lakeside Dr., Foster City, CA. 94404
  TIME: 1976 to the present with weekly updates
  COMMENT: This is a serials database of material intended largely for a lay readership. It includes non-health journals with health stories as they occur in other IAC databases such as Industry Index and Legal Resources Index.

HANDBOOKS

There are many sources that one can consult for a datum, a definition, an address, or a further reference. A sample list of interest to the S.A. professional is given below.

Abel, Ernest L. (compiler): *Dictionary of Alcohol Use and Abuse: Slang, Terms, and Terminology.* Westport, Connecticut, Greenwood Press, 1985.
——. *A Dictionary of Drug Abuse Terms and Terminology.* Westport, Connecticut, Greenwood Press, 1984.
Austin, Gregory A. and Prendergast, Michael L.: *Drug Use and Abuse: a Guide to Research Findings.* Santa Barbara, California, ABC–CLIO Information Services, 1984.
Cox, Terrence C. et al. (compilers): *Drugs and Drug Abuse: A Reference Text.* Toronto, Addiction Research Foundation, 1983.
Drug, Alcohol, and Other Addictions: a Directory of Treatment Centers and Prevention Programs Nationwide. Phoenix, Arizona, Oryx Press, 1989.
Keller, Mark, V. Efron, and Jellinek, E.M. (Eds.). *CAAL Manual: a Guide to the Use of the Classified Abstract Archives of the Alcohol Literature.* New Brunswick, New Jersey, Rutgers Center of Alcohol Studies, 1965.
Keller, Mark and McCormick, Mairi: *A Dictionary of Words About Alcohol.* New Brunswick, New Jersey, Publications Division, Rutgers Center of Alcohol Studies, 1966.
Lender, Mark Edward: *Dictionary of American Temperance Biography: from Temperance Reform to Alcohol Research, the 1600s to the 1980s.* Westport, Connecticut, Greenwood Press, 1984.
Newton, Frank, Olmedo, Esteban L. and Padilla, Amado M.: *Hispanic Mental Health Research: a Reference Guide.* Berkeley, University of California Press, 1982.

O'Brien, Robert and Chafetz, Morris (Eds.): *The Encyclopedia of Alcoholism.* New York, Facts on File, Inc., 1982.

O'Brien, Robert and Cohen, Sidney: *The Encyclopedia of Drug Abuse.* New York, Facts on File, 1984.

The 7th Edition: 1989 National Directory of Alcoholism & Addiction Treatment Programs, Including Agencies, Services, & Community Resources. Cleveland, International Publishing Group, 1982—.

Smith, Darren L. (Ed.): *Hispanic Americans Information Directory, 1990-1991.* Detroit, Gale Research Inc., 1990.

Spears, Richard A.: *The Slang and Jargon of Drugs and Drink.* Metuchen, New Jersey, Scarecrow Press, 1986.

The U.S. Journal's 1991 National Treatment Directory for Alcoholism, Drug Abuse and Other Addiction Problems. Deerfield Beach, Florida, U.S. Journal of Drug and Alcohol Dependence, 1986—.

Women's Recovery Programs: a Directory of Residential Addiction Treatment Centers. Phoenix, Arizona, Oryx Press, 1990.

GRANT INFORMATION

Funding for research is crucial, and information on funding is plentiful. How to apply for grants, write them, assess them, and incorporate them into one's work are topics covered in the selected list here below.

America's New Foundations, 4th ed. Rockville, Maryland, Taft Group, 1990.

Annual Register of Grant Support. Chicago, Marquis Academic Media, 1969—.

Bauer, David G.: *The "How To" Grants Manual: Successful Grantseeking Techniques for Obtaining Public and Private Grants.* New York, American Council on Education: Macmillan; London: Collier Macmillan, 1984.

Behling, John H.: *Guidelines for Preparing the Research Proposal.* Lanham, Maryland, University Press of America, 1984.

Corporate 500: the Directory of Corporate Philanthropy. San Francisco, Public Management Institute, 1980—.

Directory of Biomedical and Health Care Grants. Phoenix, Arizona, Oryx Press, 1985—.

Directory of Federal Aid for Health and Allied Fields: A Guide to Federal Assistance Programs for Health and Allied Fields. Santa Monica, California, Ready Reference Press, 1982.

Directory of Research Grants. Phoenix, Oryx Press, 1975—.

The Foundation Center Source Book Profiles. New York, The Foundation Center, 1983—.

The Foundation Directory. New York, The Foundation Center, 1960—.

The Foundation Grants Index. New York, The Foundation Center;

Foundation Grants to Individuals. Claude Barilleaux (Ed.). New York, The Foundation Center, 1984.

Georgi, Charlotte: *Fund-Raising, Grants, and Foundations: A Comprehensive Bibliography.* Littleton, Colorado, Libraries Unlimited, 1985.

The Grants Register. Chicago, St. James Press, 1969–70, 1973/75–.

Hispanics and Grant Makers. Washington D.C.: Council on Foundations, 1981.

Jankowski, Katherine E., editor. *Taft Guide to Corporate Giving Contacts: Over 2,650 Corporate Direct Giving Programs and Company-Sponsored Foundations.* 6th ed. Washington, D.C., Taft Corporate Information Service, 1989.

Lauffer, Armand: *Grantsmanship and Fund Raising.* Beverly Hills, Sage Publications, 1984, 1985 printing.

Margolin, Judith B.: *The Individual's Guide to Grants.* New York, Plenum Press, 1983.

Meador, Roy: *Guidelines for Preparing Proposals: A Manual on How to Organize Winning Proposals for Grants, Venture Capital, R & D Projects, Other Proposals.* Chelsea, Michigan, Lewis Publishers, 1985.

Schlachter, Gail A.: *Directory of Financial Aids for Minorities, 1984–1985.* Santa Barbara, Reference Service Press: ABC–CLIO Information Services, 1985.

Schlachter, Gail A.: *How to Find Out About Financial Aid: A Guide to Over 700 Directories Listing Scholarships, Fellowships, Loans, Grants, Awards, Internships.* Los Angeles, Reference Service Press, 1987.

Shellor, Jill R.: *Grant Seekers Guide: Funding Sourcebook/National Network of Grantmakers.* Mt. Kisco, New York, Moyer Bell, 1985.

Taft Corporate Giving Directory. Washington, D.C.: Taft Corporation, 1984–.

Where America's Large Foundations Make Their Grants. 5th ed. New York: Public Service Materials Center, 1983.

White, Virginia (Ed.). *Grant Proposals that Succeeded.* New York, Plenum Press, 1983.

JOURNALS

This section is divided into two parts. The first part has those journals considered to be especially important to S.A. professionals, thereafter is a list of titles of other journals that also publish articles of interest, but that would not be considered of primary importance.

Primary Journals:

Advances in Alcohol and Substance Abuse. New York, Haworth, V.1–, 1981–. Quarterly.

Alcohol Awareness Service. Rockville, Maryland, U.S. Alcohol, Drug Abuse, and Mental Health Administration, Office for Substance Abuse Prevention. Prepared by the National Institute on Alcohol Abuse and Alcoholism for the Office for Substance Abuse Prevention. 1987–. Bimonthly.

Alcohol Clinical Update. Hanover, New Hampshire, Project Cork at Dartmouth Medical School, V.1–, N.1–, 1982–. Bimonthly.

Alcohol Health and Research World. Rockville, Maryland, National Institute on Alcohol Abuse and Alcoholism. U.S. G.P.O., distributor, V.1–, No. 1–, 1973–. Quarterly.

American Journal of Drug and Alcohol Abuse. New York, Marcel Dekker, V.1–, 1974–. Four numbers annually

Contemporary Drug Problems. New York, Federal Legal Publications, 1971/72—. Quarterly.

Drug and Alcohol Dependence: An International Journal on Biomedical and Psychosocial Approaches. Lausanne, Elsevier Sequoia. Six issues per annum.

Hispanic Journal of Behavioral Sciences. Los Angeles, Spanish Speaking Mental Health Research Center, UCLA, V.1—, No.1—, 1979—. Quarterly.

Hospital and Community Psychiatry. Washington, American Psychiatric Association, January 1966—. Monthly.

International Journal of the Addictions. New York, Marcel Dekker, V.1—, 1966—. Monthly as of 1985.

Journal of Studies on Alcohol. New Brunswick, New Jersey, Journal of Studies on Alcohol, Inc., 6—, 1975—. Bimonthly as of 1983, title and frequency have varied.

Other journals in which relevant articles have been published include: American Anthropologist, American Journal of Epidemiology, American Journal of Psychiatry, American Journal of Public Health, Aztlan, British Journal of the Addictions, Children Today, Journal of Chronic Disease, Journal of Clinical Psychiatry, Journal of Consulting and Clinical Psychology, Journal of Drug Education, Journal of School Health, Journal of the American Medical Association, Journal of Youth and Adolescence, Medical Anthropology, Psychological Reports, Public Health Reports, Social Problems, Social Work, and Urban Health.

RESEARCH CENTERS AND OTHER INSTITUTIONS

- Addiction Research Foundation.
  33 Russell Street, Toronto Ontario M5S 2S1, Canada
  416/595-6144

- Alcohol Beverage Medical Research Foundation: Johns Hopkins University, School of Medicine
  720 Rutland Avenue, 57 Turner Auditorium, Baltimore, MD 21205
  301/955-3264

- Alcoholics Anonymous World Services, Inc.
  468 Park Avenue South, New York, NY 10016
  212/686-1100

- Alcoholism and Drug Abuse Institute.
  3937 15th Avenue, NE, Seattle, WA 98105
  206/543-0937

- California Hispanic Commission on Alcohol and Drug Abuse.
  5838 E. Beverly Blvd., Los Angeles, CA 90022
  213/722-4529

- Children of Alcoholics Foundation
  540 Madison Avenue, 23rd Floor, New York, NY 10022
  212/980-5393

- Fordham University, Hispanic Research Center
  Thebaud Hall, Bronx, NY 10458
  212/579-2629

- Hastings Center
  255 Elm Road, Briarcliff Manor, NY 10510
  914/762-8500

- National Coalition of Hispanic Health and Human Services Organizations
  1030 15th Street N.W., Suite 1053
  Washington D.C. 20005
  202/371-2100

- National Council on Alcoholism, Inc.
  12 West 21st Street, 7th Floor
  New York, NY 10017
  212/206-6770

- Project Cork Institute
  Dartmouth Medical School, Hanover, NH 03756
  603/646-7540

- Research Institute on Alcoholism.
  1021 Main Street, Buffalo, NY 14203
  716/887-2511

- Rutgers University Center of Alcohol Studies
  Smithers Hall, Busch Campus, Piscataway, NJ 08854
  908/932-4442

- UCLA Spanish Speaking Mental Health Research Center.
  A352 Franz Hall, Los Angeles, CA 90024
  310/825-8886

Appendix B

ABOUT THE CONTRIBUTORS

Anthony Michael Alcocer, Dr.P.H., is a native of Los Angeles and received his education at Loyola-Marymount University, Los Angeles, California State University, Los Angeles, and the University of California at Los Angeles where he received his doctorate in Medical Care Organization. He is a licensed therapist and has worked with substance abuse populations for over twenty-five years. Contributions to his field have been principally in the area of Hispanic populations and substance abuse. He was the co-principal investigator of the 1976 California Study on Spanish Speaking Alcoholism and continued to contribute to the literature in this field over the years. Dr. Alcocer is a Professor of Health Science at California State University, Northridge.

Manuel Barrera, Jr., Ph.D., is Professor of Psychology and Director of the Clinical Psychology Center at Arizona State University. He also has held visiting appointments with Oregon Research Institute and the Department of Psychiatry, University of California—San Francisco. He received his Ph.D. in Clinical Psychology from the University of Oregon. For the past 15 years his research and scholarship have focused on social support and Hispanic mental health topics. More recently he has applied his interests to the study of adolescents' alcohol and substance abuse.

Richard C. Cervantes, Ph.D., is Assistant Professor of Psychiatry (Psychology) at the University of Southern California, Department of Psychiatry. He also has a private practice in forensic psychology. He received his doctorate in clinical psychology from Oklahoma State University. He has done research and written extensively on psychological aspects of Hispanics.

Geertruida C. de Goede, M.L.S., has worked with the literature of social concerns at the Legislative Library, Victoria, British Columbia (1975–1981), at the Southwestern Medical Center Library, Dallas, Texas (1981–1984), and at the Central Library, The University of Texas at Arlington (1984 to present). Ms. de Goede is a member of the American Library Association, the Association of College and Research Libraries, the Northeast Texas Online Users Group, and the Tarrant County Association of Law Librarians (of which she is 1992 president).

Mario R. De La Rosa, Ph.D., is a Social Science Analyst with the Epidemiological Research Branch, National Institute on Drug Abuse. He received his doctorate in

Social Welfare Administration from Ohio State University and a Masters in Social Work from Case Western Reserve University. Dr. De La Rosa currently manages a research grant portfolio on epidemiologic studies investigating the crime/drug connection. He has been actively involved in stimulating research on substance abuse in minority population groups and encouraging minority researchers to submit grants to NIDA. Before joining NIDA he was an Assistant Professor at the University of Illinois at Urbana-Champaign. Dr. De La Rosa is the author of several papers on social support systems of Hispanics and reports on the crime/drug connection.

Melvin Delgado, Ph.D., is Professor of Social Work and Chair of the Macro-Practice Sequence, Boston University School of Social Work. His current interests in the field of AODA focus on the use of Latino natural support systems in prevention and early intervention with high-risk youth.

Carann Simpson Feazell, M.S.S.W., has worked in Human Resource Management for over ten years. She was Manager, Health Services and Benefits, for General Electric Corporation. Previous to that, she was Manager, Employee Assistance Program, Southwestern Bell Corporation. She has written articles on services to battered women, and services to ethnic minorities in the workplace. She has also presented many papers on managed health care.

M Jean Gilbert, Ph.D., is an applied anthropologist who received her doctorate at the University of California at Santa Barbara. Her research as a National Institute on Alcohol Abuse and Alcoholism (NIAAA) Scholar in Hispanic Alcohol Studies at U.C.L.A. (1984–1990) focused on alcohol use among Mexicans and Mexican Americans. In collaboration with Juana Mora, Ph.D., she has recently finished a study of alcohol use among Latinas: professionals, blue-collar workers, and homemakers. Dr. Gilbert's other research has been concerned with social epidemiology, medical belief systems across different cultural groups, maternal and child health, and health service utilization patterns among American ethnic minorities. She serves in an advisory capacity on various panels and committees for NIAAA, the National Institute on Drug Abuse and the National Institute of Medicine. Currently, she is conducting health research for Kaiser Permanente, Southern California region.

Denise Humm-Delgado, Ph.D., is Associate Professor of Social Work and Chair of the Social Policy Sequence, Simmons College School of Social Work, Boston, Massachusetts. She is interested in the development of social policies that support the national helping networks of individuals, families, and communities, and that guarantee entitlement to services, benefits, and rights for oppressed groups.

Barbara L. Kail, D.S.W., is Associate Professor of Social Work at Fordham University Graduate School of Social Work. She has published numerous works on drug use, especially among women. She is the editor of *Drug Use Among Women of Color,* published by Edwin Mellen Press, 1992.

Alberto G. Mata, Jr., Ph.D., formerly a senior advisor and research sociologist at the National Institute on Drug Abuse, is currently an Associate Professor at the University of Oklahoma in the Department of Human Relations. His recent activities involved working in implementing and monitoring community based HIV risk reduction interventions targeting intravenous drug abusers and their sexual partners. His original research began exploring and describing Mexican-American youth involvements with "street life—gang and drug use patterns in a midwestern blue collar community". Since then he has been involved in several studies of Hispanic community young adults and youth drug use, ranging from inhalant abuse to Heroin use. He served as Co-Principal investigator with UWM Professor Joan Moore on the East Los Angeles Women and Heroin Study Project. He currently serves as a board member on the National Community AIDS Partnership and the National March of Dimes Professional Services Advisory Board.

Finetta Reese, Ph.D., received her doctorate in Clinical Psychology from Arizona State University and completed postdoctoral research training at ASU's Program for Prevention Research. She is currently Assistant Professor of Psychology at Virginia Commonwealth University. Her research interests include stress and coping processes, alcohol abuse prevention, and minority mental health issues.

Arturo Rio, Ph.D., was an Assistant Professor of Psychiatry at the University of Miami Center for Family Studies and the Spanish Family Guidance Center. Dr. Rio published widely in the areas of child and adolescent mental health and education. He won numerous awards including the 1990 Outstanding Research Publication Award of the American Association of Marriage and Family Therapists. Dr. Rio passed away in October 1990.

Sylvia Rodriguez-Andrew, Ph.D., is currently an Associate Professor in the Department of Sociology and Social Work at Texas Lutheran College, in Seguin, Texas. She chairs the Department of Sociology and Social Work as well as the Division of Social Sciences. Dr. Rodriguez-Andrew is also Program Evaluation Consultant for alcohol and other drug use prevention, intervention, and treatment services at the Mexican American Unity Council in San Antonio, Texas.

Beatrice A. Rouse, Ph.D., has over 15 years experience conducting epidemiological, clinical, and experimental studies of alcohol and other drug use. Dr. Rouse's publications include co-editing books and monographs on drug abuse as well as more than 30 drug-related scientific articles. Her knowledge of national health and drug research concerns and policies has been gained through participation in various federal, scientific, and professional committees and conferences as well as her present work in drug abuse services research. In addition, Dr. Rouse serves as the Managing Editor of NIDA's *Drug Abuse Research Series* and is in charge of projects dealing with quality assurance of drug treatment and with assessing state standards and licensing, certification, and accreditation requirements for drug abuse treatment and reimbursement. Dr. Rouse is on the Leadership Council of the

APHA Section on Alcohol, Tobacco, and Other Drugs and is also on the Editorial Board of the *American Journal of Public Health*. In addition, she teaches a course on the Epidemiology of Substance Abuse at the University of Michigan School of Public Health International Graduate Summer Institute of Epidemiology.

Raymond Sanchez Mayers, Ph.D., is Associate Professor and Associate Dean at Rutgers University School of Social Work. He has written extensively on Hispanic issues and presented many papers on aspects of employee assistance programs and managed health care. He received his M.S.W. from Barry University in Miami and his doctorate in Social Welfare from Brandeis University.

Daniel Santisteban, Ph.D., is an Assistant Professor of Psychiatry at the University of Miami Center for Family Studies and the Spanish Family Guidance Center. Dr. Santisteban has specialized in the area of family factors in the etiology of substance abuse and behavior problems among Hispanic youth as well as on substance abuse program evaluation. Dr. Santisteban has published on the use of family therapy intervention with Hispanic youth and their families.

Fernando I. Soriano, Ph.D., is a psychologist and currently an Assistant Professor in the Department of Behavioral Science at the University of Missouri, Kansas City. Dr. Soriano has conducted and published research in the areas of substance abuse, delinquency, AIDS, discrimination and mental health, cultural sensitivity, program design and evaluation. He is a consultant to many private and public agencies, and serves on several national committees, including the American Psychological Association's Commission on Violence and Youth, and on the Advisory Committee on Youth Gang Drug Abuse Prevention for the Administration on Children, Youth, and Families. Before coming to Missouri, Dr. Soriano headed the Navy's in-house research project focusing on the development of support services to Navy families. He has a book out soon entitled, *Conducting Needs Assessments: A Multidisciplinary Approach* (Sage Publications).

Federico Souflee, Jr., Ph.D., is an Assistant Professor at the School of Social Work, the University of Texas at Arlington. He is the co-author of a book on the management of human service programs and has written several articles on Chicano—specific issues related to social work education and practice. A native of El Paso, Dr. Souflee received his M.S.S.W. from the University of Texas at Austin, and his doctorate in Human Services Administration from the University of Texas at Arlington. He is a former director of Social Services, Project Head Start, HEW, Washington, D.C.; Chicano Training Center, Houston; and Harris County Child Welfare Unit, Houston.

Jose Szapocznik, Ph.D., is Professor of Psychiatry and Director of the Center for Family Studies, the Spanish Family Guidance Center and the Miami World Health Organization Collaborating Center. He has published widely in the areas of Hispanic behavior, including *Breakthroughs in Family Therapy with Drug Abusing, Behavior*

Problem Youth, published by Springer. Dr. Szapocznik has won numerous awards, including the 1989 Rafael Tavares M.D. Award of the Association of Hispanic Mental Health Professionals, the 1990 Outstanding Research Publication Award of the American Association of Marriage and Family Therapists, and the 1991 Distinguished Professional Contributions Award from the American Psychological Association.

Thomas D. Watts, D.S.W., is Professor and Director of the Baccalaureate Program in Social Work at The University of Texas at Arlington. He has written extensively on the subject of alcoholism, especially among ethnic minorities. He has authored and co-edited a number of publications, including *Social Thought on Alcoholism* (Krieger, 1986), *Prevention of Black Alcoholism: Issues and Strategies* (Charles C Thomas, 1985), and many others.

PART V
BIBLIOGRAPHY

Abrams, David B.: Psychosocial assessment of alcohol and stress interactions: Bridging the gap between laboratory and treatment outcome research. In Pohorecky, Larissa A. and Brick, John (Eds.): *Stress and Alcohol Use.* New York, Elsevier Biomedical, 1983, pp. 61–86.

Ackerly, W. and Gibson, G.: Lighter fluid "sniffing." *American Journal of Orthopsychiatry, 120*(11):1056–1061, 1964.

Acosta, F.X., Yamamoto, J., and Evans, L.A.: *Effective Psychotherapy for Low-Income and Minority Patients.* New York, Plenum, 1982.

Albaugh, B. and Albaugh, P.: Alcoholism and substance sniffing among the Cheyenne and Arapaho Indians of Oklahoma. *International Journal of the Addictions, 14*(7):1001–1007, 1979.

Alcocer, Anthony M.: Quantitative Study. In Technical Systems Institute, *Drinking practices and alcohol-related problems of Spanish speaking persons in California.* Sacramento, California Office of Alcohol and Drug Problems, 1979.

Alcocer, Anthony M.: *Hispanic Alcohol Abuse: Perceptions and Realities.* A paper presented at the American Association for the Advancement of Science, Washington, DC., January, 1982.

Alcocer, Anthony M. and Gilbert, M. Jean: *Drinking Practices and Alcohol Related Problems of Spanish Speaking Persons in California.* Sacramento, California Office of Alcohol and Drug Programs, 1979.

Alexander, J.F.: Defensive and supportive communications in normal and deviant families. *Journal of Consulting and Clinical Psychology, 40:*223–231, 1973.

Alvirez, David, and Bean, Frank D.: The Mexican American family. In Mindel, C.H. and Haberstein, R.N. (Eds.): *Ethnic Families in America.* New York, Elsevier, 1976.

Amaro, H.: *Hispanic Women and AIDS: Considerations for Prevention and Research.* Paper prepared for the NIMH/NIDA Research Workshop on "Women and Aids: Promoting Healthy Behaviors," Boston, MA., 1987.

Amaro, H. Whitaker, R. Coffman, G. and Heeren, T.: Acculturation and marijuana and cocaine use. Findings from HHANES 1982–1984. *American Journal of Public Health, 80* Supplement:54–60, 1990.

American Psychiatric Association: *Diagnostic and statistical manual of mental disorders (DSM-IIIR)* (3rd ed.). Washington, DC., American Psychiatric Association, 1983.

Amsel, Z.: Introducing the concept "community prevention." In Leukefeld, C.G., Battjes, R.J. and Amsel, Z. (Eds.): *AIDS and Intravenous Drug Use: Future Direc-*

tions for Community-based Prevention Research. NIDA Research Monograph 93. Washington, D.C., U.S. Government Printing Office, 1990.

Anglin, M.D., Ryan, M.T., Booth, M.V., and Hser, Y.: Ethnic differences in narcotic addiction: Part I, Characteristics of Chicano and Anglo methadone maintenance clients. *International Journal of the Addictions, 23:*125–149, 1988.

Asnis, S.F. and Smith, R.C.: Amphetamine abuse and violence. *Journal of Psychedelic Drugs, 10:*371–377, 1978.

Atkinson, Donald R., Poston, W. Carlos, Furlong, Michael J., and Mercado, Pauline: Ethnic group preferences for counselor characteristics. *Journal of Consulting Psychology,* 36(1):68–72, 1989.

Austin, G.A., Macari, M.A., and Lettieri, D.J., (Eds.): *Research Issues Update.* Washington, D.C., National Institute on Drug Abuse, 1978.

Axinn, June and Levin, Herman: *Social welfare: A History of the American Response to Need.* New York, Harper and Row, 1982.

Bachrach, K. and Sandler, I.: A retrospective assessment of inhalant abuse in the barrio: Implications for prevention. *International Journal of the Addictions,* 20(8):1177–1189, 1985.

Ball, J.C., Shaffer, J.W., and Nurco, D.N.: The day-to-day criminality of heroin addicts in Baltimore—a study in the continuity of offence rates. *Drug and Alcohol Dependence, 12:*119–142, 1983.

Bandura, A.: *Social Foundations of Thought and Action.* Englewood Cliffs, Prentice Hall, 1986.

Barker, G. and Adams, W.: Glue sniffing. *Sociology and Social Research, 47*(3):298–310, 1963.

Barnes, G.: Solvent abuse: A review. *International Journal of the Addictions, 14*(1):1–26, 1979.

Barnes, G.M. and Welter, J.W.: Patterns and predictors of alcohol use among 7–12 grade students in New York State. *Journal of Studies on Alcohol, 47*(1):53–62, 1986

Barrera, Manuel, Jr.: Social support in the adjustment of pregnant adolescents: Assessment issues. In Gottlieb, B.H. (Ed.): *Social Networks and Social Support.* Beverly Hills, Sage, 1981, pp. 69–96.

Barrera, Manuel, Jr.: Distinctions between social support concepts, measures, and models. *American Journal of Community Psychology, 14:*413–446, 1986.

Barrera, Manuel, Jr., Zautra, A., and Baca, L.M.: Some research considerations in studying stress and distress of Mexican Americans. In Martinez, J.L., Jr. and Mendoza, R.H. (Eds.): *Chicano Psychology.* Orlando, Academic Press, 1984, pp. 223–247.

Barrett, M.E., Joe, G and Simpson, D.: Acculturation influences on inhalant use. *Hispanic Journal of Behavioral Sciences, 13:*276–296, 1991.

Bass, M.: Sudden sniffing death. *Journal of the American Medical Association, 212*(12):2075–2079, 1970.

Beck, D.F.: *Counselor Characteristics: How They Affect Outcomes.* Milwaukee, Family Service America, 1988.

Beezley, D.A., Gantner, A.B., Bailey, D.S., and Taylor, S.P.: Amphetamines and human physical aggression. *Journal Research in Personality, 21:*52–60, 1987.

Belenko, S. and Kehrer, B.: *Final Report of a Study of Drinking Patterns Among Adults and Youth in Los Angeles County.* Princeton, Mathematica Policy Research, Inc., 1978.

Belle, D. (Ed.).: *Children's Social Networks and Social Supports.* New York, Wiley, 1989.

Bengston, V.L.: *Families, Support Systems, and Ethnic Groups: Patterns of Contrast and Congruence.* Paper presented at the meeting of the Gerontological Society, New York, 1976.

Bennett, L., and Ames, G.: *The American Experience with Alcohol.* New York, Plenum, 1986.

Bonnheim, M. and Korman, M.: Family interaction and acculturation in Mexican American inhalant users. *Journal of Psychoactive Drugs, 17*(1):25–34, 1985.

Booth, M.V., Castro, F.G., and Anglin, M.D.: What do we know about Hispanic substance abuse? A review of the literature. In Glick, R. and Moore, J. (Eds.): *Drugs in Hispanic Communities.* Rutgers University Press, New Brunswick, 1990, pp. 21–43.

Borgadus, E.S.: Gangs of Mexican-American youth. *Sociology and Social Research, 25:*55–66, 1943.

Brehm, M. and Sharp, A. (Eds.): *Review of Inhalant Abuse Research.* Rockville, MD., U.S. Government Printing Office, 1977.

Brown, G.H.: *The Condition of Education for Hispanic Americans.* Washington, D.C., National Center for Education Statistics, 1980.

Brown, L., Oliver, J., Flor de Alva (Eds.): *Sociocultural and Service Issues in Working with Hispanic American Clients.* New York, Rockefeller College, 1985.

Brown, Sandra A.: Expectancies versus background in the prediction of college drinking patterns. *Journal of Consulting and Clinical Psychology, 53*(1):23–130, 1985.

Brown, Sandra A, Goldman, Mark S. and Christiansen, B.A.: Do alcohol expectancies mediate drinking patterns of adults? *Journal of Consulting and Clinical Psychology, 53*(4):512–519, 1985.

Brownell, K.D.: The addictive disorders. In G.T. Wilson, C.M. Franks, K.D. Brownell, and P.C. Kendall (Eds.): *Annual Review of Behavior Therapy: Theory and Practice.* New York, Guilford, 1984, Vol. 9, pp. 211–258.

Brozorsky, M. and Winkler, E.: Glue sniffing in children and adolescents. *New York State Journal of Medicine, 65*(15):1984–1989, 1965.

Bruno, J. and Doscher, L.: Patterns of drug use among Mexican-American potential school dropouts. In Eiseman, S. (Ed.): *Foundations for a Psychosocial Approach.* New York, Baywood, 1984, pp. 152–161.

Brunswick, A.F.: Health needs of adolescents: How the adolescent sees them. *American Journal of Public Health, 59:*1730–1745, 1969.

Burr, W.: *Theory Construction and the Sociology of the Family.* New York, Wiley, 1973.

Caetano, Raul: Drinking patterns and alcohol problems among Hispanics in the U.S.: A review. *Drug and Alcohol Dependence, 12*(1):37–59, 1983.

Caetano, Raul: Ethnicity and drinking in Northern California: A comparison among Whites, Blacks and Hispanics. *Alcohol and Alcoholism, 19*(1):31–44, 1984a.

Caetano, Raul: Hispanic drinking practices in Northern California. *Hispanic Journal of Behavioral Sciences, 6*(4):345–364, 1984b.

Caetano, Raul: Self-reported Intoxication among Hispanics in Northern California. *Journal of Studies on Alcohol,* 45(4):349–355, 1984c.

Caetano, Raul: *Drinking patterns and alcohol problems in a national sample of U.S. Hispanics.* Paper presented at the National Institute of Alcohol Abuse and Alcoholism Conference, Epidemiology of Alcohol Use and Abuse Among U.S. Minorities, Bethesda, MD., September, 1985.

Caetano, Raul: Alternative definitions of Hispanics: Consequences in an alcohol survey. *Hispanic Journal of Behavioral Sciences,* 8(4):331–344, 1986.

Caetano, Raul: Acculturation and drinking patterns among U.S. Hispanics. *British Journal of the Addictions,* 82:789–799, 1987a.

Caetano, Raul: Alcohol use and depression among U.S. Hispanics. *British Journal of Addictions,* 82 (11):1245–1251, 1987b.

Caetano, Raul: Acculturation, drinking and social settings among U.S. Hispanics. *Drug and Alcohol Dependence,* 19:215–226, 1987c.

Caetano, Raul: Alcohol use among Hispanic groups in the United States. *American Journal of Drug and Alcohol Abuse,* 14(3):293–308, 1988.

Caetano, Raul: Concepts of alcoholism among whites, blacks and Hispanics in the United States. *Journal of Studies on Alcohol,* 50(6):580–582, 1989a.

Caetano, Raul: Differences in alcohol use between Mexican-Americans in Texas and California. *Hispanic Journal of the Behavioral Sciences,* 11(1):58–69, 1989b.

Caetano, Raul and Medina-Mora, Maria E.: Acculturation and drinking among people of Mexican descent in Mexico and the United States. *Journal of Studies on Alcohol,* 49(5):462–471, 1988.

Cahalan, D.: Supplemental report. *Ethnoreligious group differences, 1974 California drinking survey.* Prepared for Office of Alcohol Program Management. Berkeley, California Social Research Group, 1975.

Cahalan, D., Cisin, I. and Crossley, H.: *American drinking practices.* Monograph No. 7. New Brunswick, Rutgers Center on Alcohol Studies, 1969.

Cahalan, D., Roizen, R. and Room, R.: *Findings of a statewide California survey on attitudes related to control of drinking problems.* Berkeley, University of California, 1974.

Cahalan, D. and Room, R.: *Problem drinking among American men.* Monograph No. 7. New Brunswick, Rutgers Center on Alcohol Studies, 1974.

Canino, I.A.: The Hispanic child: Treatment considerations. In R. M. Becerra, M. Karno and I.I. Escobar (Eds.), *Mental health and Hispanic Americans-Clinical Perspectives.* New York, Grune & Stratton, 1982.

Carrillo, G.: Changing norms of Hispanic families: Implications for treatment. In E.E. Jones and S.J. Korchin (Eds.), *Minority Mental Health* (pp. 250–266). New York, Praeger, 1982.

Carroll, E.: Notes on the epidemiology of inhalants. In C.W. Sharp and M. L. Brehm (Eds.), *Review of inhalants: From Euphoria to Dysfunction.* Rockville, MD., US Government Printing Office, 1977.

Centers for Disease Control: *HIV/AIDS Surveillance Report,* June 1991, 1–18, 1991a.

Centers for Disease Control: HIV infection in women. *CDC HIV/AIDS Prevention Newsletter,* 2(1), 3–5, 1991b.

Cervantes, Richard C., and Castro, R.G.: Stress, coping and Mexican American mental health: A systematic review. *Hispanic Journal of Behavioral Sciences, I* (1): 1–73, 1985.

Cervantes, Richard C., Gilbert, M. Jean, Salgado de Snyder, Nelly and Padilla, Amado M.: Psychosocial and cognitive correlates of alcohol use in young adult immigrant and U.S. born Hispanics. *International Journal of the Addictions, 25*(3), 1990–1991.

Cervantes, Richard C., Padilla, Amado M., and Salgado de Snyder, N.: Reliability and validity of the Hispanic Stress Inventory. *Hispanic Journal of Behavioral Sciences, 12,* (1), 76–82, 1990.

Chapel, I. and Taylor, D.: Glue sniffing. *Missouri Medicine, 65*(4):288–296, 1968.

Chassin, L.: Adolescent substance use and abuse. In Karoly, P. and Steffen, J.J. (Eds.): *Adolescent Behavior Disorders: Foundations and Contemporary Concerns.* Lexington, Lexington Books, 1984, pp. 99–152.

Chavez, E.L., Edwards, R., and Oetting, E.R.: Mexican-American and White-American dropouts, drug use health status and involvement in violence. *Public Health Reports, 104:*594–604, 1989.

Chesney, Barbara K., Rounds, Kathleen A., and Chesler, Mark A: Support for parents of children with cancer: The value of self-help groups. *Social Work with Groups, 12:*119–139, 1989.

Christiansen, Bruce A., Goldman, Mark S. and Inn, Andres: Development of alcohol-related expectancies in adolescents: Separating pharmacological from social learning. *Journal of Consulting and Clinical Psychology, 50*(3):336–344, 1982.

Clinger, O. and Johnson, N.: Purposeful inhalation of gasoline vapors. *Psychiatric Quarterly, 25:*557–567, 1951.

Coddington, R.D.: The significance of life events as etiologic factors in the disease of children: I. A survey of professional workers. *Journal of Psychosomatic Research, 16:* 7–18, 1972.

Cohen, L.: *Culture, Disease and Stress Among Latino Immigrants.* Washington D.C., Smithsonian Institution, 1979.

Cohen, R.Y.: Mobilizing support for weight loss through work-site competitions. In Gottlieb, B.H. (Ed.): *Marshaling Social Support: Formats, Processes, and Effects.* Newbury Park, Sage, 1988, pp. 241–264.

Cohen, S.: The volatile solvents. *Public Health Reviews, 11*(2):185–200, 1973.

Cohen, S.: Inhalants and solvents. In Beschner, G. and Friendman, A. (Eds.): *Youth Drug Abuse: Problems, Issues and Treatment.* Lexington, Lexington Books, 1979.

Cohen, S., Lichtenstein, E., Mermelstein, R., Kingsolver, K., Baer, J. S., and Kamarack, T. W.: Social support interventions for smoking cessation. In Gottlieb, B.H. (Ed.): *Marshaling Social Support: Formats, Processes, and Effects.* Newbury Park, Sage, 1988, pp. 211–240.

Cohen, S., and Syme, S. L.: *Social Support and Health.* Orlando, Academic Press, 1985.

Cohen, S., and Wills, T.A.: Stress, social support, and the buffering hypothesis. *Psychological Bulletin, 98,* 310–357, 1985.

Coleman, A.F.: How to Enlist the Family as an Ally. *American Journal of Drug and Alcohol Abuse.* *3:*167–173, 1976.

Collins, J. and Mardsen, M.: *Validity of self reports of drug use among arrestees.* Research Triangle Institute. Unpublished manuscript, 1990.

Cooper, E.J. and Cento, M: Group and the Hispanic prenatal patient. *American Journal of Orthopsychiatry, 47:*689–700, 1977.

Corliss, L.: A review of the evidence on glue sniffing—A persistent problem. *Journal of School Health, 35*(10):442–449, 1965.

COSSMHO: *AIDS: A Guide for Hispanic Leadership.* Washington, D.C., The National Coalition of Hispanic Health and Human Services Organizations, 1989.

Costello, Raymond M.: Hispanic alcoholic treatment considerations. *Hispanic Journal of the Behavioral Sciences,* 9(1):83–89, 1987.

Cox, T.: *Stress.* Baltimore, University Park Press, 1978.

Coyne, J.C., Wortman, C. B., and Lehman, D. R.: The other side of support: Emotional overinvolvement and miscarried helping. In Gottlieb, B.H. (Ed.): *Marshaling Social Support: Formats, Processes, and Effects.* Newbury Park, Sage, 1988, pp. 305–330.

Crites, J. and Schuckitt, M.: Solvent misuse in adolescents at a community alcohol center. *Journal of Clinical Psychiatry, 40:*39–43, 1979.

D'Augelli, A.R., Vallance, T.R., Danish, S. J., Young, C.E., and Gerdes, J. L.: The community helpers project: A description of a prevention strategy for rural communities. *Journal of Prevention, 1:*209–224, 1981.

Davis, D.I.: Family Therapy for the Drug Abuser: Conceptual and Practical Considerations. *Drug Forum, 6:*197–199, 1977–1978.

Dawson, D.A., and Hardy, A.M.: AIDS knowledge and attitudes of Hispanic Americans: Provisional data from the 1988 Health Interview Survey. *Advance Data from Vital and Health Statistics,* 166, Hyattsville, MD., Public Health Service, 1988.

De Barona, M. and Simpson, D.: Inhalant users in drug abuse prevention programs. *American Journal of Drug and Alcohol Abuse,* 10(4):503–518, 1984.

De La Cancela, V.: Minority AIDS prevention: Moving beyond cultural perspectives towards sociopolitical empowerment. *AIDS Education and Prevention,* 1(2):141–153, 1989.

De La Rosa, Mario: Natural support systems of Puerto Ricans: A key dimension of well being. *Health and Social Work, 13:*181–190, 1988.

De la Rosa, Mario: Patterns and consequences of illegal drug use among Hispanics. In Sotomayor, Marta (Ed.): *Empowering Hispanic Families: A Critical Issue for the '90s.* Milwaukee, Family Service America, 1991.

De La Rosa, Mario, Khalsa, J.H. and Rouse, Beatrice A.: Hispanics and illicit drug use: a review of recent findings. *The International Journal of the Addictions, 26:*665–691, 1990.

De La Rosa, Mario R., Lambert, E., and Gropper, B.: Introduction: Exploring the drug use and violence connection, pp. 1–8. In De La Rosa, M.R., Lambert, E., and Gropper, B. (Eds.): *Drugs and Violence: Causes, Correlates, and Consequences.* NIDA Research Monograph 103. Rockville, Maryland, 1990.

Delgado, Melvin: Hispanic cultural values: Implications for groups. *Small Group Behavior, 12:*69–80, 1981.

Delgado, Melvin: Hispanics and psychotherapeutic groups: Issues and approaches for group leaders. *Journal of Group Psychotherapy, 33:*507–520, 1983.

Delgado, Melvin: Groups in Puerto Rican Spiritism: Implications for Clinicians. In Jacobs, Carolyn, and Bowles, Dorcas D. (Eds.): *Ethnicity and Race: Critical Concepts in Social Work.* Silver Spring, National Association of Social Workers, 1988.

Delgado, Melvin and Humm-Delgado, Denise: Natural support systems: A source of strength in Hispanic communities. *Social Work, 27:*83–89, 1982.

Delgado, Melvin and Humm-Delgado, Denise: Hispanics and group work: A review of the literature. *Social Work with Groups, 7:*85–96, 1984.

Delgado, Melvin and Rodriguez-Andrew, Sylvia: *Alcohol and Other Drug Use Among Hispanic Youth.* OSAP Technical Report 4. Rockville, MD., US Government Printing Office, 1990.

Delgado, Melvin and Rodriguez-Andrew, Sylvia: *Hispanic adolescents and substance abuse.* Washington, DC., United States Government Printing Office, forthcoming.

Delgado, Melvin, and Siff, Shirley: A Hispanic adolescent group in a public school setting: An interagency approach. *Social Work and Groups, 3:*73–85, 1980.

Dembo, R., Pilaro, L., Burgos, W., Des Jarlais, D., and Schmeidler, J.: Self-concept and drug involvement among urban junior high school youths. *International Journal of the Addictions, 14*(8):1125–1144, 1979.

Des Jarlais, D.C., and Friedman, S.R.: HIV and intravenous use. *AIDS, 2*(Supplement 1):S65–S69, 1988.

Des Jarlais, D.C., Friedman, S.R., and Stoneburner, R.L.: HIV infection and intravenous drug use: Critical issues in transmission dynamics, infection outcomes, and prevention. *Review of Infectious Diseases, 10:*151–158, 1988.

DiClemente, R.J., Boyer, B.C., and Morales, E.S.: Minorities and AIDS: Knowledge, attitudes, and misconceptions among Black and Latino adolescents. *American Journal of Public Health, 78:*55–57, 1988.

Dworkin, A. and Stephens, R.: Mexican American adolescent inhalant abuse: A proposed model. *Youth and Society, 11*(4):493–506, 1980.

Dyer, M.: Inhalant abusers: A neglected aspect in substance abuse treatment. *Grassroots,* 1–2, 1984.

Eden, Stanley and Aguilar, Robert: The Hispanic chemically dependent client: Considerations for diagnosis and treatment. In Lawson, Gary and Lawson, Ann W. (Eds.): *Alcoholism and Substance Abuse in Special Populations.* Rockville, Aspen, 1989.

Elliot, D., Huizinger, D., and Ageton, S.S.: *Explaining Delinquency and Drug Use.* Beverly Hills, Sage, 1985.

Engmann, D.: *Alcoholism and Alcohol Abuse Among the Spanish Speaking Population in California: A Needs and Services Assessment.* Sacrament, California Commission on Alcoholism for the Spanish Speaking, Inc., 1976.

Estrada, A., Rabow, J. and Watts, R.H.: Alcohol use among Hispanic adolescents: A preliminary report. *Hispanic Journal of Behavioral Sciences, 4*(3):339–351, 1982.

Fagan, J. and Chin, K.: Violence as regulation and social control in the distribution of crack. In De La Rosa, M.R., Lambert, E., and Gropper, B. (Eds.): *Drugs and Violence: Causes, Correlates and Consequences.* NIDA Research Monograph 103. Rockville, Maryland, National Institute of Drug Abuse, 1990, pp. 9–44.

Fairbank, Gregman, and Baullin, Inc.: *Report on a Baseline Survey of AIDS Risk Behaviors and Attitudes in San Francisco's Latino Communities.* San Francisco: Fairbank, Bregman and Maullin, 1987.

Falicov, C.J.: Mexican families. In M. McGoldrick, J.K. Pearce, and J. Groidans (Eds.): *Ethnicity and Family Therapy.* New York, Guilford, 1982, pp. 134–163.

Farber, Anne and Rogler, Lloyd H.: *Unitas: Hispanic and Black Children in a Healing Community.* New York, Fordham University Hispanic Research Center, 1981.

Farrington, D.P.: The family backgrounds of aggressive youths. In L.A. Hersov, M. Berger, and D. Shaffer (Eds.): *Aggression and Anti-Social Behavior in Childhood and Adolescence.* Oxford, Pergamon, 1978.

Fimbres, M.F. and McKay, E.G.: *Getting Started: Becoming Part of the AIDS Solution. A Guide for Hispanic Community-based Organizations.* Washington, D.C., National Council of La Raza, 1989.

Finch, J.F., Okun, M.A., Barrera, Manuel, Jr., Zautra, A.J., and Reich, J.W.: Positive and negative social ties among older adults: Measurement models and the prediction of psychological distress and well-being. *American Journal of Community Psychology, 17:*585–605, 1989.

Fitzpatrick, J.: Drugs and Puerto Ricans in New York City. In Glick, Ronald and Moore, Joan (Eds.): *Drugs in Hispanic Communities.* New Brunswick, Rutgers University Press, 1990.

Fleming, R., Baum, A., and Singer, J.E.: Toward an integrative approach to the study of stress. *Journal of Personality and Social Psychology, 46*(4):939–949, 1984.

Foy, D.W., Sipprelle, R.C., Rueger, D.B., and Carroll, E.M.: Etiology of posttraumatic stress disorder in Vietnam veterans: Analysis of promilitary, military and combat exposure influences. *Journal of Consulting and Clinical Psychology, 52*(1):79–87, 1984.

Frias, G.: *Barrio Warriors: Homeboys of Peace.* Los Angeles, California, Diaz Publications, 1982.

Friedman, Samuel R., Sufian, Meryl, and Des Jarlais, Don C.: The AIDS epidemic among Latino intravenous drug users. In Glick, Ronald and Moore, Joan (Eds.): *Drugs in Hispanic Communities.* New Brunswick, Rutgers University Press, 1990.

Fullerton, H.N. Jr.: New labor force projections, spanning 1988 to 2000. *Monthly Labor Review, 112* (11):3–12, 1989.

Gandossy, R.P., Williams, J., Cohen, J., and Harwood, H.: *Drugs and Crime: A Survey and Analysis of the Literature.* Washington, D.C., National Institute of Justice, 1980.

Garmezy, N.: Children under stress: Perspectives on antecedents and correlates of vulnerability and resistance to psychopathology. In Rabin, A.I., Aronoff, J., Barclay, A.M. and Zucker, R.A. (Eds.): *Further Explorations in Personality.* New York, Wiley, 1981.

Garmezy, N.: Stressors of childhood. In N. Garmezy and M. Rutter (Eds.): *Stress, Coping and Development in Children.* New York, McGraw-Hill, 1983.

Gibson, M.A.: *Accommodation Without Assimilation: Sikh Immigrants in an American High School.* New York, Cornell Publications, 1988.

Gilbert, M. Jean: *Social Epidemiological Factors Underlying Contrasts in Mexican American and Anglo American Blue- and White-Collar Drinking Patterns.* Paper presented at the Annual Meeting of the American Anthropological Association, Denver, 1984.

Gilbert, M. Jean: Mexican-Americans in California: Intracultural variations in attitudes and behavior related to alcohol. In Bennett, Linda A. and Ames, Genevieve M. (Eds.): *The American Experience with Alcohol: Contrasting Cultural Perspectives.* New York, Plenum, 1985, pp. 255–277.

Gilbert, M. Jean: Alcohol consumption patterns in immigrant and later generation Mexican American women. *Hispanic Journal of the Behavioral Sciences, 9*(3):299–313, 1987a.

Gilbert, M. Jean: Programmatic approaches to the alcohol-related needs of Mexican Americans. In Gilbert, M. Jean and Cervantes, Richard (Eds.): *Mexican Americans and alcohol.* Los Angeles, Spanish Speaking Mental Health Research Center, University of California, 1987b.

Gilbert, M. Jean: Alcohol-related practices, problems and norms among Mexican-Americans: An overview. In National Institute on Alcohol Abuse and Alcoholism Monograph #18, *Alcohol Use Among U.S. Ethnic Minorities.* Washington, D.C., U.S. Government Printing Office, 1989a, pp. 115–134.

Gilbert, M. Jean: Hispanic Americans: Alcohol use, abuse and adverse consequences. In Watts, T.D. and Wright, R. (Eds.): *Alcoholism in Minority Populations.* Springfield, Thomas, 1989b, pp. 55–75.

Gilbert, M. Jean and Alcocer, Anthony M.: Alcohol use and Hispanic youth: An overview. *Journal of Drug Issues, 18:*26–39, 1988.

Gilbert, M. Jean and Cervantes, Richard C.: Alcohol services for Mexican Americans: A review of utilization patterns, treatment considerations, and prevention activities. *Hispanic Journal of Behavioral Sciences, 8*(3):191–223, 1986a.

Gilbert, M. Jean, and Cervantes, Richard C.: Patterns and practices of alcohol use among Mexican Americans: A comprehensive review. *Hispanic Journal of Behavioral Sciences, 8:*1–60, 1986b.

Gilbert, M. Jean and Gonsalves, Ricardo: *The Social Context of Mexican and Mexican American Male Drinking Patterns.* Paper presented at the Annual Meetings of the American Anthropological Association, Washington, D.C., 1985.

Glasser, H. and Massengale, O.: Glue sniffing in children: Deliberate inhalation of vaporized plastic cement. *Journal of American Medical Association, 181*(4):300–303, 1962.

Glazer, N. and Moynihan, D.P.: *Beyond the Melting Pot.* Cambridge, Harvard-MIT Press, 1963.

Glick, Ronald and Moore, Joan (Eds.): *Drugs in Hispanic Communities.* New Brunswick, Rutgers University Press, 1990.

Goldenberg, I., and Goldenberg, H.: *Family Therapy: An Overview.* Monterey, Brooks/Cole, 1980.

Goldstein, P.J.: *Drugs and Violent Crimes.* Paper presented at a workshop on drugs and crime. Available from Committee on Research on Law Enforcement and the Administration of Justice, Washington, D.C., 1986.

Goldstein, P.J. and Brownstein, H.: *Drug-Related Crime Analysis — Homicide: Executive Summary.* Report to the National Institute of Justice. Washington, D.C., 1987.

Gordon, A.J.: Alcohol and Hispanics in the Northeast: A study of cultural variability and adaptation. In Bennett, Linda A. and Ames, Genevieve M. (Eds.): *The American Experience With Alcohol: Contrasting Cultural Perspectives.* New York, Plenum, 1985, pp. 297–313.

Gossett, J., Lewis, J., and Phillips, V.: Extent and prevalence of illicit drug use as reported by 56,745 students. *Journal of the American Medical Association, 216:* 1464–1470, 1971.

Gottlieb, Benjamin H. (Ed.): *Social Networks and Social Support.* Beverly Hills, CA., Sage, 1981.

Gottlieb, Benjamin H. (Ed.): *Social Support Strategies: Guidelines for Mental Health Practice.* Beverly Hills, CA., Sage, 1983.

Gottlieb, Benjamin H. (Ed.): *Marshaling Social Support.* Newbury Park, CA., Sage, 1988.

Governor's Task Force on Inhalant Abuse. Austin, Texas Department of Community Affairs, 1984.

Grebler, L, Moore, Joan W., and Guzman, R.C.: *The Mexican-American People.* New York, Free Press, 1970.

Green, C.P.: Assessment of family stress. *Journal of Advanced Nursing, 7:* 11–17, 1982.

Green, J.: Overview of adolescent drug use. In Beschner, G.M. and Friedman, A.S. (Eds.): *Youth Drug Abuse.* Lexington, D.C. Heath, 1979.

Greer, J.: Adolescent abuse of typewriter correction fluid. *Southern Medical Journal, 77*(3):297–298, 301, 1984.

Griffith, J.: *Psychological Impairment Among Mexican Americans and Their Need for Mental Health Services.* Unpublished manuscript, 1983.

Griffith, J., and Villavicencio, S.: Relationships among acculturation, sociodemographic characteristics and social supports in Mexican American adults. *Hispanic Journal of Behavioral Sciences, 7:* 75–92, 1985.

Gropper, B.: *Probing the Links Between Drugs and Crime.* Washington, D.C., National Institute of Justice, 1985.

Gross, J.: Bleak lives: Women carrying AIDS. *The New York Times,* p. 1, August 27, 1987.

Guinn, R.: Alcohol use among Mexican-American youth. *Journal of School Health, 38*(2):90–91, 1978.

Guinn, R. and Hurley, R.S.: Comparison of drug use among Houston and Lower Rio Grande Valley secondary students. *Adolescence, 11*(43):455–459, 1976.

Gutierrez, Lorraine, Ortega, Robert M., and Suarez, Zulema E.: Self-help and the Latino Community. In Powell, Thomas J. (Ed.): *Working with Self-Help.* Silver Spring, National Association of Social Workers, 1990.

Haberman, P.W.: Denial of Drinking in a Household Survey. *Quarterly Journal of Studies on Alcohol, 31*(3):710–717, 1970.

Haberman, P.W.: Alcoholism indicators among Hispanics in New York State. *Hispanic Bulletin, 9*(2):1–7, 1986.

Hanson, C.L., Henggeler, S.W., Haefele, W.F., et al.: Demographic, individual, and family relationship correlates of serious and repeated crime among adolescents and their siblings. *Journal of Consulting and Clinical Psychology, 52:*523–538, 1984.

Hansen, D.A., and Johnson, V.A.: Rethinking family stress theory: Definitional aspects. In Burr, W.R., Hill, R., Nye, F.I. and Reiss, I.L. (Eds.): *Contemporary Theories About the Family.* New York, Free Press, 1979, Vol. 1.

Hansen, W.B., Graham, J.W., Sobel, J.L., Shelton, D. R., Flay, B.R., and Johnson, C.A.: The consistency of peer and parent influences on tobacco, alcohol and marijuana use among young adolescents. *Journal of Behavioral Medicine, 10:*559–579, 1987.

Hansen, W.B., Malotte, C.K., Collins, L., Fielding, J.E.: Dimensions and psychosocial correlates of adolescent alcohol use. *Journal of Alcohol and Drug Education, 32:*19–31, 1987.

Harrel, A. and Lisn, H.: *Drug Abuse in Rural America.* Rockville, MD., US Government Printing Office, 1981.

Hatch, J.P., Bierner, S.M., and Fisher, J.G.: The effects of smoking and cigarette nicotine content on smokers' preparation and performance of a psychosocially stressful task. *Journal of Behavioral Medicine, 6*(2):207–216, 1983.

Hecht, A.: Inhalants: Quick route to danger. *FDA Consumer,* Rockville, MD., U.S. Dept of Health and Human Services, 1980.

Heiligman, A.: A survey of drug use in a rural Minnesota senior high school. *Drug Forum, 2*(2):173–177, 1973.

Hendin, H., Pollinger, A., Ulman, R., and Carr, A.C.: *Adolescent Marijuana Abusers and Their Families.* NIDA Research Monograph 40, Washington, D.C., U.S. Printing Office, 1981.

Hernandez, A.: *Immigrant Status Children and Stress.* Unpublished manuscript, 1984.

Hershberg, Theodore: Free Blacks in antebellum Philadelphia: A study of ex-slaves, freeborn, and socioeconomic decline. In Colby, Ira C. (Ed.): *Social Welfare Policy: Perspectives, Patterns, and Insights.* Chicago, Dorsey, 1989.

Hetherington, E.M. and Martin, B.: Family interaction. In Quay, H.C. and Werry, J.S. (Eds.): *Psychopathological Disorders in Childhood.* New York, Wiley, 1979.

Hill, Reuben: *Families Under Stress.* New York, Harper, 1949.

Hirschi, T.: *Causes of Delinquency.* Berkeley, University of California Press, 1969.

Hofstede, G.: *Culture's Consequences.* Beverly Hills, Sage, 1980.

Holck, S.E., Warren, C., Smith, J. and Rochat, R.: Alcohol Consumption among Mexican American and Anglo women: Results of a survey along the U.S. Mexico border. *Journal of Studies on Alcohol, 45*(2):149–154, 1984.

Holmes, T.H., and Rahe, R.H.: The social readjustment rating scale. *Journal of Psychosomatic Research, 11:*213–218, 1967.

Honey, Ellen: AIDS and the inner city: Critical issues. *Social Casework, 69:*365–370, 1988.

Hoppe, S.K. and Heller, P.L.: Alienation, familism, and the utilization of health services by Mexican Americans. *Journal of Health and Social Behavior, 16*(3):304–314, 1975.

House, J.S.: *Work Stress and Social Support.* Reading, Addison-Wesley, 1981.

House, J.S., Umberson, D., and Landis, K.R.: Structures and processes of social support. *Annual Review of Sociology, 14:*293–318, 1988.

Hser, Y., Anglin, M.D., and Mcglothlin, W.H.: Sex differences in addict careers, 1. Initiation of use. *American Journal of Drug and Alcohol Abuse, 13:*33–57, 1987.

Huba, G.J., Wingard, J.A., and Bentler, P.M.: Framework for an interactive theory of drug use. In Lettieri, D.J. Sayers, M. and Pearson, H.W. (Eds.): *Theories on Drug Abuse: Selected Contemporary Perspectives.* NIDA Research Monograph #30. Rockville, MD., NIDA, 1980, pp. 95–101.

Hynes, Kathleen and Werbin, Jorge: Group psychotherapy for Spanish-speaking women. *Psychiatric Annals, 7:*52–63, 1977.

Inciardi J.: Personal communication, July 15, 1989.

Inciardi, J. and Pottieger, A.E.: Kids, crack and crime. *The Journal of Drug Issues, 21* (2):257–270, 1991.

Jackson, N., Carlisi, J., Greenway, C. and Zalesnick, M.: Age of initial drug experimentation among White and Non-White ethnics. *The International Journal of the Addictions, 16*(8):1373–1386, 1981.

Jackson, R., Thornhill, E. and Gonzales, R.: Glue sniffing–brief flight from reality. *Journal of the Louisiana State Medical Society, 119*(11):451–454, 1967.

Jessor, R.: *Adolescent Problem Drinking: Psychosocial Aspects and Developmental Outcomes.* Paper presented at the Alcohol Research Seminar, NIDA, 1983.

Jessor, R. and Jessor, S.L.: *Problem Behavior and Psychosocial Development: A Longitudinal Study of Youth.* New York, Academic Press, 1977.

Jessor, R., and Jessor, S.L.: A social-psychological framework for studying drug use. In Lettieri, D.J., Sayers, M. and Pearson, H.W. (Eds.): *Theories on Drug Abuse: Selected Contemporary Perspectives.* NIDA Research Monograph #30. Rockville, MD., NIDA, 1980, pp. 102–109.

Johnson, B.: Toward a theory of drug subcultures. In Lettieri, D., Sayers, M. and Pearson, H.W. (Eds.): *Theories on Drug Abuse: Selected Contemporary Perspectives.* Washington D.C., USGPO, 1980.

Johnson, Elaine M. and Delgado, Jane L.: Reaching Hispanics with messages to prevent alcohol and other drug abuse. *Public Health Reports, 104*(6):588–594, 1989.

Johnson, L.V. and Matre, M.: Anomie and alcohol use: Drinking patterns in Mexican American and Anglo neighborhoods. *Journal of Studies on Alcohol, 39*(5):894–902, 1978.

Johnston, L., Bachman, J., and O'Malley, P.: Monitoring the future survey: 1989 National High School Senior Drug Abuse Survey. Paper released at February 13, 1990 press conference. Rockville, MD., U.S. Department of Health and Human Services, 1990.

Johnston, L., O'Malley, P., and Bachman, J.: *Drug Use, Drinking and Smoking: National Survey Results from High School, College, and Young Adult Populations 1975-1988.* Rockville, MD., National Institute on Drug Abuse, 1989.

Jorquez, J.S.: Heroin Use in the barrio: Solving the problem of relapse or keeping the tecato gusano asleep. *American Journal of Drug and Alcohol Abuse, 13:*63–74, 1984.

Kahn, Arleen and Bender, Eugene I.: Self-help groups as a crucible for people empowerment in the context of social development. *Social Development Issues, 9:*4–13, 1985.

Kandel, D.: Stages in adolescent involvement in drug use. *Science, 190*(28):912–914, 1975.

Kandel, D., Single, E. and Kessler, R.C.: The epidemiology of drug use among New York State high school students: Distribution, trends, and change in rates of use. *American Journal of Public Health, 66*(1):43–53, 1976.

Kandel, D.B., Kessler, R.C., and Margulies, R.Z.: Antecedents of adolescent initiation into stages of drug use: A developmental analysis. In Kandel, D. H. (Ed.): *Longitudinal Research on Drug Use: Empirical Findings and Methodological Issues.* New York, Wiley, 1978.

Katz, A. and Bender, Eugene I.: *The Strengths in Us: Self-Help in the Modern World.* New York, Franklin Watts, 1976.

Kazdin, A.E.: *Conduct Disorders in Childhood and Adolescence.* Newbury Park, Sage, 1987.

Keefe, Susan E., and Padilla, Amado M.: *Chicano Ethnicity.* Albuquerque, University of New Mexico Press, 1987.

Keefe, Susan E., Padilla, Amado, M., and Carlos, M.L.: The Mexican American extended family as an emotional support system. In Casas, J.M. and Keefe, Susan E. (Eds.): *Family and Mental Health in the Mexican American Community, Monograph #7.* Los Angeles, Spanish Speaking Mental Health Research Center, UCLA, 1978, pp. 49–67.

Kessler, R.C., Price, R.H., and Wortman, C.B.: Social factors in psychopathology: Stress, social support, and coping processes. *Annual Review of Psychology, 36:*531–572, 1985.

Klastsky, A.L. et al.: Racial patterns of alcoholic beverage use. *Alcoholism: Clinical and Experimental Research, 7*(4):372–377, 1983.

Kneilser, T. and Heller, H.M.: *Therapeutic communities and arrests: A preliminary analysis of arrests before and after treatment,* 1974. New York City Addiction Services Agency, Department of Research and Evaluation, as cited in Reed, 1978.

Korman, M.: A psycho-social and neurological study of young inhalant users. Unpublished paper. University of Texas Health Science Center, Dallas, TX, 1977.

Korman, M., Trimboli, F. and Semler, I.: A comparative evaluation of 162 inhalant users. *Addictive Behaviors, 5:*143–152, 1980.

Kosterlitz, Julie: "Us," "Them" and AIDS. *National Journal,* 7-2-88, 1738–1742.

Kotler, Philip and Andreasen, Alan R.: *Strategic Marketing for Nonprofit Organizations* (3rd Ed.). Englewood Cliffs, Prentice-Hall, 1987.

Kozel, N.J. and Dupont, R.L.: Narcotics and crime. *International Journal of the Addictions, 7:*443–450, 1972.

Kraidman, Meri: Group therapy with Spanish-speaking clinic patients to enhance ego functioning. *Group, 4:*59–64, 1980.

Kumpfer, K.L.: Family functioning factors associated with delinquency. In K. L. Kumpfer (Ed.): *Effective Parenting Strategies Literature Review,* In Press.

Kumpfer, K.L., and DeMarsh, J.: Genetic and family environmental influences on children of drug abusers. *Journal of Children in Contemporary Society, 3*(4), 1985.

Kumpfer, K.L., Whiteside, H.O. and Jensen, J.: Impact of structural factors on family functioning. In Kumpfer, K. L. (Ed.), *Effective Parenting Strategies Literature Review,* in press.

Lang, Alan R.: Psychosocial factors in drinking performance and stress. In Pohorecky, Larissa A. and Brick, John (Eds.): *Stress and Alcohol Use.* New York, Elsevier, 1983, pp. 229–248.

Laredo Times, July 3, 1989.

Lazarus, R.S., and Folkman, S.: *Stress, Appraisal, and Coping.* New York, Springer, 1984.

Leon, Ana M., Mazur, Rosaleen, Motalvo, Elba, and Rodriguez, Miriam: Self-help support group for Hispanic mothers. *Child Welfare, 63:*261–268, 1984.

Levy, L.: Drug use on campus: Prevalence and social characteristics of collegiate drug users on campuses of the University of Illinois. *Drug Forum, 2*(2):141–171, 1973.

Lewis, C.E., Siegel, J.M., and Lewis, M.A.: Feeling bad: Exploring sources of distress among preadolescent children. *American Journal of Public Health, 74:*117–122, 1986.

Lieberman, Morton A., Borman, Leonard, D., and Associates: *Self-Help Groups for Coping with Crisis.* San Francisco, Jossey-Bass, 1979.

Litwak, E.: Complementary roles for formal and informal support groups: A study of nursing homes and mortality rates. *Journal of Applied Behavioral Science, 21:*407–425, 1985.

Loeber, R. and Dishion, T.J.: Boys who fight at home and school: Family conditions influencing cross-setting consistency. *Journal of Consulting and Clinical Psychology, 52:*759–768, 1984.

Long, G.L. and Demares, R.G.: Indicators of criminality during treatment for drug abuse. *American Journal of Drug and Alcohol Abuse, 2:*123–136, 1975.

Long, John M.: Drug use patterns in two Los Angeles barrio gangs. In Glick, Ronald and Moore, Joan (Eds.): *Drugs in Hispanic Communities.* New Brunswick, Rutgers University Press, 1990.

Lowenstein, L.: Glue sniffing and substance abuse: A tragic social phenomenon. *Contemporary Review, 224*(1421):309–313, 1984.

Lusero, G.: *Alcoholics Anonymous in a Chicano Community: An Analysis of Affiliation and Transferability.* Doctoral Dissertation, Brandeis University, 1977.

MacAndrew, Craig and Edgerton, Robert B.: *Drunken Comportment: A Social Explanation.* New York, Aldine, 1969.

Maddahian, E., Newcomb, M.D. and Bentler, P.M.: Single and multiple patterns of adolescent substance use: Longitudinal comparisons of four ethnic groups. *Journal of Drug Education, 15*(4):311–326, 1985.

Maddux, J. and Desmond, D.P.: *Careers of Opiod Users.* New York, Praeger, 1981.

Maddux, J.F. and McDonald, L.K.: Status of 100 San Antonio addicts one year after admission to methadone maintenance. *Drug Forum, 2:*239–252, 1973.

Maguire, Lambert: Natural helping networks and self-help groups. In Nobel, Milton (Ed.): *Primary Prevention in Mental Health and Social Work.* New York, Council on Social Work Education, 1981.

Malgady, R.G., Rogler, Lloyd H., and Costantino, G.: Culturally sensitive psychotherapy for Puerto Rican children and adolescents: a program of treatment outcome research, *Journal of Consulting and Clinical Psychology, 58*(6):704–712, 1990.

Manov, A. and Lowther L.A.: Health care approach for hard-to-reach adolescent runaways. *Nursing Clinics of North America, 18:*333–342, 1983.

Maril, R.L. and Zavaleta, A.N.: Drinking patterns of low-income Mexican-American women. *Journal of Studies on Alcohol, 40*(5):480–484, 1979.

Marin, Barbara Vanoss: Hispanic culture: Implications for AIDS prevention. In Boswell, J., Hexter, R. and Reinisch, J. (Eds.): *Sexuality and Disease: Metaphors, Perceptions and Behavior in the AIDS Era.* New York, Oxford University Press, 1989.

Marin, Barbara Vanoss: Drug abuse treatment for Hispanics: A culturally appropriate, community-oriented approach. In Watson, R.R. (Ed.): *Prevention and Treatment of Drug and Alcohol Abuse.* Humana Press, 1990.

Marin, Gerardo: AIDS prevention among Hispanics: Needs, risk behaviors, and cultural values. *Public Health Reports, 104*(5):411–415, 1989.

Marin, Barbara Vanoss, and Marin, Gerardo: *Information about Human Immunodeficiency Virus in Hispanics in San Francisco.* San Francisco, University of California, Center for AIDS Prevention Studies. Technical Report #4, 1989.

Marin, Barbara Vanoss, and Marin, Gerardo: Effects of acculturation on knowledge of AIDS and HIV among Hispanics. *Hispanic Journal of Behavioral Sciences, 12:*110–121, 1990.

Marin, Barbara Vanoss, Marin, Gerardo, and Juarez, R.: Differences between Hispanic and non-Hispanics in willingness to provide AIDS prevention advice. *Hispanic Journal of Behavioral of Behavioral Science, 12*(2):153–164, 1990.

Marin, Gerardo, Sabogal, F., Marin, Barbara Vanoss, Otero-Sabogal, R. and Perez-Stable, F.: Development of a short acculturation scale for Hispanics. *Hispanic Journal of Behavioral Science, 9:*183–205, 1987.

Marin, Gerardo and Triandis, II. C.: Allocentrism as a cultural characteristic of Hispanics and Latin Americans. In Diaz-Guerrero, R. (Ed.): *Cross-Cultural and National Studies in Social Psychology.* Amsterdam, Elsevier, 1985.

Markides, K.S. and Krause, N.: Alcohol consumption in three generations of Mexicans: The influence of marital satisfaction, sex-role orientation and acculturation. In Foster, B. and Salloway, J. (Eds.): *Chemical Bonds: The Socio-cultural Matrix of Alcohol and Drug Abuse.* New York, Wadsworth, 1987.

Markides, K.S., Krause, N. and Mendes de Leon, C.: Acculturation and alcohol consumption among Mexican Americans: A three generation study. *American Journal of Public Health, 78*(9):1178–1181, 1988.

Marlatt, Alan: Alcohol, expectancy and emotional states. How drinking patterns may be affected by beliefs about alcohol. *Alcohol Health and Research World, 11*(4):10–18, 1987.

Martinez, Cervando: Group process and the Chicano: Clinical issues. *International Journal of Group Therapy, 27:*225–231, 1977.

Mason, T.: *Inhalant use and treatment.* NIDA Services Research Monograph Series, Washington, DC., U.S. Government Printing Office, 1979.

Massengale, O., Glaser, H., LeLievere, R., Dodds, J., and Klock, M.: Physical and psychological factors in glue sniffing. *New England Journal of Medicine, 269:*1340–1344, 1963.

Mata, Alberto: *Inhalant Use in a Small Rural South Texas Community.* Testimony before the Governor's Task Force on Inhalant Abuse. San Antonio, TX, June, 1984.

Mata, Alberto G.: *Alcohol Use in a Small Rural South Texas Community: An Executive Summary.* A report to the Texas Commission on Alcoholism, Austin, Texas and the Frio County Alcohol Prevention Project, Pearsall, Texas. Austin, University of Texas at Austin, 1986.

Mata, Alberto and Jorquez, J.S.: Mexican-American intravenous drug users needle sharing practices: implications for AIDS prevention. (NIDA Research Monograph No. 80). Washington D.C., USGPO, 1988.

Mata, Alberto and Rodriguez-Andrew, Sylvia: Inhalant abuse in a small rural South Texas community. In Crider, R.A. and Rouse, Beatrice A. (Eds): *Epidemiology of Inhalant Abuse: An Update.* NIDA Research Monograph 85. Rockville, MD., US Government Printing Office, 1988.

Matute-Bianchi, M.E.: Ethnic identities and patterns of school success and failure among Mexican descent and Japanese-American students in a California high school: An ethnographic analysis. *American Journal of Education, 95*(1):233–255, 1986.

Mays, V.M., and Cochran, S.D.: Issues in the perception of AIDS risk and risk reduction activities by Black and Hispanic/Latina women. *American Psychologist, 43*(1):949–957, 1988.

McBride, D.C. and McCoy, C.B.: Crime and drug-using behavior. *Criminology, 19:*281–302, 1981.

McClintock, E., Bayard, M.P., and McClintock, C.G.: The socialization of social motivation in Mexican American families. In E.E. Garcia (Ed.): *The Mexican American Child: Language, Cognition, and Social Development.* Tempe, AZ., Center for Bilingual Education, Arizona State University, 1983, pp. 142–161.

McCubbin, H.I. and Figley, C.R.: *Coping with Normative Transitions—Vol. I.* New York, Brunner/Mazel, 1983.

McGough, Dixie P. and Hindman, Margaret H.: *A Guide to Planning Alcoholism Treatment.* Rockville, MD., National Institute on Alcohol Abuse and Alcoholism, Undated.

McGrath, J.: Methodological problems in research on stress. In Krohne, H. and Laux, L. (Eds.): *Achievement, Stress, and Anxiety.* Washington, D.C., Hemisphere, 1978.

McKay, E.: *The Changing Demographics of the Hispanic Family.* Washington, D.C., National Council of La Raza, 1987.

McKay, E.G.: *Changing Hispanic Demographics.* Washington, D.C., National Council of La Raza, 1988.

Meloff, W.: An exploratory study of adolescents glue sniffers. Doctoral dissertation. University of Colorado. *Dissertation Abstracts International,* 31(3-A):1391–1392, 1970.

Mendes de Leon, C.F. and Markides, K.S.: Alcohol consumption and physical symptoms in a Mexican American population. *Drug and Alcohol Dependence,* 16(4):369–379, 1986.

Menikoff, Alan: Long-term group psychotherapy of Puerto Rican women: Ethnicity as a clinical support. *Group, 3:*172–180, 1979.

Mensch, B.S. and Kandel, D.B.: Dropping out of high school and drug involvement. *Social Education, 61:*95–113, 1988.

Metcalfe, R.J.A., Dobson, C.B., Cook, A., and Michaud, A.: The construction, reliability and validity of stress inventory for children. *Educational Psychology,* 2(1):59–71, 1982.

Minuchin, Salvador: *Families and Family Therapy.* Cambridge, Harvard University Press, 1974.

Minuchin, Salvador and Fishman, H.C.: *Family Therapy Techniques.* Cambridge, Harvard University Press, 1981.

Mirowski, J., Ross, C.E.: Mexican culture and its emotional contradictions. *Journal of Health and Social Behavior, 25:*2–13, 1984.

Mizio, Emelicia: *Puerto Rican Task Force Report.* New York, Family Service Association of America, 1979.

Montiel, Miguel: The Chicano family: A review of research. *Social Work, 18*(2):22–23, 1973.

Moore, Joan W.: *Homeboys: Gangs, Drugs, and Prison in the Barrios of Los Angeles.* Philadelphia, Temple University Press, 1978.

Moore, Joan W.: Variation in violence in Hispanic gangs. In Kraus, J.F., Sorenson, S.B., and Juarez, P.D. (Eds.): *Research Conference on Violence and Homicide in Hispanic Communities,* Los Angeles, University of California, 1988, pp. 215–230.

Moore, Joan W.: Gangs, drugs and violence. In De La Rosa, M.R., Lambert, E., and Gropper, B. (Eds.): *Drugs and Violence: Causes, Correlates, and Consequences.* NIDA Research Monograph 103. Rockville, Maryland, 1990, pp. 160–176.

Moore, Joan W. and Mata, Alberto: *Women and heroin in Chicano communities.* Unpublished manuscript, 1981.

Moore, Joan W., Vigil, J.D. and Garcia, R.: Residence and territoriality in Chicano gangs. *Social Problems, 31:*182–194, 1983.

Morales, Armando: The Mexican-American gang member: Evaluation and treatment. In Becerra, R.M., Darno, M., and Escobar, J.I. (Eds.): *Mental Health and Hispanic Americans.* New York, Grune and Stratton, 1982, pp. 139–155.

Morales, Armando: Substance abuse and Mexican American youth: An overview. *Journal of Drug Issues, 14:*297–311, 1984.

Morgan, M., Wingard, D., and Felice, M.: Subcultural differences in alcohol use among youth. *Journal of Adolescent Health Care, 5:*191–195, 1984.

Morrisey, M.A. and Jensen, G.A.: Employer-sponsored insurance coverage for alcoholism and drug-abuse treatments. *Journal of Studies on Alcohol,* 49(5):456–461, 1988.

Moss N, and Hensleigh, P.: Substance use by Hispanic and white non-Hispanic pregnant adolescents: A preliminary survey. *Journal of Youth Adolescence, 17:*531–541, 1988.

Murillo, N.: The Mexican American family. In Wagner, N.N. and Haug, M.J. (Eds.): *Chicanos: Social and Psychological Perspectives.* St. Louis, C.V. Mosby, 1971, pp. 97–108.

Nader, P.R., Wexler, D.B. et al.: Comparison of beliefs about AIDS among urban, suburban, incarcerated, and gay adolescents. *Journal of Adolescent Health Care, 19:*413–418, 1989.

Nall, F.C., and Speilberg, J.: Social and cultural factors in the responses of Mexican Americans to medical treatment. *Journal of Health and Social Behavior, 8*(4):299–308, 1967.

Nash, Kermit B.: Self-help groups: An empowerment vehicle for sickle cell disease patients and their families. *Social Work with Groups, 12:*81–97, 1989.

National Center for Health Statistics: *Contraceptive use in the United States, 1982.* Data from the National Survey of Family Growth, Series 23, No. 12. Washington, D.C., U.S. Government Printing Office, 1986.

National Institute on Drug Abuse: *Services research report: An investigation of selected rural drug abuse programs.* NIDA–DHEW, Washington, D.C., U.S. Government Printing Office, 1977.

National Institute on Drug Abuse: *Demographic characteristics and patterns of drug use of clients admitted to drug abuse treatment facilities in selected States: Annual Data.* Rockville, MD., US Government Printing Office, 1985a.

National Institute on Drug Abuse: *National Household Survey on Drug Abuse: Population Estimates.* Rockville, MD., US Government Printing Office, 1985b.

National Institute on Drug Abuse: *Hispanic health and Nutrition and Examination Survey (HHANES): Use of selected drugs among Hispanics.* Rockville, MD., US Government Printing Office, 1987a.

National Institute of Drug Abuse: *Prevention Research: Deterring Drug Abuse Among Children and Adolescents.* Research Monograph no. 63., Washington, D.C., U.S. Government Printing Office, 1987b.

National Institute on Drug Abuse: *Use of selected drugs among Hispanics: Mexican-Americans, Puerto Ricans, and Cuban-Americans.* Washington, D.C., USGPO, 1987c.

National Institute on Drug Abuse: *Data from the national drug and alcoholism treatment utilization survey (NDATUS),* 1988.

National Institute on Drug Abuse, 1991.

Neff, James A.: Alcohol consumption and psychological distress among U.S. Anglos, Hispanics and Blacks. *Alcohol and Alcoholism, 21*(1):111–119, 1986.

Neff, James A., Hoppe, Sue Keir and Perea, Patricia: Acculturation and alcohol use: Drinking patterns and problems among Anglo and Mexican American male drinkers. *Hispanic Journal of the Behavioral Sciences, 9*(2):151–181, 1987.

New York Police Department: Homicide analysis. Crime Analysis Unit, New York, 1982.

Newcomb, M.D. and Bentler, P.M.: Substance use and ethnicity: Differential impact of peer and adult models. *Journal of Psychology, 120*(1):83–95, 1986.

Newsweek: Hour by hour: Crack, the junkies, the jailers, the pimps, and the tiniest addicts, pp. 64–65, November 28, 1988.

Nicholi, A.: The inhalants: An overview. *Psychosomatics, 24*(10):914–921, 1983.

Normand, William C., Iglesias, Juan, and Payn, Stephen: Brief group therapy to facilitate utilization of mental health services by Spanish-speaking patients. *American Journal of Orthopsychiatry, 44:*37–42, 1974.

Nurco, D.N., Ball, J.C., Shaffer, J.W., and Janlon, T.E.: The criminality of narcotics addicts. *Journal of Nervous Disorders and Mental Disease, 173:*94–102, 1985.

Nurco, D.N., Ball, J.C., Shaffer, J.W., Kinlock, T.W., and Lengrod, E.A.: Comparison by ethnic group and city of the criminal activities of narcotic addicts. *Journal Nervous Disorders and Mental Health, 174*(2):112–117, 1986.

Nurco, D.N., Kinlock, T.W., and Hanlon, T.: The drug-crime connection. In Inciardi, J. (Ed.): *Handbook on Drug Control in the United States.* Westport, Greenwood, in press.

Nuttal, R.L. and Nuttal, E.V.: A longitudinal study predicting heroin and alcohol use among young Puerto Ricans. In Schecter, A.S. (Ed.): *Drug Dependence and Alcoholism (Volume II): Social and Behavioral Issues.* New York, Plenum, 1981, pp. 819–831.

Nylander, I.: Thinner addiction in children and adolescents. *ACTA Psychiatry, 29*(9):273, 1962.

O'Donnell, J.A., and Clayton, R.R.: Determinants of early marijuana use. In Beschner, G.M. and Friedman, A.S. (Eds.): *Youth Drug Abuse.* Lexington, D.C. Heath, 1979.

Occupational injury and illness incidence rates by industry, United States. *Monthly Labor Review, 112*(11):138–139, Table 51, 1988.

Oetting, E.R., Edwards, R.W., and Beauvais, F.: Social and psychological factors underlying inhalant abuse. In Crider, R.A. and Rouse, B.A. (Eds.): *Epidemiology of Inhalant Abuse: An Update.* NIDA Research Monograph 85, Rockville, MD., NIDA, 1988, pp. 172–203.

Office of Substance Abuse Prevention: *Alcohol and Other Drug Use Among Hispanic Youth.* Technical Report #4, Rockville, Maryland, National Institute of Drug Abuse, 1990.

Olarte, Silvia W. and Masnik, Ruth: Benefits of long-term group therapy for disadvantaged Hispanic outpatients. *Hospital and Community Psychiatry, 36:*1093–1097, 1985.

Oxley, D., Barrera, Manuel, Jr., and Sadalla, E.K.: Relationships among community size, mediators, and social support variables: A path analytic approach. *American Journal of Community Psychology, 9:*637–651, 1981.

Padilla, Amado M., Cervantes, Richard C., and Maldonado, M.: *Psychosocial Stress in Mexican Immigrant Adolescents.* (Unpublished manuscript), 1988.

Padilla, Amado M., Cervantes, Richard C., Maldonado, M., and Garcia, R.E.:

Coping responses to psychosocial stressors among Mexican and Central American immigrants. *Journal of Community Psychology, 16:*418–427, 1988.

Padilla, Amado M., Salgado de Snyder, Nelly S., Cervantes, Richard C., and Baezconde-Garbanati, L.: Self-regulation and risk-taking behavior: Hispanic perspectives. In Lipsett, Lewis P. and Mitrick, Leonard L. (Eds.): *Self-Regulation, Impulsivity, and Risk-taking Behavior: Causes and Consequences.* Norwood, Albex (in press).

Padilla, E., Padilla, A., Morales, A., Olmedo, E., and Ramirez, R.: Inhalant, marijuana and alcohol abuse among barrio children and adolescents. *International Journal of the Addictions, 14*(7):945–964, 1979.

Padilla, E.R., Padilla, A., Ramirez, R., Morales, A. and Olmedo, E.L.: *Inhalant, Marijuana and Alcohol Abuse Among Barrio Children and Adolescents* (Occasional paper No. 4). Los Angeles, Spanish Speaking Mental Health Research Center, UCLA, 1977.

Padilla, F.: *Latino Ethnic Consciousness: The Case of Mexican Americans and Puerto Ricans in Chicago.* Notre Dame, Notre Dame University Press, 1985.

Page, J.B.: Cuban drug users in Miami. In Glick, Ronald and Moore, Joan (Eds.): *Drugs in Hispanic Communities.* New Brunswick, Rutgers University Press, 1990.

Page, J.B., Rio, L., Sweeney, L. and McKay, C.: Alcohol and adaption to exile in Miami's Cuban population. In Bennett, L. and Ames, G. (Eds.): *The American Experience With Alcohol: Contrasting Cultural Perspectives,* New York, Plenum, 1985, pp. 315–332.

Paine, H.J.: Attitudes and patterns of alcohol use among Mexican Americans. *Quarterly Journal of Studies on Alcoholism, 38:*544–554, 1977.

Patterson, G.R.: *Coercive family process.* Eugene, Castalia, 1982.

Pearlin, L.I., and Schooler, C.: The structure of coping. *Journal of Health and Social Behavior, 19:*2–21, 1978.

Perez, R.: Effects of stress, social support and coping style on adjustment to pregnancy among Hispanic women. *Hispanic Journal of Behavioral Sciences, 5*(2):141–161, 1983.

Perez, R., Padilla, A., Ramirez, A., Ramirez, R. and Rodriguez, M.: *Correlates and Changes Over Time in Drug and Alcohol Use Within a Barrio Population* (Occasional paper No. 9). Los Angeles, Spanish Speaking Mental Health Research Center, UCLA, 1979.

Perez, R., Padilla, A., Ramirez, A., Ramirez, R. and Rodriguez, M.: Correlates and changes over time in drug and alcohol use within a barrio population. *Journal of Community Psychology, 8:*621–638, 1980.

Pointer, J.: Typewriter correction fluid inhalation: A new substance of abuse. *Journal of Toxicology Clinical Toxicology, 19*(5):493–499, 1982.

Pomales, J. and Williams, V.: Effects of level of acculturation and counseling style on Hispanic students' perceptions of counselor. *Journal of Consulting Psychology, 36*(1):79–83, 1989.

Ponce, F.Q. and Atkinson, D.R.: Mexican-American acculturation, counselor ethnicity, counseling style, and perceived counselor credibility. *Journal of Counseling Psychology, 36*(2):203–208, 1989.

Press, E. and Done, A.: Solvent sniffing: Physiological effects and community control measures for intoxication from the intentional inhalation of organic solvents I. *Pediatrics, 39*(3):451–461, 1967a.

Press, E. and Done, A.: Solvent sniffing: Physiological effects and community control measures for intoxication from intentional inhalation of organic solvents II. *Pediatrics, 39*(4):611–622, 1967b.

Prockop, L.: Multifocal nervous system damage from inhalation of volatile hydrocarbons. *Journal of Occupational Medicine, 19*(2):139–140, 1977.

Rachal, J.V., Maisto, S.A., Guess, L. and Hubbrad, R.L.: Alcohol use among youth. In NIAAA: *Alcohol Consumption and Related Problems* (Alcohol and Health Monograph No. 1), Washington, DC., U.S. Government Printing Office, 1982, pp. 55–95.

Rachal, J.V., Williams, J.R., Behan, M.L., Cavanaugh, B., Moore, R.P. and Eckerman, W.C.: *A National Study of Adolescent Drinking Behaviors, Attitudes and Correlates.* Research Triangle Park, NC., Research Triangle Institute, Center for the Study of Social Behavior, 1975.

Radloff Lenore S.: The CES–D scale: A self report depression scale for research in the general population. *Applied Psychological Measurement, 1:*385–401, 1977.

Ramirez, D.G.: *A Review of the Literature on the Underutilization of Mental Health Services by Mexican Americans: Implications For Future Research and Service Delivery.* San Antonio, Intercultural Development Research Association, 1980.

Ramirez, Oscar, and Arce, Carlos: The contemporary Chicano family: An empirically based review. In Baron, Jr., A. (Ed.): *Exploration in Chicano Psychology.* New York, Praeger, 1981.

Rio, A., Santisteban, D.A., and Szapocznik, Jose: Treatment approaches for Hispanic drug abusing adolescents. In Glick, R. and Moore, J. (Eds.): *Drug Abuse in Hispanic Communities.* New Brunswick, Rutgers University Press, 1990.

Roberts, R., and Vernon, S.: Minority status and psychological distress reexamined: The case of Mexican Americans. In Greenley, J. (Ed.): *Research in Community and Mental Health.* London, Jais, 1984, Vol. 4, pp. 131–164.

Robles, R., Martinez, R. and Moscoso, M.: Drug use among public and private secondary school students in Puerto Rico. *The International Journal of the Addictions, 14*(2):243–258, 1979.

Rodriguez, O.: Progress report of Grant No. DA5630. Rockville, Maryland, National Institute on Drug Abuse, 1990.

Rodriguez-Andrew, Sylvia: Inhalant abuse: An emerging problem among Mexican American adolescents. *Children Today, 14*(4):23–25, 1985.

Rodriguez-Andrew, Sylvia, Gilbert, M. Jean and Trotter, Robert T.: Mexican American cultural norms related to alcohol use as reflected in drinking settings and language use. In Gilbert, M. Jean (Ed.): *Alcohol Consumption Among Mexicans and Mexican-Americans: A Binational Perspective.* Los Angeles, Spanish Speaking Mental Health Research Center, University of California, 1988.

Rogler, Lloyd H., Cortes, D.E. and Malgady, R.G.: Acculturation and mental health status among Hispanics. *American Psychologist, 46:*585–597, 1991.

Rogler, Lloyd H., Malgady, R.G., Costantino, G., and Blumenthal, R.: What do culturally sensitive mental health services mean? The case of Hispanics. *American Psychologist, 42:*565–570, 1987.

Rouse, Beatrice: Substance Abuse in Mexican Americans. In *Mental Health Issues of the Mexican Origin Population in Texas.* Rodriguez, Reymundo and Coleman, Marion T. (Eds.): Austin, Hogg Foundation for Mental Health, University of Texas, 1986.

Rouse, Beatrice A., Kozel, N., and Richards, L.G. (Eds.): *Self Reports Methods of Estimating Drug Use: Meeting Current Challenges to Validity.* NIDA Research Monograph 57, Rockville, Maryland, National Institute on Drug Abuse, 1985.

Rutter, M. and Guiller, H.: *Juvenile Delinquency — Trends and Perspectives.* New York, Penguin, 1983.

Sabagh, G.: Fertility planning status of Chicano couples in Los Angeles. *American Journal of Public Health, 70:*56–61, 1980.

Sabogal, F., Marin, G., Otero-Sabogal R., Marin, B.V. and Perez-Stable, E.J.: Hispanic familism and acculturation: What changes and what doesn't? *Hispanic Journal of Behavioral Sciences, 9*(4):397–412, 1987.

Sanchez-Dirks, R.: Drinking practices among Hispanic youth. *Alcohol Health and Research World,* Winter, 21–27, 1978.

Sandler, I., Gersten, J.C., Reynolds, K., Kallgren, C.A., and Ramirez, R.: In Gottlieb, B.H. (Ed.): *Marshaling Social Support: Formats, Processes, and Effects.* Newbury Park, Sage, 1988, pp. 305–330.

Santisteban, D., and Szapocznik, J.: Substance abuse disorders among Hispanics: A focus on prevention. In Becerra, R.M., Karno, M. and Escobar, J.I. (Eds.): *Mental Health and Hispanic Americans: Clinical Perspectives.* New York, Grune & Stratton, 1982.

Santostefano, S., and Rieder, C.: Cognitive controls and aggression in children: The concept of cognitive-affective balance. *Journal of Consulting and Clinical Psychology, 52*(1):46–56, 1984.

Sarason, I.G., Levine, H.M., Basham, R.B., and Sarason, B.R.: Assessing social support: The social support questionnaire. *Journal of Personality and Social Psychology, 44,* 127–139, 1983.

Sarason, I.G. and Sarason, B.R. (Eds.): *Social Support: Theory, Research, and Applications.* Dordrecht, The Netherlands, Martinus Mijhoff, 1985.

Schaefer, Diana, S. and Pozzaglia, Daniella: Hispanic parents of children with cancer. In Gittermann, Alex and Shulman, Larry (Eds.): *Mutual Aid Groups and the Life Cycle.* Itasca, Peacock, 1986.

Schilling, R.F., Schinke, S.P., Nichols, S.E., Zayes, L.H., Miller, S.O., Orlandi, M.A., and Botvin, G.J.: Developing strategies for AIDS prevention research with Black and Hispanic drug users. *Public Health Reports, 104*(1):2–11, 1989.

Schilling, R.F., Schinke, S.P. and Weatherly, R.: Service trends in a conservative era: Social workers rediscover the past. *Social Work, 33:*5–9, 1988.

Selnow, G.W., and Crano, W.D.: Formal vs. informal group affiliations: Implications for alcohol and drug use among adolescents. *Journal of Studies on Alcohol, 47:*48–52, 1986.

Shapiro, D., and Goldstein, J.B.: Biobehavioral perspectives on hypertension. *Journal of Consulting and Clinical Psychology, 50*(6):841–858, 1982.

Sharp, C. and Brehm, M. (Eds.): *Review of Inhalants: Euphoria to Dysfunction.* NIDA Research monograph 15, Washington, DC., U.S. Government Printing Office, 1977.

Sharp, D. and Korman, M.: Volatile substances. In Lewinson, J. and Ruiz, P. (Eds.): *Substance Abuse: Clinical Problems and Perspectives.* Baltimore, Williams and Wilkens, 1980.

Shedler, J., and Block, J.: Adolescent drug use and psychological health: A longitudinal inquiry. *American Psychologist, 45*(5):612–630, 1990.

Shulman, Larry: The dynamics of mutual aid. *Social Work with Groups, 8:*51–60, 1985/86.

Simons, R.L., Conger, R.D., and Whitbeck, L.B.: A multistage social learning model of the influences of family and peers upon adolescent substance abuse. *Journal of Drug Issues, 18:*293–315, 1988.

Singer, Merrill: Indigenous treatment of alcoholism: The case of Puerto Rican spiritualism. *Medical Anthropology, 8:*246–273, 1984a.

Singer, Merrill: Spiritual healing and family therapy: Common approaches to treatment of alcoholism. *Family Therapy, 11:*155–162, 1984b.

Singer, Merrill, Davison, Lani, and Yalin, Fuat (Eds.): *Conference Proceedings: Alcoholic Use and Abuse Among Adolescent Adolescents.* Hartford, Hispanic Health Council, 1987.

Skager, R. and Maddahian, E.: *A survey of substance use and related factors among secondary school students in grades 7, 9, and 11 in the County of Orange, Fall 1983.* Los Angeles, Center for the Study of Evaluation, School of Education, UCLA, 1984.

Skager, R., Stecher, B. and Maddahian, E.: *Report of the Spring, 1985 substance use survey of five Ventura County school districts, grades 7, 9, and 11.* Unpublished report, 1986.

Smith-Peterson, C.: Substance abuse treatment and cultural diversity. In Bennet, G., Vaurakis, C., and Woolf, D. (Eds.): *Substance Abuse Pharmacologic, Developmental and Clinical Perspectives.* New York, Wiley, 1983.

Solomon, M.Z., and DeLong, W.: Recent transmitted disease prevention efforts and their implications for AIDS health education. *Health Education Quarterly, 13:*301–316, 1986.

Soriano, Fernando I.: AIDS and Hispanics: A challenge to Hispanic families. In Sotomayor, Marta (Ed.): *Empowering Hispanic Families: A Critical Issue for the 90's.* Milwaukee, Family Service America, 1991.

Soriano, Fernando I. and De La Rosa, Mario R.: Cocaine use and criminal activities among Hispanic juvenile delinquents in Florida. In Glick, R. and Moore, J. (Eds.): *Drugs in Hispanic Communities.* New Brunswick, Rutgers University Press, 1990, pp. 55–73.

Sotomayor, Marta: The Mexican American family and interaction with social systems. In Munoz, F.U. and Endo, R. (Eds.): *Perspectives on Minority Group Mental Health.* Washington, D.C., University Press of America, 1982, pp. 71–81.

Spence, R.T., Fredlund, E. and Kavinsky, J.: *1988 Texas Survey of Substance Use Among Adults.* Austin, Texas Commission on Alcohol and Drug Abuse, 1989.

Stanton, M.D.: Drugs and the family: A review of the recent literature. *Marriage and Family Review, 2:*1–10, 1979a.

Stanton, M.D.: Family treatment of drug problems: A review. In Dupont, R.L., Goldstein, A. and O'Donnell, J. (Eds.): *Handbook of Drug Abuse.* Washington, D.C., U.S. Government Printing Office, 1979b.

Stanton, M.D. and Todd, T.C.: Engaging resistant families in treatment. *Family Process, 20:*261–293, 1981.

Staples, R., and Mirande, A.: Racial and cultural variations among American families: A decennial review of the literature on minority families. *Journal of Marriage and the Family, 42*(4):887–903, 1980.

Stoneburner, R.L., Des Jarlais, D.C., Benezra, D., Gorelkin, L., Sotheran, J.L., Friedman, S.R., Schultz, S., Marmor, M., Mildvan, D., and Maslansky, R.: A larger spectrum of severe HIV-1-Related disease in intravenous drug users in New York City. *Science, 242:*916–919, 1988.

Stybel, L., Allen, P., and Lewis, F.: Deliberate hydrocarbon inhalation among low socioeconomic adolescents not necessarily apprehended by the police. *International Journal of the Addictions, 11*(2):345–361, 1976.

Sue, S., and Zane, N.: The role of culture and cultural techniques in psychotherapy: A critique and reformulation. *American Psychologist, 42:*37–45, 1987.

Sutherland, E.H. and Cressey, D.R.: *Criminology.* (10th Ed.) Philadelphia, Lipincott, 1978.

Swaim, R., Beauvais, F., Edwards, R. and Oetting, E.: Adolescent drug use in three small rural communities in the Rocky Mountain region. *Journal of Drug Education, 16*(1):57–73, 1986.

Szapocznik, Jose, Daruna, P., Scopetta, M., and de los Angeles, A.: The characteristics of Cuban immigrant inhalant abusers. *American Journal of Drug and Alcohol Abuse, 4*(3):377–389, 1977.

Szapocznik, Jose, Foote, F., Perez-Vidal, A., Hervis, O., and Kurtines, William M.: *One Person Family Therapy.* Dept. of Psychiatry, University of Miami, Miami, Florida, 1985.

Szapocznik, Jose and Kurtines, William: Acculturation, biculturalism and adjustment among Cuban Americans. In Paddila, Amado M. (Ed.): *Acculturation Theory, Models and Some New Findings.* Boulder, Westview, 1980.

Szapocznik, Jose, Kurtines, William M., and Contributors: *Breakthroughs in Family Therapy with Drug-Abusing and Problem Youth.* New York, Springer, 1989.

Szapocznik, Jose, Kurtines, William M., and Fernandez, T.: Bicultural involvement and adjustment in Hispanic-American youths. *International Journal of Intercultural Relations, 4:*353–365, 1980.

Szapocznik, Jose, Kurtines, William M., Hervis, O., and Spencer, F.: One person family therapy. In Lubin, E. and O'Connor, W.A. (Eds.): *Ecological Approaches to Clinical and Community Psychology.* New York, Wiley, 1984, pp. 335–355.

Szapocznik, Jose, Lasaga, J., Perry, P., and Solomon, J.: Outreach in the Delivery of Mental Health Services to Hispanic Elders. *Hispanic Journal of Behavioral Sciences. 1:*21–40, 1979.

Szapocznik, Jose, Perez-Vidal, A., Brickman, A.L., Foote, F., Santisteban, D., Hervis,

O., and Kurtines, William: Engaging adolescent drug abusers and their families into treatment: A Strategic Structural Systems Approach. *Journal of Consulting and Clinical Psychology, 56*(4):552–557, 1988.

Szapocznik, Jose, Rio, Arturo T. and Kurtines, William M.: Brief Strategic Family Therapy for Hispanic problem youth. In Beutler, L.E. and Crago, M. (Eds.): *Psychotherapy research: An international review of programmatic studies.* Washington, D.C., American Psychological Association, 1991.

Szapocznik, Jose, Rio, Arturo T., Hervis, O.E., Mitrani, V.B., Kurtines, William M. and Faraci, A.M.: Assessing change in family functioning as a result of treatment: The Structural Family Systems Rating Scale (SFSR). *Journal of Marital and Family Therapy, 17*(3):295–310, 1991.

Szapocznik, Jose, Santisteban, David, Kurtines, William M., Perez-Vidal, A. and Hervis, O.E.: Bicultural effectiveness training: A treatment intervention for enhancing intercultural adjustment. *Hispanic Journal of Behavioral Sciences, 6*(4):317–344, 1984.

Szapocznik, Jose, Santisteban, David A., Perez-Vidal A., and Brickman, A.: *Drug Abuse Syndrome: A Procedure for Early Identification of Adolescent Drug Abusers.* Unpublished Manuscript, University of Miami, 1989.

Szapocznik, Jose, Santisteban, David, Rio, Arturo, Perez Vidal, A., Kurtines, William M. and Hervis, O.E.: Bicultural effectiveness training (BET): An intervention modality for families experiencing intergenerational/intercultural conflict. *Hispanic Journal of Behavioral Sciences, 6*(4):303–330, 1986.

Szapocznik, Jose, Santisteban, David, Rio, Arturo, Perez Vidal, A., Santisteban, Daniel and Kurtines, William M.: Family Effectiveness Training: An intervention to prevent drug abuse and problem behavior in Hispanic adolescents. *Hispanic Journal of Behavioral Sciences, 11*(1):3–27, 1989.

Szapocznik, Jose, Santisteban, David, Rio, Arturo, Perez-Vidal, A. and Kurtines, William M.: Family Effectiveness Training for Hispanic families: Strategic Structural Systems intervention for the prevention of drug abuse. In Lefley, H.P. and Pedersen, P.B. (Eds.): *Cross-Cultural Training for Mental Health Professions.* Springfield, Thomas, 1986.

Szapocznik, Jose, Scopetta, M.A., and King, O.E.: Theory and practice in matching treatment to the special characteristics and problems of Cuban immigrants. *Journal of Community Psychology, 6:*112–122, 1978.

Szapocznik, Jose, Scopetta, M.A., Aranalde, M., and Kurtines, William: Cuban value structure: Treatment implications. *Journal of Consulting and Clinical Psychology, 46*(5):961–970, 1978.

Texas Commission on Alcohol and Drug Abuse: *1990 Texas School Survey of Substance Abuse.* Austin, 1990.

The New York Times: War against drugs: Scorn on besieged streets. September 8, 1989.

Thornberry, T.: Progress report of Grant No. DA5512. National Institute on Drug Abuse, Rockville, Maryland, 1990.

Tims, F. and Ludford, J.: *Drug Abuse Treatment Evaluation: Strategies, Progress, and Prospects.* NIDA Research Monograph 51. Rockville, Maryland, National Institute on Drug Abuse, 1984.

Triandis, Harry C., Marin, Gerardo, Betancourt, Hector, Lisansky, Judith, and Chang, B.: *Dimensions of Familism Among Hispanic and Mainstream Navy Recruits*, Technical Report No. 14, Department of Psychology, University of Illinois, Champaign, 1982.

Triandis, Harry C., Marin, Gerardo, Lisansky, Judith, and Betancourt, Hector: "Simpatia" as a cultural script of Hispanics. *Journal of Personality and Social Psychology, 47:*1363–1375, 1984.

Trotter, Robert T.: Ethnic and sexual patterns of alcohol use: Anglo and Mexican American college students. *Adolescence, 17*(66):305–325, 1982.

Trotter, Robert T.: Mexican American experience with alcohol: South Texas examples. In Bennett, Linda A. and Ames, Genevieve M. (Eds.): *The American Experience with Alcohol: Contrasting Cultural Perspectives.* New York, Plenum, 1985, pp. 279–296.

U.S. Bureau of the Census: *Persons of Spanish Origin in the United States.* Current Population Reports. Series P-20, No. 403, Washington, D.C., U.S. Department of Commerce, 1985.

U.S. Bureau of the Census: *Projections of the Hispanic Population: 1983–2080.* Current Population Reports, Series P-25, No. 995. Washington, D.C., U.S. Government Printing Office, 1986.

U.S. Bureau of the Census: *The Hispanic Population in the United States: 1988 (Advance Report).* Current Population Reports, Series P-20, No. 431. Washington, D.C., U.S. Government Printing Office, 1988.

U.S. Bureau of the Census: *The Hispanic Population in the United States: March 1988.* Current Population Reports, Series P-20, No. 438. Washington, D.C., U.S. Government Printing Office, 1989.

U.S. Bureau of the Census: *The Hispanic Population in the United States: March 1989.* Current Population Reports, Series P-20, No. 444. Washington, D.C., U.S. Government Printing Office, 1990.

U.S. Bureau of the Census: *The Hispanic Population in the United States: March 1990.* Current Population Reports, Series P-20, No. 449. Washington, D.C., U.S. Government Printing Office, 1991.

U.S. Department of Justice: Bureau of Statistics. *Survey of Inmates in State Correctional Facilities.* Washington, D.C., Unpublished report, 1986.

U.S. Public Health Service: Cross-cutting issues: Women and AIDS. *Journal of the U.S. Public Health Service, 103,* 88–90, 1988.

URSA Institute: *Youth environment study. A street-based early intervention demonstration project with young drug users.* (Contract No. D-0025-2). Sacramento, California Department of Alcohol and Drugs, 1983.

Valdez, A.: Personal communication, Hispanic Research Center, University of Texas at San Antonio, San Antonio, Texas, October 31, 1990.

Valle, Ramon and Bensussen, Gloria: Hispanic social networks, social support, and mental health. In Vega, William A. and Miranda, Manuel R. (Eds.): *Stress and Hispanic Mental Health.* Rockville, MD., National Institute of Mental Health, 1985, pp. 147–173.

Valle, Ramon and Mendoza, Lydia: *The Elder Latino.* San Diego, Campanile Press, 1978.

Valle, Ramon and Vega, William A.: *Hispanic Natural Support Systems.* Department of Mental Health, State of California, 1980.

Vaux, A.: Variations in social support associated with gender, ethnicity, and age. *Journal of Social Issues, 41:*89–110, 1985.

Vaux, A.: *Social Support: Theory, Research, and Intervention.* New York, Praeger, 1988.

Vega, William: Progress report Grant No. DA5912. National Institute on Drug Abuse, Rockville, Maryland, 1990.

Vega, William A., Hough, R.L., and Romero, A.: Family life patterns of Mexican Americans. In Powell, G.J., Yamamoto, J. Romero, A.L. and Morales, A. (Eds.): *The Psychosocial Development of Minority Group Children.* New York, Brunner/Mazel, 1983, pp. 194–215.

Vega, William A., and Kolody, B.: The meaning of social support and the mediation of stress across cultures. In W.A. Vega and M.R. Miranda (Eds.): *Stress and Hispanic Mental Health: Relating Research to Service Delivery.* Rockville, MD., NIMH, 1985, pp. 48–75.

Vega, William A., Kolody, B., Valle, Ramon, and Hough, R.: Depressive symptoms and their correlates among immigrant Mexican women in the United States. *Social Science and Medicine, 22:*645–652, 1986.

Vega, William A., Valle, Ramon, Kolody, B., and Hough, R.: The Hispanic social network prevention intervention study: A community-based randomized trial. In Munoz, R.F. (Ed.): *Depression Prevention: Research Directions.* New York, Hemisphere, 1987, pp. 217–231.

Verdugo, R.R.: *The Hispanic labor force: An analysis of selected topics: 1980-1987.* Working paper. Claremont, The Tomas Rivera Center, 1988.

Vigil, J.D.: Chicano gangs: One response to Mexican Urban adaptation in the Los Angeles area. *Urban Anthropology, 12:*45–75, 1983.

Vigil, J.D.: Street socialization, locura behavior, and violence among Chicano gang members. In Kraus, J., Sorenson, S. and Suarez, P. (Eds.): *Research Conference on Violence and Homicide in Hispanic Communities.* Los Angeles, University of California, 1988, pp. 231–243.

Watts, W.D. and Wright, L.S.: The drug use—violent delinquency link among adolescent Mexican-Americans. In De La Rosa, M.R., Lambert, E., and Gropper, B. (Eds.): *Drugs and Violence: Causes, Correlates, and Consequences.* NIDA Research Monograph 103, Rockville, Maryland, 1990, pp. 136–159.

Weber, George H.: Self-help beliefs. In Weber, George H. and Cohen, Lucy M. (Eds.): *Beliefs and Self-Help.* New York, Human Sciences, 1982.

Weeks, J., and Cuellar, Jose: The role of family members in the helping networks of older people. *Gerontologist, 21:*388–394, 1981.

Weidman, A.A.: Engaging the families of substance abusing adolescents in family therapy. *Journal of Substance Abuse Treatment, 2:*97–105, 1985.

Weissman, J.C., Marr, S.W., Katsampes, P.L.: Addiction and criminal behavior: A continuing examination of criminal addicts. *Journal of Drug Issues, 6:*153–165, 1976.

Wermuth, L., and Scheidt, S.: Enlisting Family Support in Drug Treatment. *Family Process,* 25:25–34, 1986.

White, O.Z., Chambers, C.D., and Inciardi, J.: *Mexican-American criminals: A Comparative study of heroin using and non-using felons.* Unpublished manuscript, San Antonio, Texas, Department of Sociology, Trinity University, no date.

Whitehead, W.E. and Bosmajian, L.S.: Behavioral medicine approaches to gastrointestinal disorders. *Journal of Consulting and Clinical Psychology, 50*(6):972–983, 1982.

Wilde, C.: Aerosol metallic paints: Deliberate inhalation. A study of inhalation and/or ingestion of copper and zinc particles. *International Journal of the Addictions, 10*(1):127–134, 1975.

Williamson, G.: Out of the garbage rises the truth. *San Francisco Chronicle,* February 12, 1976.

Wilsnack, R. and Wilsnack, S.: Sex roles and drinking among adolescent girls. *Journal of Studies on Alcohol, 39*(11):1855–1874, 1978.

Wortman, C.B. and Lehman, D.R.: Reactions to victims of life crises: Support attempts that fail. In Sarason, I.G. and Sarason, B.R. (Eds.): *Social Support: Theory, Research, and Applications.* Dordrecht, The Netherlands, Martinus Mijhoff, 1985, pp. 463–489.

Wyse, D.: Deliberate inhalation of volatile hydrocarbons: A review. *Canadian Medical Association Journal, 108:*71–74, 1973.

Yamamoto, J., and Silva, J.A.: Do Hispanics underutilize mental health services? In Gaviria, M. and Arana, J.D.: *Health and Behavior: Research Agenda for Hispanics.* The Simon Bolivar Research Monograph Series No. 1, University of Illinois at Chicago, 1987.

Yamamoto, K.: Children's ratings of the stressfulness of experiences. *Developmental Psychology, 15*(5):581–582, 1974.

Yankofsky, Lon, Wilson, G. Terence, Adler, Jamie L., Jay, William L. and Vrana, Scott: The effect of alcohol on self-evaluation and perceptions of negative interpersonal feedback. *Journal of Studies on Alcohol, 47*(1):26–33, 1986.

Yeaworth, R., York, J., Hussey, M., Ingel, M., and Goodwin, T.: The development of an adolescent life change event scale. *Adolescence, 15:*19–97, 1980.

Zapata, J.T., and Jaramillo, P.T.: Research on the Mexican American family. *Journal of Individual Psychology, 37:*72–85, 1981.

Zastrow, Charles: *Social Work with Groups.* Chicago, Nelson-Hall, 1989.

INDEX